PRAISE FOR *FORENSIC SCIENCE IN COURT*

"You couldn't fi ____ onting the field of forensic ____ As a trial judge, Donald ____ its most critical perspecti ____ us? Judge Shelton provides ____ reas of forensic science, f ____ and in the justice system, from judges to attorneys to expert witnesses, should read this book."—**Katherine Ramsland**, DeSales University; author of *Beating the Devil's Game: A History of Forensic Science and Criminal Investigation*

"This important book stands at the intersection of law, science, and technology, and it is essential reading for lawyers, judges, jurors, investigators, policy-makers, and citizens who care about their court system. In this highly readable book, Judge Shelton vividly illustrates that all too often forensic evidence does not meet the test of scientific validity."—**Nancy S. Marder**, Chicago–Kent College of Law

"The book offers a searching examination of some of the most sacred of the sacred cows in the scientific evidence field, including fingerprints, firearms comparisons, psychiatric evaluation, and so on. Former trial lawyer and current judge Donald Shelton has successfully put together an overview of the scientific issues that demand attention in light of modern legal principles. *Forensic Science in Court* will be a uniquely useful working tool for judges, lawyers, investigators, and anyone who aspires to join those professions. It is thoroughly researched, thoughtfully presented, and completely readable."—**Nick Rine**, University of Michigan Law School

"Judge Shelton's book hits the right balance: it clearly communicates the basic procedures used in each technique but does not dwell too much in any one area. For a very difficult subject matter, it is fairly easy to read, and the case studies really make the issues come alive. Judge Shelton is not afraid to point out the weaknesses, both legally and scientifically, of some of the procedures."—**Ron Bretz**, Thomas M. Cooley Law School

"Judge Shelton's book is a very readable, entertaining, concise, and enlightening account of the history of the use of forensic science evidence in criminal trials. This book is a valuable resource for lawyers, judges, and students. I highly recommend it."—**Thomas K. Clancy**, director, National Center for Justice and the Rule of Law, University of Mississippi School of Law

FORENSIC SCIENCE
IN COURT

ISSUES IN CRIME & JUSTICE

Series Editor
Gregg Barak, Eastern Michigan University

As we embark upon the twentieth-first century, the meanings of crime continue to evolve and our approaches to justice are in flux. The contributions to this series focus their attention on crime and justice as well as on crime control and prevention in the context of a dynamically changing legal order. Across the series, there are books that consider the full range of crime and criminality and that engage a diverse set of topics related to the formal and informal workings of the administration of criminal justice. In an age of globalization, crime and criminality are no longer confined, if they ever were, to the boundaries of single nation-states. As a consequence, while many books in the series will address crime and justice in the United States, the scope of these books will accommodate a global perspective and they will consider such eminently global issues such as slavery, terrorism, or punishment. Books in the series are written to be used as supplements in standard undergraduate and graduate courses in criminology and criminal justice and related courses in sociology. Some of the standard courses in these areas include: introduction to criminal justice, introduction to law enforcement, introduction to corrections, juvenile justice, crime and delinquency, criminal law, white collar, corporate, and organized crime.

TITLES IN SERIES:

FORENSIC SCIENCE IN COURT

Challenges in the Twenty-first Century

Donald E. Shelton

ROWMAN & LITTLEFIELD PUBLISHERS, INC.

Lanham • Boulder • New York • Toronto • Plymouth, UK

Published by Rowman & Littlefield Publishers, Inc.
A wholly owned subsidiary of The Rowman & Littlefield Publishing Group, Inc.
4501 Forbes Boulevard, Suite 200, Lanham, Maryland 20706
http://www.rowmanlittlefield.com

Estover Road, Plymouth PL6 7PY, United Kingdom

British Library Cataloguing in Publication Information Available

Library of Congress Cataloging-in-Publication Data

Shelton, Donald E.
  Forensic science in court : challenges in the twenty-first century / by Donald E. Shelton.
    p. cm.—(Issues in crime & justice)
  Includes bibliographical references and index.
  ISBN 978-1-4422-0187-3 (cloth : alk. paper)—ISBN 978-1-4422-0188-0 (pbk. : alk. paper)—ISBN 978-1-4422-0189-7 (electronic)
  1. Evidence, Expert—United States. 2. Forensic sciences—United States. 3. Evidence, Criminal—United States. I. Title.
  KF9674.S54 2011
  345.73'067—dc22

                                                                              2010016853

♾™ The paper used in this publication meets the minimum requirements of American National Standard for Information Sciences—Permanence of Paper for Printed Library Materials, ANSI/NISO Z39.48-1992.

Printed in the United States of America

Much of the research for this book was originally done as part of my doctoral dissertation at the Grant Sawyer Center for Justice Studies at the University of Nevada, Reno, under the able and patient direction of Dr. James T. Richardson.

I am grateful to him and the other scholars whose reviews were an essential part of this work, including Drs. Gregg Barak, Monica K. Miller, Mara S. Merlino, and Judge Frederic Rodgers. I also appreciate the invaluable research and editing assistance of Ms. Christine Tait and attorney Kelly Roberts.

Personally, I dedicate this work to my wife, Marjorie. Perhaps because she truly knows me after forty-six years of marriage, she never once questioned why I would undertake this project and continued to support and encourage me throughout the process. And finally, to the ones who made me break into a smile even when I was so totally engrossed that I was in danger of forgetting what is truly important in life—Elizabeth, Madison, Mackenzie, and Makayla.

Contents

Figures

Introduction

IN CRIMINAL CASES JURORS ARE THE FINDERS of fact. To determine those facts, they are presented with evidence from witness testimony about what the witness observed or heard. It is for the jury to decide whether that testimony proves, either directly or circumstantially, beyond a reasonable doubt that the defendant committed the crime with which he or she is charged. Additionally, however, the jury is allowed to hear testimony from persons who are regarded as experts as to their conclusions and opinions based on the same observations. Those persons are not allowed to give opinion testimony as to the ultimate issue of the defendant's guilt or innocence. They may give opinion testimony when those opinions would assist the jury in reaching that ultimate issue. The testimony is limited to areas that are beyond the normal or common experience of jurors and where an expert's special knowledge will help the jury understand the import of the factual evidence it hears.

Testimony from scientific experts is the classic form of such expert testimony. Forensic science evidence is the observation and opinion of a trained person and is designed to aid the jury in understanding the meaning or conclusions that are suggested by the factual evidence. The expert may testify as to whether a particular event occurred, who the person was who caused the event to occur, or how the event occurred. These basic questions of "who," "whether," and "how" are the subjects of the variety of scientific evidence examined in this study. Who committed an act is the subject of such areas as deoxyribonucleic acid (DNA), fingerprint, handwriting, hair, and bite-mark analysis. The question of how an event occurred is often addressed in such areas as tool-mark analysis; firearm and bullet comparisons; fire, explosion, and arson testimony; and bloodstain pattern analysis. The question of whether an event occurred is one of the primary functions of social science expertise.

The rapid development of emerging scientific methods, especially the increased understanding of DNA, has had and will undoubtedly continue to have an almost stunning impact on our forensic evidence in the justice system, particularly at the trial level. The forensic applications of these new scientific discoveries have been most dramatically seen in the criminal trial court. This book addresses those new and old forms of scientific forensic evidence that have sufficient validity to be used in a criminal proceeding. It also addresses the "gatekeeping" role assigned to trial judges under what has become known as the *Daubert trilogy* of cases in which the Supreme Court defined that role and rejected the former *Frye* test for admissibility of scientific evidence in federal cases. This includes an examination of the *Daubert* trilogy cases themselves and the subsequent case law that has further defined and refined the standards for evaluating proposed scientific evidence. Since the *Frye* test is still used in some state courts, that standard is also reviewed in the context of the various forms of proffered scientific evidence.

Advanced technology also presents a new variety of pretrial issues in the criminal justice system, especially as they relate to DNA. In a review of existing case law, this book addresses the constitutional questions posed by the development of extremely large DNA databases, including Fourth and Fifth Amendment search and incrimination issues that are presented by how these databases are collected. It also addresses the extent to which these databases lead to the adoption or application of new statutes of limitation. Those new statutes are parsed and the emerging case law under them is reviewed. This book examines how new technology, particularly DNA, poses significant postconviction issues for the criminal justice system. These issues include whether and which convicts will be allowed access to DNA or other technologies that had not been discovered, or were not available, at the time of their trial. Case law, especially recent pronouncements from the Supreme Court, is reviewed and focuses on how the judicial desire for finality weighs against the judicial struggle for truth and certainty.

As the defense responds to new government technology in criminal cases, new forms of pretrial relief have been sought, particularly in the form of pretrial discovery and requests for expert assistance. This book examines how these new forms of scientific evidence may change the nature of pretrial discovery motions and how such requests for expert assistance, particularly for indigent defendants, will pose significant problems for an already backlogged and underfunded criminal justice system.

A significant portion of this work is designed to determine whether various forms of new and old scientific evidence meet the standards of *Daubert*. To do so, the book reviews the history and scientific basis of the most common forms of forensic scientific evidence, and the qualifications of persons who offer expert testimony in each field or discipline. An initial examination is made of common social science evidence, including eyewitness expert testimony and several "abuse syndromes." It then goes on to examine, in addition to DNA, fingerprint, handwriting, hair comparison, bite-mark, and tool-mark analyses; firearms and bullet lead comparison; fire, explosion, and arson evidence; and bloodstain pattern evidence. In each of these fields, the scientific basis is examined and then compared with the criteria for validity established under *Daubert*. Several of these forms of scientific evidence may not meet the strict standards of *Daubert*, but courts may not strictly apply those standards in the face of traditional legal admissibility rulings and in the face of prosecution demands for admission.

Through the media and through their own life experiences jurors know about, or at least they think they know about, much of this new technology. This study examines how juror expectations and demands for scientific evidence and the pressure of that so-called *CSI* effect may alter criminal trials. To do so, the book reviews the nature of juror expectations about scientific evidence as it has been gleaned from the empirical and other research that has so far been performed. The case law that has developed involving judicial efforts to cope with the *CSI* effect and juror expectations and demands is reviewed. The book identifies a variety of issues relating both to attorney conduct and to funding scientific evidence laboratories that are posed by such increased juror expectations and demands. It was hypothesized that the *CSI* effect is not related solely to television watching, but that juror expectations are culturally based phenomena to which the criminal justice system must adapt.

CASE STUDY

America's First Reported Wrongful Murder Conviction Case: The Colvin "Murder" by Rob Warden, Executive Director of the Center on Wrongful Convictions (originally posted at http://www.law.northwestern.edu/wrongfulconvictions/ exonerations/vtBoornSummary.html)

When Russell Colvin disappeared from Manchester, Vermont, in 1812, suspicion of foul play understandably fell upon his brothers-in-law, Jesse and Stephen Boorn, who had worked with him on their father's farm. The Boorn brothers had made no secret of their disdain for their sister's spouse. In fact, they had complained often that Colvin,

FIGURE I.1.
Artist's depiction of
the alleged murder of
Russell Colvin in 1812
in Manchester, Vermont,
which led to the first
wrongful conviction
in the United States.
The illustration is from
a popular nineteenth-
century novel based
on the case, *The Dead
Alive* by Wilkie Collins,
published by Shepard and
Gill, Boston, in 1874.
Northwestern Law Bluhm Clinic
Center on Wrongful Convictions.

a habitué of the local public house, was sloughing off on the job and freeloading off the family.

Despite the widespread suspicion that the Boorns had slain Colvin, nothing happened in the case until seven years later when Amos Boorn, an uncle of the suspects, claimed that Colvin had appeared at his bed-side during a recurring dream. The ghost confirmed, just as had been widely assumed, that he had been slain. He did not identify his killers, but did say that his remains had been put into an old cellar hole in a potato field on the Boorn farm.

In light of the dream, the cellar hole was excavated. In it were found pieces of broken crockery, a button, a penknife, and a jackknife—but no human remains. Russell Colvin's wife, Sally Boorn Colvin, sister of the suspects, promptly identified the items as having been her husband's.

However, she had a motive to say that, whether true or not. It was in her interest to have Russell proven dead because—more than a gestation period after his disappearance—she had given birth to a child. Because the law presumed a child born to a married woman to have been fathered by her lawful husband, Sally was ineligible for support from the child's actual father. For her to collect, Russell needed to be dead. Moreover, Sally may not have realized when she identified the items that furthering her interest in collecting support would be so potentially detrimental to her brothers' interest in remaining alive and free.

Soon after the excavation of the cellar hole, a mysterious fire destroyed the sheep barn on the Boorn place, giving rise to rumors that the fire was somehow related to the crime. Then, a few days after that, from beneath a nearby stump, a dog unearthed several bone fragments, which three area physicians pronounced human. Now the rumor mill began confabulating a plausible sequence of events: The brothers initially had buried Colvin in the cellar hole, but for an unknown reason moved the remains a couple of years later, burying them in the barn, only to be moved a second time recently, again for an unknown reason, to the location where the dog found them. Under this scenario, the killers had torched the barn to destroy evidence of the murder. Based on this speculation, Jesse Boorn was arrested and a warrant issued for the arrest of Stephen Boorn, who recently had moved to New York.

In jail, Jesse shared a cell with a forger, Silas Merrill, who promptly began cooperating with the authorities. Merrill claimed that Jesse had confessed after a visit from his father, Barney Boorn. According to Merrill, Jesse confided that Stephen clubbed Colvin to the ground during an argument. Barney Boorn happened along and, seeing that Colvin was still alive, cut his throat with Stephen's pen knife. The three then buried Colvin in an old cellar hole, but two or three years later inexplicably dug up the remains and buried them in the barn. After fire destroyed the barn, they again moved Colvin's bones, this time burying them near the stump, precisely where the dog found them. In the manner of modern jailhouse snitches, Merrill agreed to testify against the brothers in exchange for his immediate release. State's Attorney Calvin Sheldon accepted the deal, and Merrill was set free.

Facing a likely death sentence, Jesse took a desperate step, no doubt calculated to save his life: He confessed, minimizing his own culpability and exculpating his father, who never would be charged in the case. Jesse's confession conveniently placed the blame principally on Stephen, whom Jesse may have assumed to be safely beyond the reach of Vermont authorities. But when a constable from Manchester called on him in New York, Stephen voluntarily returned, vowing to clear his name, whereupon Jesse recanted, contending that he had falsely confessed in a misguided effort to save his and his father's lives.

No mind was paid to the recantation. In fact, if anything, it strengthened State's Attorney Sheldon's resolve to seek the death penalty. In the ensuing days, witnesses came forward to recall, seven years after the fact, that they had heard the Boorn brothers threaten to kill Colvin. Other witnesses belatedly recalled that, after Colvin's disappearance, the Boorns had said things suggesting they knew he was dead.

In the face of the increasingly damning evidence, Stephen suddenly took the same desperate step that had so disastrously backfired on Jesse: Stephen, too, confessed, but insisted that he had acted in self-defense—a contention that, if believed, could mitigate against his hanging.

Before trial, the largest of the bones that the dog had found was compared with an actual human leg bone that had been preserved after an amputation in a nearby county. The bones were so obviously dissimilar that the physicians who previously had been certain that the ones found on the Boorn farm were human changed their minds, agreeing now that the bones were of animal origin. By this time, however, the physicians' earlier unfounded opinion had done its damage. But for the bones, Jesse and Stephen would not have been arrested, Merrill would have been denied the opportunity to implicate them, and the brothers would not have made the incriminating statements that veritably sealed their fate at trial.

There were, however, serious problems with the confessions that should have cast doubt on their veracity. First, they were not corroborated by any solid facts. Second, it was unlikely that Stephen, a man of unquestionable low intelligence and little formal education, was the sole author of his confession, which was written in precise language, with an unmistakable emphasis on mitigation. Rather it appears likely, in retrospect, that Stephen was aided and abetted by counsel. His defense lawyers, Richard Skinner and Leonard Sargeant, were distinguished and learned, but they—like virtually everyone else—assumed their clients guilty.

The miscarriage of justice also would not have occurred, of course, had not the community superstitiously attributed Amos Boorn's account of his alleged dreamy visits from Colvin's ghost to divine agency. Nor would it have occurred absent jailhouse snitch Merrill's false claim, which by the time of trial had been rendered superfluous by the brothers' confessions and, thus, was not brought into evidence.

The principal evidence introduced at trial to corroborate the confessions was the testimony of purported eyewitnesses who claimed, seven years after the fact, to have seen the Boorns and Colvin arguing on the day the latter disappeared. The jury had no trouble reaching a guilty verdict, and the judges presiding the case—Vermont law then required the three members of the state supreme court to sit as a panel in any potential capital trial—sentenced both to death. The Vermont General Assembly convened a special session to consider a plea for clemency. Because Jesse appeared less culpable, his sentence was commuted to life in prison, but Stephen was denied relief.

The journalistic event that turned the tide for the Boorns was an item in the *New York Evening Post* of November 26, 1819, marveling that divine intervention had brought Colvin's killers to justice. The item was read aloud in the lobby of a New York hotel, where a traveler from New Jersey, Tabor Chadwick, happened to be staying. Chadwick knew a man who went by the name Russell Colvin, who often had spoken of Vermont and who had been employed for the last several years as a farmhand in Dover, New Jersey. Chadwick immediately dispatched two letters relating the foregoing, one to the *Post*, the other to the Manchester postmaster. The letters described Colvin as "a man of rather small stature—round forehead—[who] speaks very fast, has two scars on his head, and appears to be between 30 and 40 years of age."

Chadwick's letter to Manchester had no effect—perhaps a telling commentary on the quality of the defense that the Boorns received, for the postmaster who received the letter was none other than their junior trial counsel, Leonard Sergeant. The *Post*, however, published the letter on December 6, 1819. In yet another serendipitous turn of events, the letter was read by one James Whelpley, a native of Manchester now living in New York. Whelpley immediately left for Dover, where he found a living, breathing, but uncooperative Colvin, who refused to return to Vermont.

Time being of the essence—Stephen's execution was scheduled for January 28, 1820—Whelpley reportedly enlisted a young woman to entice Colvin to accompany her to New York City. Colvin reportedly accepted the invitation, but when they arrived in the city, the woman immediately deserted him. Whelpley then told Colvin that, because British ships were offshore, they would have to take a circuitous route back to New Jersey. With this subterfuge, Whelpley coaxed Colvin onto a stagecoach bound for Manchester.

When they arrived on December 22, 1819, Colvin and Whelpley were greeted by a curious crowd, alerted to their impending arrival by a telegram from Whelpley. The crowd included several of Colvin's former neighbors, thereby establishing that rumors of his murder, as Mark Twain might have said, had been greatly exaggerated.

The exoneration of the Boorns received prominent play in newspapers throughout New England. In Vermont, the reporting was reasonably accurate, but elsewhere the facts seldom stood in the way making a good story better. One error that frequently made it into print was that the Boorns' convictions had rested primarily upon testimony by Amos Boorn concerning his spectral visits from Colvin. In fact, there had been no such testimony, for the court had excluded it based on time-honored rules of evidence.

The mistaken impression to the contrary, unfortunately, prompted editorial demands for the exclusion of superstition-based testimony—a safeguard already in place and irrelevant to the Boorns' conviction. The editorials, meanwhile, were oblivious to genuine issues, such as junk science and jailhouse snitch allegations that had led to false confessions and how the justice process had been polluted by widespread knowledge of Amos Boorn's alleged dream.

As a consequence of the media missing the point, moreover, commentators learned in the law focused heavily on correcting the misinformation, rather than on possible reforms that might correct what had gone wrong. The public was left with the impression that the case was nothing more than a regrettable but freakish accident in an otherwise functioning criminal justice system. As a result, there was no constituency for reform.

Further Reading

McFarland, Gerald M. *The Counterfeit Man: The True Story of the Boorn-Colvin Murder Case.* Amherst: University of Massachusetts Press, 1990.

Moulton, Sherman R. *The Boorn Mystery: An Episode from the Judicial Annals of Vermont.* Montpelier: Vermont Historical Society, 1937.

Spargo, John. *The Return of Russell Colvin.* Bennington: Historical Museum and Art Gallery of Bennington, Vermont, 1945.

1

The History and Development of Forensic Scientific Evidence

THE HISTORY OF THE USE OF FORENSIC SCIENCE in criminal cases in the United States is well over a century old.[1] The search for scientific answers to age-old human questions that gripped the Western world in the nineteenth and twentieth centuries was extended to many aspects of American society, including the criminal justice system. The courts allowed "experts" to give opinions about issues that had previously been left exclusively to the jury, such as identification through fingerprints and details of death or injury through medical testimony. As the use and pursuit of science increased, there were corresponding increases in both the areas of claimed expertise and the technological innovations that were used or developed to apply them.

Courts initially exhibited some reluctance to accept some of this claimed expertise as scientific, in handwriting analysis, for example. However, courts eventually established a pattern of almost routine acceptance of expert witnesses offered by the prosecution as an aid to the jury in finding guilt. Courts required little if any scientific foundation to be laid by the prosecution for such testimony. In a distinctly nonscientific approach, the case law developed with the application of the *Frye* doctrine, which required only that such testimony be "generally accepted." That standard is almost self-perpetuating. As more courts admitted testimony from any particular forensic science field, other courts used those admissibility decisions to bolster the idea that the field became more "generally accepted." There was rarely any defense challenge to the empirical basis, or scientific reliability, of prosecution-generated forensic science evidence.

The areas of claimed expertise offered in criminal cases by the government expanded and was almost unquestioned by defense counsel or the courts. Prosecutors offered expert testimony based on the conclusions of criminal investigators, many of whom had little or no scientific training. In addition to fingerprints, courts allowed identification testimony (the "who" question) based on the experience and presumed expertise of witnesses in such areas as handwriting comparisons, microscopic hair comparisons, blood comparisons, and bite-mark comparisons. The conclusion in such testimony was rarely couched in terms of probability. Not only was such testimony admitted, but these experts often were allowed to testify that the claimed crime scene or related item—be it fingerprints, hair, writing, bite marks, or whatever other residue investigators found—was a "match" for a similar item from the defendant and even that it was a unique match so that the defendant was the only person who could have generated the crime scene item.

Experts in other scientific areas were allowed to testify to conclusions about the origin of materials used in the commission of a crime (the "how" question) in order to tie those materials to similar items in the defendant's control. Comparison microscope examination was used as the basis for testimony that scene bullets and test bullets were fired from the same gun, or that a particular screwdriver or other tool was used to make the marks that were left at a scene, or even that the lead from a bullet at the scene came from the same batch of bullets connected to the defendant. Still other investigators were allowed to give opinion testimony about the origins or mechanism of events at a crime scene (the "how" question). They gave opinions about such things as how a fire started based on pieces of the residue that had not been destroyed in a fire, or reconstruction of the details of how a wound was inflicted based on their observations of bloodstain patterns at the scene or on the defendant.

The routine acceptance of forensic expert testimony expanded beyond areas of physical science or physical examination. Social science testimony, as distinct from physical evidence, was created and offered by the prosecutor to bolster the government's claim that an act of alleged sexual abuse had occurred (the "whether" question). Psychologists, sociologists, social workers, and even counselors or police officers were allowed by courts to give their opinion that the testimony, or other conduct, of a complainant was consistent with the testimony and behavior of other persons who had been abused in the manner similar to that described by the complainant. The clear purpose of that testimony, regardless of any instructional limitation given by the judge, was not only that the alleged abuse occurred, but that the complainant was telling the truth about how it occurred. On the other end of that spectrum, however, courts were not allowing social scientists proffered by the defense to testify as to the unreliability of eyewitness testimony, either generally or under conditions similar to those that existed at the scene of an alleged crime.

Some forensic science and technology developments were created specifically for use in criminal justice investigation and adjudication. Fingerprint and firearm comparisons are good examples. Other forensic evidence originated in scientific and technical fields, particularly medicine, and later found often unexpected applications in the criminal justice arena. Blood typing and DNA are two obvious examples.

Fingerprint comparison has been accepted as evidence in criminal prosecutions for over one hundred years. Early visual analysis gave way to a range of techniques for finding and enhancing prints, and for locating comparison prints from a computerized database. Comparison of handwriting samples is also one of the earliest types of forensic evidence. Although it was offered in courts even before the twentieth century, it was not widely accepted as scientific evidence until it became part of the cornerstone of the prosecution case in *State v. Hauptmann*,[2] the Lindbergh kidnapping case.

DNA profiling started as a method of determining paternity. The first use of DNA in a successful U.S. criminal prosecution was in *Andrews v. State*[3] and the admission of DNA evidence in a criminal case was first approved by a state supreme court in *State v. Woodall*.[4] Properly collected and analyzed DNA evidence is now routinely admitted in every jurisdiction. DNA is probably the most important forensic science development in the twentieth century. DNA has become the "gold standard" of forensic scientific evidence and DNA typing is now universally recognized as the standard against which many other forensic individualization techniques are judged.

The development of DNA as the most important type of forensic science evidence has had a significant impact on other forms of scientific evidence. DNA testing also has the remarkable ability, in the right circumstances, to provide conclusive exculpatory evidence after conviction when specimens were not tested at the time of trial. The postconviction power of DNA testing is attributable to the same characteristics of the technology that has made it so valuable during investigation and trial. The durability of DNA permits reliable testing years after the incident, and the polymorphism of DNA sequence systems greatly increases the probability of a conclusive exculpatory result. The highly publicized Innocence Project reports that, as of the end of 2009, there have been 248 postconviction exonerations by DNA testing in the United States.[5]

While the emergence of forensic DNA evidence has proven to be a dramatically positive aspect of new breakthroughs in science and technology, one unanticipated effect is that those same new scientific analyses have cast doubt on some of the more traditional types of forensic scientific evidence that trial judges have long treated as reliable and generally accepted. New scientific methods have caused some courts to reassess the validity of such things as serology testing, comparative bullet lead analysis, bite-mark identification, handwriting analysis, hair and fiber analysis, and tool-mark and ballistics testimony. Postconviction DNA testing itself has resulted in proof of wrongful convictions that were based on seemingly reliable non-DNA forensic scientific evidence.[6] For example, 22 percent of the first two hundred postconviction DNA exonerations were from convictions that had been based on false hair or fiber comparisons, and almost 40 percent had been based on serology evidence.[7] Perhaps most disturbing is new scientific evidence that fingerprint comparison may not be entitled to the weight that courts and jurors have long ascribed to it.

These exonerations are undisputable proof of the "documented ills" of other forms of scientific evidence, including such traditionally admitted forms of evidence as fingerprints. They have provided some of the impetus for the reexamination of those disciplines in light of the *Daubert* criteria.

  CASE STUDY

The First American Court to Admit DNA Evidence: *Tommy Lee Andrews v. State of Florida,* 533 So.2d 841 (1988)

Opinion by Judge Orfinger, on appeal:

"In the early morning hours of February 21, 1987, the victim was awakened when someone jumped on top of her and held what felt like a straight edge razor to her neck. The intruder, who the victim could only identify at trial as a strong, black male, held his hand over her mouth, told her to keep quiet and threatened to kill her if she saw his face. The victim struggled with the intruder and for her efforts was cut on her face, neck, legs and feet.

The intruder then forced vaginal intercourse with the victim, following which he stole her purse containing about $40, and then left the house. A physical examination made after the attack was reported to the police [and] revealed the presence of semen in the victim's vagina.

A crime lab analyst testified that both the victim and appellant 843 were blood type O but that appellant like a majority of the population is a secretor (secretes his blood type in his saliva and other body fluids) while the victim was not. Blood type O was found in the vaginal swabs taken from the victim, though the analyst conceded that while this result could have come from the semen found in the victim's vagina, it also could have come from the victim's blood picked up by the swab. The analyst concluded that appellant was included in the population (which he stated constituted 65% of the male population) that could be the source of the semen.

A crime scene technician testified that on the morning following the crime one of the windows of the victim's house was open, and the screen was missing. The victim had testified that this window had been broken previously and was held together with wire from a coat hanger. A screen was found on the ground and fingerprints were lifted from it. A fingerprint expert testified that two of the prints lifted from the screen matched appellant's right index and middle finger.

Over objection, the state presented DNA print identification evidence linking appellant to the crime. The DNA test compared the appellant's DNA structure as found in his blood with the DNA structure of the victim's blood and the DNA found in the vaginal swab, taken from the victim shortly after the attack. The test was conducted by Lifecodes Corp., a corporation specializing in DNA identity testing. Dr. Baird of Lifecodes testified to a match between the DNA in appellant's blood and the DNA from the vaginal swab, stating that the percentage of the population which would have the DNA bands indicated by the samples would be 0.0000012%. In other words, the chance that the DNA strands found in appellant's blood would be duplicated in some other person's cells was 1 in 839,914,540."

The Florida Appeals Court unanimously held:

"The trial court did not abuse its discretion in ruling the test results admissible in this case. In contrast to evidence derived from hypnosis, truth serum and polygraph, evidence derived from DNA print identification appears based on proven scientific principles. Indeed, there was testimony that such evidence has been used to exonerate those suspected of criminal activity. Given the evidence in this case that the test was administered in conformity with accepted scientific procedures so as to ensure to the greatest degree possible a reliable result, appellant has failed to show error on this point."

CASE STUDY

The First DNA Exoneration: Kirk Bloodsworth*

On July 25, 1984, a nine-year-old girl was found dead in a wooded area in Baltimore County, Maryland. She had been beaten with a rock, sexually assaulted, and strangled. Based on a tip from an anonymous caller, police arrested an honorably discharged former Marine, Kirk Bloodsworth. On March 8, 1985, he was convicted of sexual assault, rape, and first-degree premeditated murder. He was sentenced to death.

At his trial, five witnesses testified that they had seen Bloodsworth with the little girl. A witness identified Bloodsworth from a police sketch compiled by the five witnesses. There was evidence that Bloodsworth had told acquaintances he had done something "terrible" that day that would affect his marriage. Police testified that in his first interrogation, Bloodsworth mentioned a "bloody rock," even though no weapons were known of at the time. Testimony was given that a shoe impression found near the victim's body was made by a shoe that matched Bloodsworth's shoe size but that there were no other distinguishing features.

On appeal in 1986 Bloodsworth claimed that he mentioned the bloody rock only because the police had one on the table next to him while they interrogated him, that the "terrible" thing mentioned to friends was that he had failed to buy his wife a taco salad as he had promised, and that police had withheld information from his defense that they also had another suspect. The Maryland Court of Appeals overturned Bloodsworth's conviction in July 1986 because of the withheld information and ordered a new trial. At the second trial, a jury convicted him again. This time Bloodsworth was sentenced to two consecutive life terms. His appeal from the second conviction was denied.

Bloodsworth's attorney then requested to have the physical evidence released for more sophisticated testing than was available at the time of trial. The prosecution agreed, and in April 1992 the victim's pant-

*Based on *Convicted by Juries, Exonerated by Science: Case Studies in the Use of DNA Evidence to Establish Innocence After Trial* (Washington, D.C.: U.S. Department of Justice, Office of Justice Programs, National Institute of Justice, 1996), available online at http://www.ojp.usdoj.gov/nij/pubs-sum/161258 .htm; Susan Levine, "Ex-Death Row Inmate Hears Hoped-for Words: We Found Killer," *Washington Post*, September 6, 2003, A01; Nick Madigan, "Brobst, known as tough prosecutor, named Baltimore County circuit judge," *Baltimore Sun*, December 17, 2009, available online at http://www.baltimoresun .com/news/maryland/baltimore-county/bal-md.co.brobst17dec17,0,261340.story.

ies and shorts, a stick found near the murder scene, reference blood samples from Bloodsworth and the victim, and an autopsy slide were sent to Forensic Science Associates for DNA testing. The lab report was issued on May 17, 1993, and concluded that Bloodsworth's DNA did not match any of the evidence received for testing but the lab requested a fresh sample of Bloodsworth's blood for retesting. On June 3, 1993, the lab issued a second report that restated its findings that Bloodsworth could not be responsible for the semen stain on the victim's underwear. On June 25, 1993, the FBI conducted its own test of the evidence and discovered the same results.

Prosecutors joined a petition with Bloodsworth's attorneys to grant Bloodsworth a pardon. A Baltimore County circuit judge ordered

FIGURE 1.1.
Kirk Bloodsworth.
National Library of Medicine.

Bloodsworth released from prison on June 28, 1993. Maryland's governor pardoned Bloodsworth in December 1993. Bloodsworth had served almost nine years of the second sentence, including two years on death row.

Almost ten years later, in May of 2003, a police laboratory biologist again looked at the physical evidence and almost immediately identified new semen stains for analysis. A private lab tested the new sample and the results were entered into the national DNA database. The evidence matched the DNA of a man named Kimberly Shay Ruffner, who had been arrested on charges of robbery and attempted rape and murder a few weeks after Bloodsworth's arrest in 1984. It appeared that the real murderer had been, in effect, hiding behind bars since a month after the crime. It turned out that during several of those years, Bloodsworth and Ruffner lived only one floor and a couple of cells apart in one of the state's maximum security prisons and in fact had lifted weights together. The two never talked about why Bloodsworth was in prison, but Bloodsworth is sure Ruffner knew.

On May 20, 2004, Ruffner pled guilty to the murder for which Bloodsworth had been wrongfully convicted. The prosecutor who twice convicted Bloodsworth was subsequently appointed by the Maryland governor to be a trial judge in Baltimore County. Of Bloodsworth, she said, "He served years of his life in prison for a crime he didn't commit. And that's wrong, but it made me a better prosecutor then, and it's going to make me a better judge now because, of all people, I am mindful of how serious a business this is and how greatly it impacts lives."

Bloodsworth has become a program officer for The Justice Project's Campaign for Criminal Justice Reform and The Justice Project Education Fund. He was an ardent supporter of the "Innocence Protection Act," which was signed into law on October 30, 2004, as part of the larger "Justice for All Act" of 2004. It established the "Kirk Bloodsworth Post-Conviction DNA Testing Program," which helps states defray the costs of postconviction DNA testing. He has become a national spokesperson educating the public on issues surrounding wrongful convictions and an advocate against capital punishment.

Further Reading

Junkin, Tim. *Bloodsworth: The True Story of the First Death Row Inmate Exonerated by DNA*. New York: Shannon Ravenel Books, 2004.

2

The Problem of Junk Science:
Frye and the *Daubert Trilogy*

T HE ROLE OF THE TRIAL JUDGE AS THE GATEKEEPER to determine which forms of scientific forensic evidence are appropriate for consideration by the jury is now firmly entrenched in our law. Although states differ as to the implementation of that role, all have adopted the gatekeeper concept. Some states still use the test established in *Frye v. United States*,[1] which proposed that scientific evidence needed to be sufficiently established so that it had gained "general acceptance" in the relevant scientific community.[2] Federal courts and many states, however, use a revised admissibility standard first announced by the Supreme Court of the United States in *Daubert v. Merrell Dow Pharmaceuticals, Inc.*[3] *Daubert* and two subsequent Supreme Court amplifications, *General Electric Co. v. Joiner*[4] and *Kumho Tire Co. v. Carmichael*,[5] are commonly referred to as the *Daubert trilogy* and speak directly to the court's role in the admissibility of scientific evidence as expert testimony.

In *Daubert*, the Supreme Court of the United States held that the newly enacted federal rules of evidence superseded *Frye's* general acceptance test, and the Court directed the courts to examine the principles and methodology of proffered scientific evidence and not just whether its conclusions were accepted in the scientific community.[6] The Court held that when faced with a proffer of expert scientific testimony under Rule 702, the trial judge must make a preliminary assessment of whether the testimony's underlying reasoning or methodology is scientifically valid and can be properly applied to the facts at issue. The Court suggested that the criteria for making that decision included whether the proffered theory has been tested, whether it "has been subjected to peer review," its error rate, the existence of standards controlling its operation, and whether it has acceptance within the relevant scientific community. The Court made it clear that the focus is on the principles and methodology of the scientific proposition and not on the proffered conclusions.

Subsequently, however, Justice Rehnquist seemed to muddy the waters of the standards. In *Joiner,* the trial judge rejected the testimony of plaintiff's proffered experts that linked his cancer to polychlorinated biphenyls (PCBs) manufactured by the defendants and granted summary judgment.[7] The plaintiff claimed that the judge had focused on the experts' conclusions, rather than on their methodology, contrary to the clear admonitions of *Daubert.* The Court disagreed and upheld the trial judge's decision:

> Respondent points to *Daubert's* language that the "focus, of course, must be solely on principles and methodology, not on the conclusions that they generate. . . ." He claims that because the District Court's disagreement was with the conclusion that the experts drew from the studies, the District Court committed legal error and was properly reversed by the Court of Appeals. But conclusions and methodology are not entirely distinct from one another. Trained experts commonly extrapolate from existing data. But nothing in either *Daubert* or the Federal Rules of Evidence requires a district court to admit opinion evidence that is connected to existing data only by the *ipse dixit* of the expert. *A court may conclude that there is simply too great an analytical gap between the data and the opinion proffered.*[8]

Thus, *Joiner* clearly indicates that the trial judge gatekeeper has the discretion to totally reject and disallow an expert's opinion, even if based on an accepted methodology, if the judge finds that the expert's conclusion is not reliably based on that methodology.

In *Kumho,* the Court expanded its *Daubert* ruling and again indicated that significant deference was to be given to trial judges in the exercise of their gatekeeping role. In this defective tire case, the trial court granted summary judgment for defendants after finding that the opinions of plaintiff's expert engineer were not based on a method that the judge found to be "sufficiently reliable."[9] In its opinion, the Court first made it clear that the *Daubert* analysis was to be applied to evidence proffered by all experts, not only by scientists.[10] Second, the Court reinforced the *Joiner* holding that trial judges are permitted to examine whether an expert's conclusions are sufficiently reliable, even if based on a proper and accepted methodology.

Unfortunately, *Daubert's* application in criminal cases has raised serious issues about whether the courts apply the standards as rigorously when prosecutors introduce forensic evidence to prove guilt as when plaintiffs in civil cases use it to prove civil liability. And there may be some demonstrable validity to the charge.[11] The National Research Council of the National Academy of Sciences recently completed a congressionally authorized study of the use of forensic science in the criminal justice system.[12] After examining the current use of forensic evidence in criminal prosecutions and the *Daubert* reliance on the adversarial process for determining the admissibility of such evidence, the researchers were extremely critical of the current system and stated:

> The report finds that the existing legal regime—including the rules governing the admissibility of forensic evidence, the applicable standards governing appellate review of trial court decisions, the limitations of the adversary process, and judges and lawyers who often lack the scientific expertise necessary to comprehend and evaluate forensic science—is inadequate to the task of curing the documented ills of the forensic science disciplines.[13]

Adequate or not, *Daubert* is nevertheless the process that most criminal court trial judges must use, at least for the time being.

Rules of Evidence and Tests Applied by States[14]

State	State Rule	Admissibility Test
Alabama	Ala. R. Evid. Rule 702	*Daubert* for DNA; *Frye* for all else
Alaska	Alaska R. Evid. 702	*Daubert*
Arizona	Ariz. R. Evid. R. 702	*Frye*
Arkansas	A.R.E. 702	*Daubert*
California	Cal. Evid. Code §720	*Kelly/Frye*
Colorado	C.R.E. 702	*Daubert*
Connecticut	Conn. Code Evid. §7-2	*Daubert*
D.C.	N/A	*Frye*
Delaware	Del. Uniform R. Evid. 702	*Daubert*
Florida	Fla. Stat. § 90.702	*Frye*
Georgia	O.C.G.A. § 24-9-67.1	*Daubert*
Hawaii	Haw. Rev. Stat. Ann. § 702	Some *Daubert* factors
Idaho	I.R.E. Rule 702	*Daubert*
Illinois	There is no substantial equivalent to Fed. R. Evid. 702	*Frye*
Indiana	Ind. R. Evid. 702	*Daubert*
Iowa	Iowa R. Evid. 702	*Daubert*
Kansas	K.S.A. § 60-456	*Frye*
Kentucky	Ky. R. Evid. 702	*Daubert*

(*continued*)

Rules of Evidence and Tests Applied by States (*continued*)

State	State Rule	Admissibility Test
Louisiana	La. C.E. Art. 702	*Daubert*
Maine	Me. R. Evid. 702	Some *Daubert* factors
Maryland	Md. R. Evid. 5-702	*Frye*
Massachusetts	N/A	*Daubert*
Michigan	Mich. R. Evid. 702	*Daubert*
Minnesota	Minn. R. Evid. 702	*Frye/Mack*
Mississippi	Miss. R. Evid. Rule 702	*Daubert*
Missouri	Mo. Rev. Stat. § 490.065(1)	Unique test for civil; *Frye* for criminal
Montana	Mont. R. Evid. 702	*Daubert*
Nebraska	Neb. Rev. Stat. § 27-702	*Daubert*
Nevada	Nev. Rev. Stat. Ann. §50.275	*Daubert* "may provide persuasive authority"
New Hampshire	N.H. R. Evid. 702	*Daubert* (although N.H. courts have applied Frye to DNA evidence)
New Jersey	N.J. R. Evid. 702	*Daubert* for toxic tort cases, certain medical causation cases, Frye other civil cases; Frye for criminal cases
New Mexico	N.M. R.E. 11-702	*Daubert*
New York	N.Y. C.P.L.R. §4515	*Frye*
North Carolina	N.C. Gen. Stat. § 8C-1	Some *Daubert* factors
North Dakota	N.D. R. Evid. 702	*Frye*
Ohio	Ohio R. Evid. 702	*Daubert*
Oklahoma	12 Okl. St. § 2702	*Daubert*
Oregon	Oregon R. Evid. 40.410	Applies a multifactor test that includes the *Daubert* factors
Pennsylvania	Penn. R. Evid. 702	*Frye*
Rhode Island	R.I. R. Evid. 702	*Daubert*
South Carolina	Rule 702, SCRE	*Daubert* factors
South Dakota	S.D. R. Evid. 702 (SDCL § 19-15-2)	*Daubert*
Tennessee	Tenn. R. Evid. Rule 702	*Daubert* factors
Texas	Tex. Evid. R. 702	Some *Daubert* factors
Utah	Utah R. Evid. Rule 702	Unique test
Vermont	Vermont R. of Evid. 702	*Daubert*
Virginia	Va. Code Ann. §8.02-401.1	Unique test
Washington	Wash. R. Evid. 702	*Frye*
West Virginia	W. Va. R. Evid. 702	*Daubert*
Wisconsin	Wis. Stat. Ann. § 907.02	Unique test
Wyoming	Wyo. R. Evid. 702	*Daubert*

CASE STUDY

A Short Polygraph Case Becomes a Landmark Rule of Forensic Evidence

The so-called *Frye test* of "general acceptance" was the standard for the admissibility of scientific evidence in both federal and state courts for over seventy years and is still used in several state courts. Surprisingly, this landmark standard was not established by the United States Supreme Court or even a state Supreme Court. It arose from a decision of an intermediate District of Columbia court of appeals decision in a murder prosecution. At his trial the defendant attempted to introduce the results of an early version of a lie detector, or polygraph, test, known as a *systolic blood pressure deception test,* to prove his innocence. The trial judge did not allow the jury to hear the evidence and the defendant appealed his murder conviction on that basis. The entire opinion is less than 650 words long, but had a long-lasting impact on the future of scientific evidence in court.

Frye v. United States, 54 App. D. C. 46, 293 F. 1013 (1923)

Court of Appeals of District of Columbia

Before SMYTH, Chief Justice, VAN ORSDEL, Associate Justice, and MARTIN, Presiding Judge of the United States Court of Customs Appeals.

VAN ORSDEL, Associate Justice. Appellant, defendant below, was convicted of the crime of murder in the second degree, and from the judgment prosecutes this appeal.

A single assignment of error is presented for our consideration. In the course of the trial, counsel for defendant offered an expert witness to testify to the result of a deception test made upon defendant. The test is described as the *systolic blood pressure deception test.* It is asserted that blood pressure is influenced by change in the emotions of the witness, and that the systolic blood pressure rises are brought about by nervous impulses sent to the sympathetic branch of the autonomic nervous system. Scientific experiments, it is claimed, have demonstrated that fear, rage, and pain always produce a rise of systolic blood pressure, and that conscious deception or falsehood, concealment of facts, or guilt of crime, accompanied by fear of detection when the person is under examination, raises the systolic blood pressure in a curve, which corresponds exactly to the struggle going on in the subject's mind, between fear and attempted control of that fear, as the examination touches the vital points in respect of which he is attempting to deceive the examiner.

In other words, the theory seems to be that truth is spontaneous, and comes without conscious effort, while the utterance of a falsehood requires a conscious effort, which is reflected in the blood pressure. The rise thus produced is easily detected and distinguished from the rise produced by mere fear of the examination itself. In the former instance, the pressure rises higher than in the latter, and is more pronounced as the examination proceeds, while in the latter case, if the subject is telling the truth, the pressure registers highest at the beginning of the examination, and gradually diminishes as the examination proceeds.

Prior to the trial defendant was subjected to this deception test, and counsel offered the scientist who conducted the test as an expert to testify to the results obtained. The offer was objected to by counsel for the government, and the court sustained the objection. Counsel for defendant then offered to have the proffered witness conduct a test in the presence of the jury. This also was denied.

Counsel for defendant, in their able presentation of the novel question involved, correctly state in their brief that no cases directly in point have been found. The broad ground, however, upon which they plant their case, is succinctly stated in their brief as follows:

> The rule is that the opinions of experts or skilled witnesses are admissible in evidence in those cases in which the matter of inquiry is such that inexperienced persons are unlikely to prove capable of forming a correct judgment upon it, for the reason that the subject-matter so far partakes of a science, art, or trade as to require a previous habit or experience or study in it, in order to acquire a knowledge of it. When the question involved does not lie within the range of common experience or common knowledge, but requires special experience or special knowledge, then the opinions of witnesses skilled in that particular science, art, or trade to which the question relates are admissible in evidence.

Numerous cases are cited in support of this rule. Just when a scientific principle or discovery crosses the line between the experimental and demonstrable stages is difficult to define. Somewhere in this twilight zone the evidential force of the principle must be recognized, and while courts will go a long way in admitting expert testimony deduced from a well-recognized scientific principle or discovery, *the thing from which*

the deduction is made must be sufficiently established to have gained
general acceptance in the particular field in which it belongs.

We think the systolic blood pressure deception test has not yet gained
such standing and scientific recognition among physiological and psychological authorities as would justify the courts in admitting expert
testimony deduced from the discovery, development, and experiments
thus far made.

The judgment is affirmed.

[emphasis added]

CASE STUDY

The Judge as Gatekeeper: *Daubert v. Merrell Dow Pharmaceuticals,* 509 U.S. 579 (1993)

In the 1950s, American doctors began prescribing an antinausea drug
called *Bendectin* to pregnant women who were experiencing morning
sickness. Benedictin was prescribed to more than thirty-five million
American women between 1956 and 1983, when it was withdrawn
from the market. The drug was manufactured by Merrell Dow Pharmaceutical Company. Many children of women who had taken Bendectin
were born with serious birth defects and their parents believed that the
defects were caused by the drug.

Jason Daubert and Eric Schuller were two of the children who were
born with serious birth defects. They and their parents sued Merrell
Dow, alleging that their birth defects had been caused by their mothers'
ingestion of Bendectin. The company moved for summary judgment,
claiming that there was no admissible evidence that Bendectin caused
birth defects. Merrell Dow submitted an affidavit of a well-credentialed
physician epidemiologist, Steven H. Lamm. He stated that he had reviewed all the literature in the area—more than thirty published studies
involving over 130,000 patients—and that no study had found Bendectin to be capable of causing birth defects. The plaintiffs did not deny
that the previously published studies were as Lamm characterized them.
Instead, they submitted the testimony of eight well-credentialed experts
of their own who testified that Bendectin can cause birth defects. Their
conclusions were based upon animal studies, pharmacological studies

FIGURE 2.1.
Justice Harry A. Blackmun.
Library of Congress.

of the chemical structure of Bendectin, and the reanalysis of some of the prior published epidemiological studies.

The trial judge applied the "general acceptance" *Frye* test and granted the motion for summary judgment. The judge held that plaintiffs' expert testimony based on the animal studies and the recalculations of previous human study data was not admissible because it had not been published in professional journals. The plaintiffs appealed but the Ninth Circuit Court of Appeals affirmed the ruling for the defendant and held that the plaintiffs' evidence was not admissible because it was "unpublished, not subjected to the normal peer review process and generated solely for use in litigation."

On further appeal, the Supreme Court held that the recently adopted Federal Rules of Evidence superseded and replaced the *Frye* "general acceptance" test. Rule 702 states:

> If scientific, technical, or other specialized knowledge will assist the trier of fact to understand the evidence or to determine a fact in issue, a witness qualified as an expert by knowledge, skill, experience, training, or education, may testify thereto in the form of an opinion or otherwise.

Justice Blackmun wrote:

> Nothing in the text of this Rule establishes "general acceptance" as an absolute prerequisite to admissibility. Nor does respondent present any clear indication that Rule 702 or the Rules as a whole were intended to incorporate a "general acceptance" standard. The drafting history makes no mention of *Frye*, and a rigid "general acceptance" requirement would be at odds with the "liberal thrust" of the Federal Rules and their "general approach of relaxing the traditional barriers to 'opinion' testimony."

But he quickly added:

> That the *Frye* test was displaced by the Rules of Evidence does not mean, however, that the Rules themselves place no limits on the admissibility of purportedly scientific evidence. Nor is the trial judge disabled from screening such evidence. To the contrary, under the Rules the trial judge must ensure that any and all scientific testimony or evidence admitted is not only relevant, but reliable.

Rather, the Court said that the judge must decide "whether the reasoning or methodology underlying the testimony is scientifically valid" and "whether that reasoning or methodology properly can be applied to the facts in issue." The Court suggested several factors to be considered, including whether the reasoning and methodology has been or can be scientifically tested, its known error rate, and whether it has published in professional journals (although the Court clearly stated that publication "is not a *sine qua non of admissibility*"). Because the lower courts had not applied the proper test of admissibility, the Supreme Court sent the case back to them "for further proceedings consistent with this opinion."

The plaintiffs' victory in the Supreme Court was short lived. On remand, rather than sending the case back to the trial court for a jury trial, the Ninth Circuit decided to reconsider its earlier opinion and apply what the authoring judge, Judge Kozinski, interpreted as the new Supreme Court test. Emphasizing the fact, not discussed by the Supreme Court, that the plaintiffs' expert evidence was prepared for litigation rather than being the result of benign research, he again affirmed the trial court's summary judgment for the pharmaceutical company. The Supreme Court refused to hear an appeal of that ruling. In spite of the Supreme Court's earlier decision, the result was that the plaintiffs were never allowed to have a jury decide whether their birth defects were caused by Bendectin.

3

DNA: The New Gold Standard

Admissibility of DNA at Trial

DNA IS THE MOLECULAR STRUCTURE IN ALL living things that contains their genetic information.[1] DNA evidence is very durable and can be extracted from the smallest of remains many years after a crime.[2] Equally significant is its "polymorphism," meaning that, depending on the method used for its extraction, it is unique among humans and can identify the donor of the specimen with overwhelming accuracy. DNA testing can be extremely precise and can often demonstrate that only one person in billions could have been the source of the specimen evidence.[3]

DNA profiling started "as a method of determining paternity."[4] The first use of DNA in a successful U.S. criminal prosecution was in *Andrews v. State,*[5] a case in which police matched DNA samples from semen to the defendant's blood in a rape case.[6] The admission of DNA evidence in a criminal case was first approved by a state supreme court in *State v. Woodall.*[7] Subsequently, properly collected and analyzed DNA evidence has been routinely admitted.[8] DNA test results are now admissible in virtually every jurisdiction.[9] DNA matching has almost totally replaced blood typing for identification purposes and is probably the most important forensic science development in the twentieth century.[10] Thirteen states have even adopted statutes authorizing admission of DNA evidence.[11]

While the National Academy of Sciences report was critical of the basis for some other types of forensic evidence, there is no remaining doubt about the reliability of properly performed DNA analysis. The report found that "[a]mong existing forensic methods, only nuclear DNA (nDNA) analysis has been rigorously shown to have the capacity to consistently, and with a high degree of certainty, demonstrate a connection between an evidentiary sample and a specific individual or source." DNA evidence is now universally admitted by courts in the United States because of its reliability and the fact that, absent fraud or an error in labeling or handling, the probabilities of a false positive are miniscule.[12]

Other than issues of laboratory procedures and safeguards, which present themselves in all forensic science cases, the admissibility questions concerning DNA that remain today arise mainly from the development and discovery of new methods of DNA analysis. We are in what has been described as the "fifth phase" of the judicial evaluation of DNA admissibility.[13] The nDNA method is the most discriminating test, while mitochondrial DNA testing is less so.[14] DNA testing does not really produce a match between two samples, but instead describes the statistical likelihood that the evidence sample came from someone other than the defendant. Three common methods are used to generate DNA profiles: restriction fragment length polymorphism, polymerase chain reaction (PCR), and short tandem repeats test.[15]

Results obtained through PCR-based DNA methods are being offered regularly, and the only remaining question for trial judges is whether those methods have a solid scientific foundation or are generally accepted in the scientific community. Current opinions are almost unanimous that PCR-based laboratory procedures satisfy standards of admissibility under *Frye* or *Daubert* evaluations.[16] Courts in more than thirty-five states have specifically admitted evidence based on the PCR method of amplifying DNA.[17] Use of the now common "product rule" for testing the frequency of genotypes in the population in PCR-based tests is widely recognized as both scientifically sound and generally accepted. More than twenty-five states have admitted evidence of accompanying population frequency statistics.

The value of DNA evidence goes beyond proving identity. DNA evidence may be used by the prosecutor to prove or corroborate many elements of the charged crime. Prosecutors have been urged to use DNA evidence "just as any other form or type of evidence—to corroborate, validate and/or impeach evidence or testimony."[18] The location of a tested specimen of blood or other evidence may corroborate a complainant's description of where the offense occurred or could be used to refute a defense claim of alibi. The location of DNA tested samples may show single sources or mixed DNA from both the complainant and the defendant and may demonstrate a sequence of events. DNA evidence may even be offered by the prosecutor to show purpose or intent. DNA evidence may also be offered as impeachment of a defendant's testimony or earlier statements or to enhance the credibility of a complainant.

Although DNA profiling is clearly scientifically superior to other forensic identification evidence, it is not infallible.[19] DNA evidence and its underlying methodology are, of course, subject to human error. False-positive DNA results have occurred and will undoubtedly continue to be part of the DNA testing landscape.[20] Proffered evidence may still, as with other forensic science evidence, be the result of mistakes or contamination in its collection, testing, or interpretation.[21] As the technology and methodology of DNA testing has progressed, it is the human errors that may present the biggest evidentiary challenges for trial judges. DNA evidence has been recently challenged on a variety of factors, including poor laboratory proficiency testing, contamination, lack of proper laboratory protocols or accreditation, improper techniques, lack of quality control, and broken chains of custody. Laboratory temperature variances are a source of challenge because DNA is very sensitive to environmental conditions and can "start to degrade depending on the sample's exposure to extreme temperatures, oxygen, water, sweat, and breath."[22] If the sample evidence is contaminated before PCR amplification, the identity of the donor may be masked by overamplification.[23] Before and at the laboratory, DNA testing errors result from sample mislabeling, or otherwise switching samples, or from cross-contamination between samples in the same or different cases.[24]

Currently, the immense demand for DNA testing by police and prosecutors may inadvertently pose the most serious threat to its use in criminal trials. The overwhelming demand may be resulting in poor laboratory practices by inexperienced or overworked technicians to the degree that confidence in DNA test results is affected. For example, the Department of Justice Inspector General officially reported that the Federal Bureau of Investigation laboratory still "was riddled with flawed scientific practices that had potentially tainted dozens of criminal cases, including the bombings of the Federal Building in Oklahoma City and the World Trade Center in New York."[25] Suspected and documented cases of poor practices and false reports by forensic scientists at various state and local crime laboratories have been rampant.[26]

The reality is that there are few accepted standards for the performance and practices of forensic science laboratories, either public or private. The National Academy of Sciences report recommends significant strengthening of the oversight of crime laboratories in light of the fact "that there are no requirements, except in a few states (New York, Oklahoma, and Texas), for forensics laboratories to meet specific standards for quality assurance or for practitioners to be certified according to an agreed set of standards." Trial judges are the primary guardians of the integrity of scientific evidence that is sought to be introduced to prove guilt. When it comes to DNA evidence, the gatekeeper role assigned to trial judges may find its most important function not in an evaluation of the reliability or general acceptance of new scientific theory, but rather in the very traditional functions of ensuring that proffered evidence meets basic standards of authenticity, relevance, and reliability in the particular application of a scientific theory.

Deficiencies in a particular application may be found to go more to weight than admissibility. Nevertheless, when it comes to human error, particularly of the types recently reported, the application may indeed be "so altered" as to skew the results beyond the limits of admissibility. It would be a mistake to assume, as the public is wont to do, that all proffered DNA evidence is genuine, reliable, and admissible. As the Gallup poll reported in 2005:

> More than 8 in 10 Americans (85%) think DNA evidence is either completely (27%) or very (58%) reliable. A majority considered it reliable when Gallup first asked the question in 2000; the percentage backing the reliability of DNA has increased since then.[27]

DNA evidence, like other types of forensic evidence, is subject to laboratory and other errors. In performing the gatekeeper role, trial judges will need to demand more than mere testimony of a genetic match and not disregard the apparently distinct possibility of human error.[28]

Postconviction DNA Testing

The availability of DNA testing has given rise to numerous postconviction requests for DNA testing on the basis that it could produce important exculpatory evidence. Many states have responded with legislation addressing the standards for those requests, and courts will continue to deal with such requests for some time.

DNA testing has a remarkable ability, in the right circumstances, to provide conclusive exculpatory evidence after conviction in cases in which specimens were not tested at the time of trial.[29] The postconviction power of DNA testing is attributable to the same characteristics of the technology that has made it so valuable during investigation and trial: The durability of DNA permits reliable testing years after the incident, and the polymorphism of DNA sequence systems greatly increases the probability of a conclusive incriminating or exculpatory result.[30]

In 1999, the Department of Justice conducted a thorough study of the question of postconviction DNA testing.[31] The report of the study suggests that the requests can be viewed in the following categories: (1) "cases in which biological evidence was collected . . . still exists, [and if] subjected to DNA testing or retesting, exclusionary results will exonerate the petitioner";

(2) "cases in which biological evidence was collected . . . still exists, [and if] subjected to DNA testing or retesting, exclusionary results would support the petitioner's claim of innocence, but reasonable persons might disagree as to whether the results are exonerative"; (3) "cases in which biological evidence was collected . . . still exists, [and if] subjected to DNA testing or retesting, favorable results will be inconclusive"; (4) "cases in which biological evidence was never collected, or cannot be found despite all efforts, or was destroyed, or was preserved in such a way that it cannot be tested"; or (5) "cases in which a request for DNA testing is frivolous."[32] Trial judges will usually encounter cases in the first two categories.

Neither common law standards nor existing court rules or statutes regarding postconviction relief are considered adequate to address the prospect of postconviction DNA testing. First, those standards and rules assume that the defendant already has what is regarded as newly discovered evidence, whereas DNA motions seek relief in the form of conducting tests to obtain such evidence. Second, DNA poses the distinct possibility of completely exonerating a defendant. Third, the durability of DNA suggests that arbitrary time rules or statutory limits on postconviction motions may not be appropriate to requests for DNA testing. As a result of those concerns, the federal government and a number of states have recently enacted statutes to specifically address postconviction DNA testing motions.[33] At the federal level, the Justice For All Act[34] strengthened the right to postconviction DNA testing if convicts assert their innocence, if DNA testing would support that innocence, and if the "testing would create a reasonable probability that the applicant did not commit the offense."[35]

In states without specific DNA testing statutes or rules, the courts must rely on the general procedures governing motions for postconviction relief. Initially, the defendant in these situations is seeking postconviction discovery in the form of evidentiary samples and testing of those samples. Some courts have held that the right to some postconviction relief necessarily implies a right to postconviction discovery.[36] Other state courts have held that *Brady v. Maryland,* guaranteeing a defendant the constitutional right to be informed of exculpatory evidence,[37] carries with it the concomitant right to obtain such evidence even after conviction.[38]

The United States Supreme Court recently considered the question of whether there is a federal constitutional right to postconviction DNA testing, a matter that is especially important in states that have not enacted statutes or rules regulating postconviction DNA testing. In *District Attorney's Office v. Osborne,*[39] the Supreme Court specifically held that *Brady v. Maryland* does not apply to postconviction issues and that the federal due process clause does not guarantee postconviction DNA testing. The Supreme Court found

Alaska's general rules regarding postconviction discovery and newly discovered evidence were "not constitutionally inadequate." The result of the *Osborne* decision is to leave the procedures for access to postconviction DNA testing entirely to the states.

The track record of DNA's impact on the criminal justice process indicates that it will continue to play an important role in postconviction as well as preconviction procedures. Justice Stephen Breyer recently surveyed DNA's impact on our criminal justice system and stated:

> DNA evidence promises not only to make future criminal trials more reliable, but also to permit the reevaluation of past convictions, perhaps convictions that were secured many years ago. When should those convictions be reexamined? Are present reopening procedures adequate, in light of both the added certainty that DNA evidence can provide and of the numbers of closed cases in which potentially determinative DNA evidence might be obtained? Must the boundaries of preexisting legal rights be reshaped better to avoid the risk of imprisoning a defendant who is in fact innocent? Are new statutes needed?[40]

Access to potentially exonerating postconviction DNA testing pits our need for judicial efficiency (motivated by a desire for finality) against our constitutionally and humanely motivated desire for certainty of guilt.

CASE STUDY

DNA and "Cold Cases": *People v. Gary Leiterman*

In 1969, Washtenaw County, Michigan, had witnessed a series of murders of young women in what became known as the "Michigan Murders." On March 19, 1969, Jane Mixer was a twenty-three-year-old first-year law student at the University of Michigan. She had arranged to meet her boyfriend at her parent's home in Muskegon, Michigan, some two and a half hours away from the Ann Arbor law school, where they would announce their wedding plans. In what was a common practice at the time, she posted a note on a "ride board" in the basement of the law library seeking a ride to Muskegon. She told her boyfriend that a man who identified himself as "David Johnson" had responded to the posting and was going to pick her up at 6 p.m. on his way to Muskegon. On that evening, however, she called her boyfriend and said that Johnson had not yet appeared and she was trying to contact him from her dorm room. At approximately 10 p.m., the roommate of a fellow student named David Johnson received a telephone call from a woman who identified herself as "Janie Mixer" and inquired whether Johnson still intended to drive her to Muskegon. The roommate told the caller that Johnson was on stage performing in a campus play at that moment and was not going to Muskegon that evening.

Jane Mixer never made it to Muskegon. The next day her body was found on top of a grave in a cemetery a few miles from Ann Arbor. She had been strangled with a stocking and shot twice in the head with a .22-caliber gun. Her pantyhose had been pulled down but there was no evidence of a rape.

The public assumed that it was another of the serial murders. Subsequently, a young man named John Norman Collins was arrested and convicted of one of the earlier murders and the killings stopped. Police were not so sure.

During the Mixer investigation, state police examined her dorm room and found a phone book open to the page with listings for "David Johnson." Police determined that all of the David Johnsons associated with the university had alibis. During the investigation, one of the officers went to the area of the law library basement where the "ride board" was located. Because he also happened to be working on another case involving pay telephone fraud, he went into a pay telephone booth near the board. He saw a telephone book in the booth with the handwritten words "Mixer—Muskegeon" on the cover. He collected the phone book as evidence. The investigation, however, went nowhere and the police had no leads as to the killer. There was no DNA analysis available in 1969 and the Mixer case remained unsolved for thirty-five years.

In 2004, state police working in a "cold case" unit found the old box of evidence from the Mixer murder, including the victim's pantyhose. Some of the evidence was sent to the laboratory. On the pantyhose, the state police lab found five stains of a substance they believed was either sweat or saliva. DNA analysis from the lab was run through the Combined DNA Index System (CODIS) database and it came back with a "hit." The DNA on Mixer's pantyhose matched a sample from a Gary Leiterman, a sixty-two-year-old former nurse from the western side of Michigan who was in the national database because of a 2002 conviction for prescription fraud. The odds that the DNA on the stockings had come from someone other than Leiterman were 170 trillion to one.

The trial of Leiterman attracted the attention of the national media, and the trial was covered daily by the print media and by Court TV, which carried the entire trial live on its website. CBS covered the case

FIGURE 3.1.
Gary Leiterman.
Leiterman Case Exhibits.

nationally and later aired a one-hour episode of *48 Hours Mystery* based on the case.

Although the DNA evidence linking Leiterman to the killing was overwhelming, the prosecution had a significant problem. Photos of the Mixer body at the cemetery showed a small drop of what appeared to be blood on her forearm. Police had scraped the small remnants of the blood into an evidence envelope. When the state police lab analyzed those remnants they found DNA that they testified also found a match in the CODIS system—but not to Gary Leiterman. According to the lab, the blood spot matched the DNA of a man named John Ruelas. In 2004, Ruelas was serving a life sentence in a Michigan prison for the murder of his mother, but Ruelas was only four years old at the time of the Mixer murder and was obviously not the murderer. It turned out that the police lab was examining Ruelas's DNA in connection with his mother's murder at the same time they were analyzing the scraping from the blood spot on Jane Mixer's arm. Nevertheless, the laboratory steadfastly denied that it had contaminated the blood scraping with the Ruelas sample. The defense presented its own DNA expert who testified that he believed the samples had been cross-contaminated.

There was other evidence against Leiterman, however. The phone-book found in the law library basement had been discarded but a photograph of the cover with the handwriting on it had been saved. A govern-

FIGURE 3.2.
Blood spot analyzed as Ruelas's DNA.
Leiterman Case Exhibits.

ment handwriting expert compared the handwritten words "Mixer" and "Muskegeon" with several 1969 samples of the defendant's handwriting. He testified that it was "highly probable" that defendant wrote the words on the phonebook cover. The defense offered a handwriting expert who testified that Leiterman's samples did not match the phonebook writing.

Leiterman had lived and worked in the Ann Arbor area at the time of the killing. A former roommate testified that around that time he found a stack of newspapers kept by Leiterman on the floor of his bedroom closet. The newspapers the defendant saved all featured articles about John Norman Collins and the details of the serial "Michigan Murders." The roommate also testified that Leiterman owned a revolver and had even set up a firing range in the basement of their home. State records confirmed that in 1967 Leiterman had purchased and registered a six-shot .22-caliber Ruger revolver, which he later reported as having been stolen. During a December 2004 search of defendant's house, however, the police seized a revolver cylinder that a state police firearms expert testified was "consistent with" the construction and design of such a Ruger pistol. A state police ballistics expert testified that bullet fragments removed from Mixer's brain were "similar" to several bullets found in the 2004 search and "could have been" fired from a .22-caliber, six-shot Ruger revolver. The ballistics expert did admit, however, that there are more than three dozen models of guns capable of firing similar bullets.

Thirty witnesses testified during the two-week trial. Leiterman did not take the stand. The jury found him guilty of first-degree murder after deliberating for a few hours. The defendant hired a new lawyer and sought a new trial but the trial judge refused.

On appeal to the Michigan Court of Appeals, Leiterman claimed that the evidence of contamination was so strong that the DNA evidence was inadmissible under the *Daubert* standards used in Michigan. The defense offered the affidavit of a new DNA expert, a Dr. Kessis, who again asserted that the contamination of the blood spot scrapings made DNA evidence from the pantyhose stains unreliable. The appellate court disagreed:

> We need not, however, address the merits of Kessis' challenges to the testing conducted by the state police crime lab as to the reliability and, therefore, its admissibility. Indeed, the Court in *Daubert* specifically counseled courts to respect the differing functions of judge and jury—stating that the focus of the reliability inquiry "must be upon the principles and methodology, not on the conclusions that they generate." . . . Thus, we join those courts that have concluded that because challenges such as those raised by Kessis concern the manner in which a method is applied in a particular case rather than the validity of the method, they affect the weight that should be given to the evidence rather than its admissibility. . . .
>
> Because the type of testing employed in this case has received general acceptance as reliable, . . . any objection to its results are relevant to the weight of the testimony and not its admissibility. Indeed, the alleged errors identified by Kessis, and relied on by defendant in seeking a new trial in this matter, are insufficient to skew the otherwise reliable PCR methodology used in this case. Rather, the alleged errors strike at the weight of the evidence introduced by the prosecution. There was, therefore, no error in the admission of the testimony at trial, and the trial court did not abuse its discretion in denying defendant's motion for a new trial on that ground.

Leiterman also appealed that the handwriting analysis testimony was inadmissible under *Daubert*. Because no objection to it had been made at trial, the defense had to show that its admission was "plainly erroneous." The Court of Appeals again rejected the defense argument:

The courts of this state have long received handwriting analysis testimony as admissible evidence. See, e.g., Domzalski v Jozefiak, 257 Mich 273, 279; 241 NW 259 (1932) (noting that, while various authorities disagree on the value of handwriting comparison testimony, "all agree that it is evidence, the weight of which is for the trier of the facts"). And, [u]nder Daubert, a trial judge need not expend scarce judicial resources reexamining a familiar form of expertise every time opinion evidence is offered. In fact, if a given theory or technique is "so firmly established as to have attained the status of scientific law," then it need not be examined at all, but instead may properly be subject to judicial notice." . . .

Given the history of general acceptance of handwriting comparison testimony by the courts of this state and the absence of any express, binding authority to the contrary, we cannot conclude that the admission of such testimony at defendant's trial was plainly erroneous.

The Court also rejected Leiterman's claim that his retained trial attorney had been ineffective to the extent that a new trial was required. The conviction was affirmed. Leiterman's application for leave to appeal to the Michigan Supreme Court was denied on January 8, 2008, and he is serving a mandatory prison term of life without parole.

4

The "Who" Question

Fingerprint Evidence

FINGERPRINT COMPARISON HAS BEEN ACCEPTED as evidence in criminal prosecutions for over one hundred years.[1] Courts have accepted the proposition
that each person's fingerprint is unique and that fingerprint comparison is
almost infallible as a means of forensic identification. Fingerprint experts
often declare a positive identification, rather than a probability of identity.
Recently, that assumption of infallibility has been seriously undermined by
new scientific analysis. Postconviction DNA testing has resulted in proof of
wrongful convictions that were based on seemingly reliable non-DNA forensic scientific evidence and most disturbing is new scientific evidence that
fingerprint comparisons may not be entitled to the weight that courts and
jurors have long ascribed to it.

Analysis of the images left by prints on the fingers, palms, or soles is more
properly known as *friction ridge analysis.* Simply put, it is an examiner's comparison of impressions left by ridges on the skin in two samples. It has traditionally been used to make an identification of a person, such as during an
arrest or death investigation, or to prove that an individual touched a surface
where one of the ridge impressions was left. Early work was by a simple visual
analysis of patent, or obvious, prints left at the scene of a crime.

Skin is never completely dry or clean. Dirt, oil, or even sweat create prints
whenever a solid surface is touched. If hands are stained, they will leave a
patent (visible) print. Latent fingerprints are invisible to the naked eye, but
the forensic scientist can visualize them though a variety of means, originally

called *dusting*. Modern forensic scientists now have a range of techniques for finding latent prints, cleaning up and enhancing print images, and rapidly finding a match from a database using computer technology. Friction ridge analysis is usually performed in crime laboratories, which may or may not be accredited. The training of latent print analysts varies greatly, from a formal training program to a one- or two-week course to simple on-the-job training. No specific certification or training is required. There are manuals for training of analysts.[2]

The Fingerprint Process

Fingerprints are reproduced images of the ridged surfaces on the skin that result when oil is transferred from the skin onto the surface that was touched. Such impression evidence at the scene is generally latent (invisible to the naked eye) or patent (visible).[3] The quality of impression evidence and its eventual analysis depend a great deal on the procedures used to collect, preserve, and enhance the evidence discovered at the scene.

There are many techniques for fingerprint detection, but only about twenty are currently in use in fingerprint laboratories. There are generally three types of techniques for making latent fingerprints visible: physical, chemical, and instrumental techniques. The basic physical process for visualizing fingerprints at a scene is "dusting" the suspected area with a powder that then adheres to the oils or other matter left by the ridges. This process is most effective on smooth surfaces that do not absorb the oils. The prints revealed by the dusting can be photographed directly as shown in figure 4.1. More often the prints are "lifted" from the surface using tape and that taped image is then pressed onto and transferred to a printed card.

A common chemical technique is called *cyanoacrylate fuming*, or, more colloquially, "superglue fuming."[4] Fingerprints leave traces of amino acids, fatty acids, and proteins that will react to the fumes produced when superglue is heated. That reaction forms a sticky, white material that clings to the ridges of fingerprints, making them visible. Items to be tested are placed inside an airtight chamber, a few drops of superglue are placed into a heating tray inside the chamber, and the reaction leaves white outlines of the ridges, which can then be photographed directly or dusted, lifted, and transferred. This chemical process is especially effective on textured or other surfaces that are not very susceptible to physical visualization. The reaction is not permanent, so the print must be photographed or transferred soon after development. A print visualized by a superglue fuming technique is shown in figure 4.2.

Other chemicals also react with the chemical in the fingerprint residue and the most common chemical technique for porous surfaces today involves

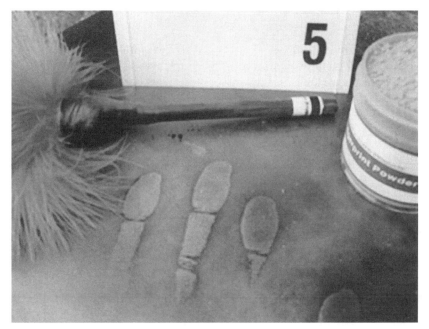

FIGURE 4.1.
Photograph of a dusted fingerprint.
Drake Group. Used by permission.

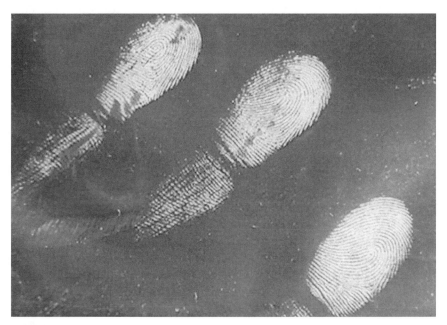

FIGURE 4.2.
Photograph of a fingerprint revealed by fuming.
Evident, Inc. Used by permission.

ninhydrin.[5] The reaction reveals prints in a high-contrast purple tone. Ninhydrin development occurs slowly at room temperature and humidity. Various treatments are then used to enhance the prints, including treatment with metal-based reagents to intensify the prints.

Other techniques have been developed and tested and each may be more appropriate in a given case depending on the conditions and the materials. For example, a recent development of an instrumental technique for fingerprint detection involves the use of a scanning Kelvin microprobe.[6] That device maps the changes in electrical impulses left when the skin comes into contact with some surfaces and displays the electrochemical images of the patterns of that contact. It requires no physical or chemical change in the suspected surface. Another even more recent development is micro-x-ray fluorescence.[7] Body salts excreted in sweat contain sodium, potassium, and chlorine that are deposited along the patterns present in a fingerprint. An image of the fingerprint can be visualized by shining a thin x-ray beam onto it without disturbing the sample. The chemical elements emit radiation at a "signature" frequency revealed in a spectrograph. An example of the images produced with this technique is shown in figure 4.3.

The other part of the fingerprinting process involves imaging and recording fingerprints of a known individual for later comparison. Inked fingerprint cards have long been accepted as the standard means for recording and storing fingerprint data. Fingerprint cards have evolved into an accepted international standard for the exchange of fingerprint identification between criminal justice agencies. The Federal Bureau of Investigation (FBI), working with the American National Standards Institute, has developed detailed specifications for taking fingerprints that are used by virtually all police agencies in the United States.[8] The techniques for taking and recording the prints are important and have also been described in detail by the FBI.[9] The impressions are recorded on a standard fingerprint identification card. The upper ten impressions—thumb, index, middle, ring, and little fingers of each hand—are taken individually. These are referred to as the *rolled* impressions because the fingers are rolled from one side of the fingernail to the other, in order to obtain all available ridge detail. The impressions at the bottom of the card are taken simultaneously without rolling, printing all of the fingers of each hand at a forty-five-degree angle, and then the thumbs. These are referred to as *plain, slapped,* or *flat* impressions. The plain impressions are used to verify the sequence and accuracy of the rolled impressions.

More recently, the FBI and many local agencies use an inkless digital system for recording fingerprints called *LiveScan*. Fingerprints are scanned into digital images, which can be electronically transmitted to the FBI and or other investigating agencies. The technology replaces the process of recording an

FIGURE 4.3.
Micro-x-ray fluorescent fingerprint images.
Courtesy of Ed Vigil, Los Alamos National Laboratory.

individual's fingerprint patterns through the ink-rolling process. It can avoid common problems with ink fingerprints such as smudging, smearing, and using too much or too little ink. The FBI has developed complex standards for digital scanning devices.[10] The federal government uses the LiveScan process exclusively, and states are slowly moving to it as well. An example of digital acquisition of fingerprints is shown in figure 4.4.

Digital devices are not without their own problems. Different types of digital scanners are available. The scanners measure the difference between the ridges and valleys using various elements such as optical or thermal differences. However, when a finger touches or rolls onto a surface, the skin may deform based on the pressure applied by the user and on skin conditions. There is also concern that the projection of an irregular, three-dimensional finger onto a two-dimensional scanner may introduce distortion. Noncontact

FIGURE 4.4.
Digital fingerprinting.
National Institute of Standards and Technology.

three-dimensional fingerprint scanners have been developed that compensate for many of these problems.[11] The FBI manages the nation's fingerprint identification system and database, which is called the *Integrated Automated Fingerprint Identification System (IAFIS)*.[12] The IAFIS maintains the largest biometric database in the world, containing the fingerprints of more than fifty-five million persons. The fingerprints and corresponding criminal history information are submitted by state, local, and federal law enforcement agencies, now mostly in digital format.

Fingerprint Analysis

The forensic science community regards friction ridge analysis as a method for assessing "individualization," the conclusion that the fingerprint impression comes unambiguously from a single person.[13] The technique used to examine fingerprints is called *Analysis, Comparison, Evaluation, and Verification (ACE-V)*.[14]

The analysis phase of the unknown print requires the examiner to consider the many factors that may affect the detail in the latent print, including the condition of the skin (aging, damage to the skin, scars, diseases, and masking attempts), the type and amount of residue (sweat, oil, blood, paint, etc.), the mechanics of the touch (pressure on the surface of the skin, flexibility of the ridges, furrows, and creases, etc.), the surface that was touched (texture, rigidity, shape, condition, and background), the development technique, the capture technique (photograph or lifting material), and the percentage of the surface available for comparison. The examiner also analyzes the known prints for factors that can affect its quality. If either print does not have sufficient detail for either identification or exclusion, the prints are considered to be "of no value" or "not suitable" for comparison.

The comparison phase is visually measuring and comparing the corresponding details in the two prints. The observations might include "the overall shape of the latent print, anatomical aspects, ridge flows, ridge counts, shape of the core, delta location and shape, lengths of the ridges, minutia location and type, thickness of the ridges and furrows, shapes of the ridges, pore position, crease patterns and shapes, scar shapes, and temporary feature shapes."

The evaluation phase requires the examiner to consider the extent of the agreement of the ridge formations in the two prints and the sufficiency of the detail present to establish an identification ("source determination").[15] A "source determination" is made when the examiner concludes that there is sufficient quantity and quality of detail in agreement between the latent print and the known print. A "source exclusion" is made when there is sufficient disagreement between the latent and known prints. If the detail is insufficient for either, it is deemed an "inconclusive comparison."

The verification phase requires that another qualified examiner repeat the observations and come to the same conclusion. However, the standard practice allows the second examiner to be aware of the conclusion of the first examiner.

In spite of the seeming formality of the fingerprint analysis process adopted by qualified examiners, the reality is that the assessment of fingerprint identification is nevertheless a subjective human interpretation. As the National Academy of Sciences report stated:

> Although some Automated Fingerprint Identification Systems (AFIS) permit fully automated identification of fingerprint records related to criminal history (e.g., for screening job applicants), the assessment of latent prints from crime scenes is based largely on human interpretation. Note that the ACE-V method does not specify particular measurements or a standard test protocol, and examiners must make subjective assessments throughout. In the United States, the threshold for making a source identification is deliberately kept subjective, so that the examiner can take into account both the quantity and quality of comparable details. As a result, the outcome of a friction ridge analysis is not necessarily repeatable from examiner to examiner. . . .

This subjectivity is intrinsic to friction ridge analysis, as can be seen when comparing it with DNA analysis. . . . For these reasons, population statistics for fingerprints have not been developed, and friction ridge analysis relies on subjective judgments by the examiner. Little research has been directed toward developing population statistics, although more would be feasible.[16]

Fingerprint examiners consider that their expertise is a matter of qualitative rather than quantitative analysis. They claim that the ability to see details in prints and the ability to compare features in prints is an "acquired skill" gained through experience and a lengthy apprenticeship.[17] They deny that it is possible to establish numerical scores or thresholds based on corresponding features because they do not determine which features are relevant until they make their initial "analysis and comparison."

Latent print examiners report a positive identification when they conclude that two different persons could not have produced the latent print. This is a subjective assessment. Although it has been suggested that examiners would be more accurate to use statistics to assign match probabilities based on population distributions of certain friction ridge features, current examiners generally refuse to do so. They claim that published statistical models only count corresponding minutiae and do not incorporate elements of clarity. The fingerprint examiner community discourages its members from testifying in terms of the probability of a match and they testify with absolute certainty that the prints could not possibly have come from two different individuals.

Fingerprint Testimony under *Frye* and *Daubert* Analyses

The challenge of *Daubert* is significant if it is to be applied to fingerprinting. On the one hand, most, if not all, of the claims made by or on behalf of fingerprint examiners enjoy unquestioning belief among the lay public, including the bench and the bar. On the other hand, little conventional science exists to support the generally accepted claims regarding fingerprint identification. Although there is debate about the number of points of similarity in fingerprints that are sufficient to declare a match, there is no generally accepted scientific or court-recognized minimum standard.[18] Proficiency testing simply does not support the zero error rate claimed by fingerprint examiners. In fact, many of the most basic tenets of fingerprint identification have never been subjected to empirical analysis. Most modern researchers who have looked into fingerprinting comparison have concluded that the broad claims of fingerprint identification accuracy cannot be substantiated.[19] As one commentator put it, the "gold standard" of fingerprinting identification may be more akin to "fool's gold."[20]

The summary assessment of fingerprint analysis on the National Academy of Sciences report was somewhat less critical but certainly casts doubt on the ready acceptance of fingerprint expert testimony:

> Historically, friction ridge analysis has served as a valuable tool, both to identify the guilty and to exclude the innocent. Because of the amount of detail available in friction ridges, it seems plausible that a careful comparison of two impressions can accurately discern whether or not they had a common source. Although there is limited information about the accuracy and reliability of friction ridge analyses, claims that these analyses have zero error rates are not scientifically plausible.
>
> ACE-V provides a broadly stated framework for conducting friction ridge analyses. However, this framework is not specific enough to qualify as a validated method for this type of analysis. ACE-V does not guard against bias; is too broad to ensure repeatability and transparency; and does not guarantee that two analysts following it will obtain the same results. For these reasons, merely following the steps of ACE-V does not imply that one is proceeding in a scientific manner or producing reliable results. . . .
>
> Better documentation is needed of each step in the ACE-V process or its equivalent. At the very least, sufficient documentation is needed to reconstruct the analysis, if necessary. By documenting the relevant information gathered during the analysis, evaluation, and comparison of latent prints and the basis for the conclusion (identification, exclusion, or inconclusive), the examiner will create a transparent record of the method and thereby provide the courts with additional information on which to assess the reliability of the method for a specific case. Currently, there is no requirement for examiners to document which features within a latent print support their reasoning and conclusions.
>
> Error rate is a much more difficult challenge. Errors can occur with any judgment-based method, especially when the factors that lead to the ultimate judgment are not documented. Some in the latent print community argue that the method itself, if followed correctly (i.e., by well-trained examiners properly using the method), has a zero error rate. Clearly, this assertion is unrealistic, and, moreover, it does not lead to a process of method improvement. The method, and the performance of those who use it, are inextricably linked, and both involve multiple sources of error (e.g., errors in executing the process steps, as well as errors in human judgment). Some scientific evidence supports the presumption that friction ridge patterns are unique to each person and persist unchanged throughout a lifetime. Uniqueness and persistence are necessary conditions for friction ridge identification to be feasible, but those conditions do not imply that anyone can reliably discern whether or not two friction ridge impressions were made by the same person. Uniqueness does not guarantee that prints from two different people are always sufficiently different that they cannot be confused, or that two impressions made by the same finger will also be sufficiently similar to be discerned as coming from the same source. The impression left by a given

finger will differ every time, because of inevitable variations in pressure, which change the degree of contact between each part of the ridge structure and the impression medium. None of these variabilities—of features across a population of fingers or of repeated impressions left by the same finger—has been characterized, quantified, or compared.[21]

Haber and Haber were less diplomatic in their review of fingerprint analysis and the comparison of multiple fingerprint conclusions, stating, "We have reviewed available scientific evidence of the validity of the ACE-V method and found none."[22] And Professor Jennifer Mnookin summarized the claims of absolute certainty by fingerprint examiners in light of *Daubert*:

> Given the general lack of validity testing for fingerprinting, the relative dearth of difficult proficiency tests, the lack of a statistically valid model of fingerprinting, and the lack of validated standards for declaring a match, such claims of absolute, certain confidence in identification are unjustified. . . . Therefore, in order to pass scrutiny under *Daubert*, fingerprint identification experts should exhibit a greater degree of epistemological humility. Claims of "absolute" and "positive" identification should be replaced by more modest claims about the meaning and significance of a "match."[23]

It seems logical that states that still use the *Frye* analysis will have little difficulty with new fingerprinting information because fingerprint identification is certainly "generally accepted" and has been for a long time. Most of the claims made by fingerprint examiners enjoy widespread belief among members of both the public and the bar. In a sense, this points up the significant limitation of the *Frye* test, in that the criminal justice systems using that test take a very long time to react to changes in science, which often can take place in a short time.

However, fingerprinting may face some challenges in *Frye* states. In the capital case of *Maryland v. Rose*,[24] the state trial judge applied Maryland's version of the *Frye* rule and, in a very detailed opinion, held that fingerprint testimony was not admissible and that the ACE-V methodology "was the type of procedure *Frye* was intended to banish, that is, a subjective, untested, unverifiable identification procedure that purports to be infallible." The Court in that case held a lengthy evidentiary hearing on admissibility, rejecting the prosecution argument that no hearing was necessary under *Frye*:

> The State's primary argument is that history favors acceptance of latent print identifications. Indeed, such identifications have been admitted for nearly one hundred years. So established is such evidence that the State opposed the Defendant's request for a *Frye-Reed* hearing. Moreover, the State requested that the Court take judicial notice of the reliability of latent print identification evidence.

The State is correct that fingerprint evidence has been used in criminal cases for almost a century. While that fact is worthy of consideration, it does not prove reliability. For many centuries, perhaps for millennia, humans thought that the earth was flat. The idea has a certain intuitive appeal. Indeed, there still exists a Flat Earth Society for people who cling to the idea the earth is not an orb. But science has proved that the earth is not flat; and it is the type of fact of which a court can take judicial notice.[25]

Daubert should clearly be a more difficult admissibility test for fingerprinting. That has not been the case. Following the state judge's exclusion of fingerprint evidence in the *Rose* case, the federal prosecutor had Rose indicted by a grand jury in federal court, where the *Daubert* standard would apply. In her brief ruling granting the government's motion *in limine* seeking to admit fingerprint evidence, even without a *Daubert* evidentiary hearing, the federal district court judge relied primarily on the Fourth Circuit holding in *United States v. Crisp*[26] and held that "fingerprint identification evidence based on the ACE-V methodology is generally accepted in the relevant scientific community, has a very low incidence of erroneous misidentifications, and is sufficiently reliable to be admissible under Fed. R. Ev. 702 generally and specifically in this case."[27]

The judge in that case had the benefit of the NAS report but found that the report "did not conclude that fingerprint evidence was unreliable such as to render it inadmissible under Fed. R. Ev. 702"[28] and she specifically rejected the Haber study error rate results, holding that "there is nothing to contradict the conclusion reached by many courts and other experts that the incidence of error in the sense of erroneous misidentification . . . is extremely rare."[29] Perhaps, as recently suggested by Professor Simon Cole, the *Frye* standard may prove to be a more stringent test for fingerprinting than *Daubert*.[30]

Indeed, the courts that have reexamined fingerprint identification under *Daubert* have either held that it passed *Daubert* muster[31] or have just continued to give it a superficial review and approval.[32] Very few have rejected or limited fingerprint examiner testimony after a *Daubert* review.[33] In *New Hampshire v. Langill*,[34] the New Hampshire Supreme Court held that the failure to conduct a blind verification phase under ACE-V was not a basis upon which fingerprint testimony could be excluded. In *United States v. Llera Plaza I*,[35] which was vacated and superseded on reconsideration in *United States v. Llera Plaza II*,[36] the federal district judge did an interesting about-face in his *Daubert* analysis of fingerprint evidence.[37] However, in view of the mounting scholarly evidence that fingerprinting may lack scientific validation, some courts have found the issue of the reliability of fingerprint comparisons is at least admissible as a jury question.[38]

It may be that the strong pro-prosecution bias of judges evaluating fingerprint admissibility in criminal cases will continue to allow fingerprint testimony to be admitted in spite of its scientific shortcomings. The rather blind acceptance of fingerprint evidence is the product of years of assumptions about its validity. Any change may only result from published DNA exonerations of persons convicted on the basis of fingerprint identification. One such case was the FBI's total misidentification of fingerprints in a multiple-murder terrorism case as those of an Oregon attorney, Brandon Mayfield, only to find later that foreign police had properly identified the prints as those of an Algerian terrorist.[39] Indeed, the federal judge in the *Rose* case felt it necessary to dismiss the *Mayfield* case as "extremely rare" and even claimed that it demonstrates the validity of ACE-V because the Spanish police caught the error.[40] The Innocence Project has disclosed other wrongful convictions based at least in part on erroneous fingerprint evidence.[41]

Any erosion of the admissibility of fingerprint evidence is likely to be slow. However, the federal courts and those state courts that have adopted *Daubert* will eventually face the necessity to reevaluate the scientific basis for assumptions about fingerprint uniqueness and then reexamine the question of whether fingerprint comparison, without scientific standards of point similarity, is perhaps more art than science. States still using the *Frye* analysis may take longer to reassess fingerprint evidence. By definition, the "general acceptance" of fingerprinting will only erode as even more scientists begin to doubt its validity and as *Daubert* courts start to doubt its admissibility.

CASE STUDY

The First U.S. Fingerprint Case: *People v. Jennings,* **252 Ill. 534, 96 N.E. 1077 (1911)**

Clarence Hiller's wife woke him in the middle of the night and said that the gas lamp outside their daughter's bedroom was not burning properly. While investigating, Hiller got up and came across an intruder at the head of the stairs. They wrestled and Hiller was fatally shot twice. Nearby, four off-duty police officers saw a man running down the street. They stopped Thomas Jennings and saw that he had bloodstains on his clothes, which he claimed he got in a fall from a streetcar, and that he was carrying a revolver.

It just so happened that the back veranda of the Hiller house had just been painted and the intruder had entered the house through a rear window close to a railing on the veranda. Police found the imprint of four fingers of a left hand in the fresh paint on the railing. They photographed the prints and removed the railing for evidence. Jennings was arrested after also being identified by several other witnesses. By coincidence, Jennings had earlier been fingerprinted by the police and the police believed they had a perfect match.

At the trial, four fingerprint witnesses testified for the state, including experts from the Chicago police, the Canadian police, and a private expert who had studied at Scotland yard. They each testified as to the basis of the fingerprint classification system. They all opined that the fingerprints on the railing were made by Jennings. Jennings was convicted and sentenced to death.

On appeal, Jennings claimed that there was no scientific basis for the fingerprint testimony that helped convict him. The Court of Appeals disagreed and stated:

> This class of evidence is admitted in Great Britain. In 1909 the Court of Criminal Appeals held that finger prints might be received in evidence, and refused to interfere with a conviction below though this evidence was the sole ground of identification. In re Castleton's Case, 3 Crim. App. 74. While the courts of this country do not appear to have had occasion to pass on the question, standard authorities on scientific subjects discuss the use of finger prints as a system of identification, concluding that experience has shown it to be reliable. . . . These authorities state that this system of identification is of very ancient origin, having been used in Egypt when the impression of the monarch's thumb was used as his sign manual, that it has been used in the courts of India for many years and more recently in the courts of several European countries; that in recent years its use has become very general by the police departments of the large cities of this country and Europe; that the great success of the system in England, where it has been used since 1891 in thousands of cases without error, caused the sending of an investigating commission from the United States, on whose favorable report a bureau was established by the United States government in the war and other departments. . . .
>
> From the evidence in this record we are disposed to hold that the classification of finger print impressions and their method of identification is a science requiring study. While some of the reasons which guide an expert to his conclusions are such as may be weighed by any intelligent person with good eyesight from such exhibits as we have here in the record, after being pointed out to him by one versed in the study of finger prints, the evidence in question does not come within the common experience of all men of common education in the ordinary walks of life, and therefore the court and jury were properly aided by witnesses of peculiar and special experience on this subject.

CHICAGO, Nov. 10.—Convicted almost solely on finger-print evidence, Thomas Jennings, a negro, was found guilty to-day of the murder of Clarence A. Hiller on Sept. 19. The jurors felt so confident of the guilt of Jennings that the first ballot resulted in a unanimous vote for conviction, with eleven of the jurors demanding the death penalty and one life imprisonment. On the third ballot the sentence of death was made unanimous.

Counsel for Jennings asked for a new trial on the ground that the finger-print evidence should not have been allowed. As a result it is probable that the Supreme Court will be asked to rule on the use of such evidence in criminal cases. Judge Kavanagh, who presided at the Jennings trial, declared, when objection was first made to the evidence, that in his opinion the murderer of Hiller wrote his signature when he rested his hand on a freshly painted porch railing at the Hiller home.

Following the murder of Hiller, the porch railing was taken to Detective Headquarters, where photographs were made of the finger prints in the paint and enlarged. Following Jennings's arrest, the imprints were compared with new imprints of his left hand. Finger-print experts testified at the trial that there were thirty-three points of similarity on the first three fingers of the left hand of the murderer of Hiller and that of Jennings.

Hiller, who was Chief Clerk in the Chicago offices of the Rock Island Railroad, was shot to death in the front hall of his suburban residence, at Washington Heights, Ill., by a negro burglar. Hiller encountered the burglar in an upper hall. The two grappled and fought down a stairway to the first floor. When the police took hold of the investigation it was only known that a negro had killed Hiller. Jennings was arrested less than half an hour after the shooting.

FIGURE 4.5.
Jennings newspaper account.
New York Times, November 11, 1910.

Thomas Jennings was executed by hanging on February 16, 1912, for the murder of Clarence Hiller.

Handwriting Comparison

Comparison of handwriting samples, or *questioned document examination* as its practitioners call it, is one of the oldest types of forensic evidence. It broadly involves the comparison of documents, printing, and writing to identify persons who are the source of the writing, to reveal alterations, or to identify the source of typewritten marks.[42] This section focuses primarily on handwriting analysis. The science is based on "the asserted ability to determine the authorship *vel non* of a piece of handwriting by examining the way in which the letters are inscribed, shaped and joined, and comparing it to exemplars of a putative author's concededly authentic handwriting."[43] Handwriting examiners claim that no two people write alike and that no one person writes the same way twice.[44] They argue, therefore, that no two writings are ever identical.[45] Although it was offered in courts even before the twentieth century, it was not widely accepted as scientific evidence until it became part of the cornerstone of the prosecution case in *State v. Hauptmann*, the Lindbergh kidnapping case.[46]

In America, the handwriting analysis system was developed and promoted by Albert S. Osborne in the early 1900s and it has remained virtually unchanged since.[47] After the *Hauptmann* case, it appears to have been almost unanimously accepted as reliable and admissible.[48] As with several other such routinely accepted types of forensic scientific evidence, *Daubert* has led scientists and the courts to reexamine questions of the reliability and admissibility of handwriting comparison expert testimony.

Questioned Document Principles and Procedures

Handwriting analysis involves the comparison of a questioned item with a item of known origin. Certain requirements must be met before a handwriting comparison can be made.[49] The writing must be of the same type (i.e., handwritten or hand-printed), and the text must be of a comparable sort (i.e., similar letter and word combinations). Special situations involve *forgery*, which is an attempt to imitate another's writing, and *disguise*, which is an attempt to change writing style to prevent identification. The bases for comparison are the features or attributes that are common to both samples. The characteristics of the writings are also identified as class characteristics (the style that the writer was taught), individual characteristics (the writer's personal style), and other gross or subtle characteristics. The attributes used for comparison of handwriting are twenty-one so-called discriminating elements.[50] The comparison is based on the principal that, although individuals have variations within their own writing, no two persons write the same way. The analysis compares variability among writers and variability within a single person's writing, as shown in the samples. Determining that two samples were written by the same person means concluding that the degree of variability is more consistent with individual writing variations than with variations between two different persons.

Beyond these basic principles, there is no dispute and no claim that there is an identified or accepted system for analyzing handwriting, and that the analysis and conclusions are subjective evaluations made by handwriting examiners.[51] The emphasis, therefore, has been on training and testing persons to be considered handwriting experts. The American Society for Testing and Materials has developed a number of standards.[52] The American Board of Forensic Document Examiners is a trade organization that provides certification.[53] Although that organization requires an undergraduate degree in some field, there is no formal educational or training requirement otherwise, and most handwriting analysts are trained in forensic laboratories.

Professor D. Michael Risinger summed up the contentions of the handwriting analysts as follows:

> Handwriting identification experts believe they can examine a specimen of adult handwriting and determine whether the author of that specimen is the same person as or a different person than the author of any other example of handwriting, as long as both specimens are of sufficient quality and not separated by years or the intervention of degenerative disease. They further believe that they can accomplish this result with great accuracy, and that they can do it much better than an average literate person attempting the same task. They believe they can obtain these accurate findings as the result of applying an analytical methodology to the examination of handwriting, according to certain principles which are reflected in the questioned documents literature. They believe that this literature explains how to examine handwriting for identifying characteristics, and that by applying the lessons taught by this literature in connection with their experiences in various training exercises and in real world problems, they learn to identify handwriting dependably.[54]

Risinger and others disagree.

Scientific Concerns with Handwriting Analysis Testimony

The basic principles of handwriting analysis, that no two people write exactly alike and that no one person writes the same word exactly the same way twice, are generally accepted as plausible scientific hypotheses. However, scientists point out that this plausibility is based on intuition rather than scientifically established evidence. They point out that these conclusions are accepted as axiomatic by handwriting examiners although they have never been thoroughly tested using scientific methods. Determining whether each person's handwriting is truly unique would necessitate a study of a large number of randomly chosen persons and the categorization and measurement of the multitude of possible variations.[55] There are no standardized measurements and there is not even a public record of handwriting samples that can be scientifically used to develop such measurements or to test the basic underlying theories of handwriting analysis.[56] No formal empirical testing has been completed.[57] The scant studies that have been undertaken do not provide statistical support for uniqueness.[58]

Criticism of the claimed expertise of handwriting examiners is more intense and has been the subject of heated debate among scholars and scientists. In 1989, D. Michael Risinger and two other law professors published the results of their literature search, which asserted that there was no reliable study that established that document examiners can accurately identify or exclude authorship by handwriting comparison.[59] The conclusion was hotly disputed by handwriting examiner organizations, but no contrary study was found.[60]

The Forensic Sciences Foundation designed and administered handwriting examiner proficiency tests for government crime laboratories. The original tests were criticized as unscientific because they were administered only to a select group of volunteer laboratories and did not use original documents.[61] The 1975 tests resulted in 89 percent of the laboratories correctly identifying the writer of a specimen letter.[62] The proficiency tests were again undertaken in 1984 and 74 percent of the responding twenty-three volunteer laboratories reached the correct result.[63] Tests in 1985, 1986, and 1987 revealed correct identification in only 41 percent, 13 percent, and 52 percent of the responses, respectively.[64] The examiner organization disputes the interpretation of these results.[65] Two subsequent Forensic Sciences Foundation tests were administered in 1987 and 1989. Risinger interpreted the unpublished 1987 test results as showing that 94 percent to 97 percent of the "easy" identifications were correctly made by the respondents, while only 41 percent of the "harder" identifications were correctly made.[66] Risinger interpreted the unpublished 1989 results showing 41 percent of respondents made false-positive identifications.

In 1994, the FBI sponsored handwriting examiner proficiency studies, which were conducted by Professor Moshe Kam and his colleagues. The first study was designed to test whether a small group of FBI document examiners could more correctly identify handwriting authors than a group of college students with no handwriting training. The results showed overwhelmingly good results by the trained examiners "indicating that handwriting identification expertise exists."[67] Subsequently, Kam and his colleagues designed a proficiency test and administered it to professional examiners, trainees, and laypersons. The results were only published in the aggregate but Kam claimed that the results "lay to rest the debate over whether or not the professional document examiners possess writer-identification skills absent in the general population."[68] However, the study still showed that the professional declared an erroneous identification in 6.5 percent of the cases. There were significant criticisms of the study. The criticisms included the use of monetary incentives for the layperson subjects, aggregation of results, and other concerns.[69] A further study was conducted by Kam and colleagues in 1998 to explain the effect that monetary incentives may have had on the test results.[70] One final Kam study was undertaken, which most closely approximated a typical identification task and compared results between professional examiners and laypersons. The reported results indicated that trained examiners performed significantly better in identifying the genuineness of signatures than laypersons and that the error rates exhibited by the professionals were much smaller than those of the laypersons.[71]

A study examining proficiency in determining the genuineness of signatures was conducted in 2002 and found that professional examiners were wrong in 3.4 percent of the cases.[72] Perhaps the most significant scientific advancement in handwriting analysis legitimacy comes from a recent study funded by the Department of Justice. Professor Sargar Srihari and his colleagues collected handwriting samples from 1,568 persons and analyzed them using computer algorithms to extract common features.[73] They concluded that the computer was able to distinguish writers with a high degree of confidence. This scientific method may lead to a much more definitive scientific basis for the expertise claimed in handwriting analysis.

The National Academy of Sciences report found value in handwriting comparison testimony but recommended further scientific study:

> The scientific basis for handwriting comparisons needs to be strengthened. Recent studies have increased our understanding of the individuality and consistency of handwriting and computer studies and suggest that there may be a scientific basis for handwriting comparison, at least in the absence of intentional obfuscation or forgery. Although there has been only limited research to quantify the reliability and replicability of the practices used by trained document examiners, the committee agrees that there may be some value in handwriting analysis.[74]

Handwriting Analysis Under *Daubert*

Daubert started a reevaluation of handwriting testimony, which led to even more inquiries after *Kumho*. Some courts are no longer so sure about the admissibility of handwriting analysis evidence. In the pre-*Kumho* case of *United States v. Starzecpyzel*,[75] the court held an extensive *Daubert* hearing on the reliability of handwriting comparison evidence. After a detailed analysis, the judge rejected the claim that handwriting analysis has a scientific basis and stated, "Were the Court to apply *Daubert* to the proffered FDE [forensic document examiner] testimony, it would have to be excluded. This conclusion derives from a straightforward analysis of the suggested *Daubert* factors—testability and known error rate, peer review and publication, and general acceptance." However, the judge went on to hold that "while scientific principles may relate to aspects of handwriting analysis, they have little or nothing to do with the day-to-day tasks performed by FDEs" and that because it is not a "science," handwriting expert testimony is not subject to the *Daubert* requirements. He allowed the handwriting expert to testify as a technical or experience-based expert.

After *Kumho*, in *United States v. Fujii*, an American court excluded handwriting analysis testimony for the first time since the Lindbergh case,[76] and it was followed in *United States v. Saelee*.[77] While other courts have begun to express some reservations, they have not excluded handwriting analysis testimony altogether.[78] Notwithstanding the doubts about the scientific basis for handwriting comparison testimony, courts have still found it admissible for the most part. In 2003, the Fourth Circuit expressly ruled that handwriting comparison testimony was admissible under *Daubert* in *United States v. Crisp*.[79] The court there held, "The fact that handwriting comparison analysis has achieved widespread and lasting acceptance in the expert community gives us the assurance of reliability that *Daubert* requires. Furthermore, as with expert testimony on fingerprints, the role of the handwriting expert is primarily to draw the jury's attention to similarities between a known exemplar and a contested sample." The court seemed to almost abdicate the "gatekeeper" role for trial judges when it concluded, "To the extent that a given handwriting analysis is flawed or flimsy, an able defense lawyer will bring that fact to the jury's attention, both through skillful cross-examination and by presenting expert testimony of his own." In *United States v. Mooney*,[80] the First Circuit reached a similar result without much explanation. For the most part, courts have continued, on one basis or another, to allow handwriting comparison testimony, although the testimony of particular witnesses has been excluded.[81]

Much like fingerprint testimony, the court system appears reluctant to actually apply a *Daubert* analysis to handwriting evidence, which has been a standard tool in the prosecution's evidence arsenal for such a long time. It may well take a highly publicized postconviction DNA exoneration of a person who was convicted based on handwriting examiner testimony to change the trend. In the meantime, however, the good news is that the handwriting examiner community appears to be taking its scientific obligations more seriously and seeking to establish a true scientific basis for the claimed expertise. The principal prospect for such evidence may lie in recent efforts to use computer analysis to compile reliable databases of handwriting samples and quantifiable features and characteristics.

CASE STUDY

The Lindbergh Kidnapping: *State v. Hauptmann*, 180 A. 809 (N.J. 1935)

Following his historic one-man, nonstop flight from New York to Paris in 1927, Charles Lindbergh became an almost instantaneous American hero and one of the most famous persons in the world. His marriage two years later and the birth of his first son, Charles, were big news. However, in 1932, twenty-month-old Charles was kidnapped from the Lindbergh home and the case was quickly dubbed the "Crime of the Century." Over two years later, a German immigrant, Bruno Richard Hauptmann, was arrested. In a "media circus trial," the likes of which would not be seen again until the O.J. Simpson trial, much of the prosecution case hinged on the testimony of experts in the fledgling forensic science field of handwriting comparison.

On March 1, 1932, using a homemade ladder, someone climbed into the second-story nursery of the Lindbergh home in New Jersey and abducted the infant. A three-piece wooden ladder, a chisel, and a handwritten ransom note demanding $50,000 were left at the scene. Five days later, a second ransom note was received increasing the ransom demand to $70,000. A third ransom note was received by the Lindbergh's attorney and a fourth ransom note was received by a person who had publicly offered to act as an intermediary, a Dr. Condon. A fifth ransom note was delivered to him by a taxicab driver, who received it from an unidentified stranger. A sixth note led the intermediary to meet an unidentified man at a New York City cemetery. The stranger eventually gave Dr. Condon a baby's sleeping suit, which was identified by the Lindberghs.

Negotiations continued and a total of thirteen ransom notes were delivered. Finally, the intermediary met an unidentified man and gave him $50,000 in exchange for the thirteenth note, which contained instructions on where to find the child. Most of the money was paid in "gold certificates," a form of U.S. currency still used at the time, and the numbers on the certificates had been recorded. The Lindbergh baby was

WANTED

INFORMATION AS TO THE WHEREABOUTS OF

CHAS. A. LINDBERGH, JR.

OF HOPEWELL, N. J.

SON OF COL. CHAS. A. LINDBERGH

World-Famous Aviator

This child was kidnaped from his home in Hopewell, N. J., between 8 and 10 p. m. on Tuesday, March 1, 1932.

DESCRIPTION:

Age. 20 months   Hair, blond, curly
Weight, 27 to 30 lbs.   Eyes, dark blue
Height, 29 inches   Complexion, light
Deep dimple in center of chin
Dressed in one-piece coverall night suit

ADDRESS ALL COMMUNICATIONS TO
COL. H. N. SCHWARZKOPF, TRENTON, N. J., or
COL. CHAS. A. LINDBERGH, HOPEWELL, N. J.

ALL COMMUNICATIONS WILL BE TREATED IN CONFIDENCE

COL. H. NORMAN SCHWARZKOPF
March 11, 1932   Supt. New Jersey State Police, Trenton, N. J.

FIGURE 4.6.
Kidnapping poster.
Federal Bureau of Investigation.

not where the kidnapper had indicated. On May 12, 1932, the child's partially decomposed remains were found in a shallow grave just two miles from the Lindbergh home.

Over two years later, one of the $10 gold certificates from the ransom money was used at a gas station in New York and the attendant noted the car's license plate number. The car was traced to Bruno Hauptmann, who also had a ransom bill in his possession when he was arrested. In a subsequent search of Hauptmann's garage, police found $14,000 more of the ransom money.

The sensational trial took place in a New Jersey state court in 1935 and lasted six weeks. Eight government handwriting experts testified, including Albert Osborn, the man who had championed handwriting analysis as a forensic science.

They testified that Hauptmann had written the ransom notes, although they did not identify him as the writer of the original note left at the scene. They claimed that Hauptmann's handwriting had many points of similarity with the ransom notes. For example, both Hauptmann's handwriting and that found on the ransom notes had backward capital *N*s, unclosed lowercase *O*s, the same-shaped lowercase *T*s, and the same curls to the lowercase *Y*s. They also testified that Hauptmann misspelled many of the same words that were misspelled in the ransom notes. For example, Hauptmann and the author of the ransom notes both misspelled "where" as "were," "our" as "ouer," "later" as "latter," and "boat" as "boad."

The qualifications of the government handwriting witnesses were challenged, as shown in this portion of the transcript of the testimony of John F. Tyrrell, a government handwriting expert:

> Q. Now, Mr. Tyrrell, I show you the ransom notes and ask you if you made an examination of those?
> A. Yes.
> Q. I show you the request and conceded writings and ask if you have made an examination of those.
> A. Yes.
> Q. In addition have you made an examination of any other documents of Bruno Richard Hauptmann which are evidence in this case?
> A. Yes.
> Q. What other documents, please?
> A. Documents having to do with automobile licenses.
> Q. What was the purpose of your examination, sir?
> A. To determine whether or not there was an identity existing between the normal or automobile writings, the request writings and the ransom notes.
> Q. As the result of your examination and comparison, have you reached an opinion concerning them?
> A. Yes.
> Q. Are you prepared to express it?
> A. Yes.
> Q. What is that opinion?
> A. That the writers are identical, that they are all written by the one writer.

On cross-examination, the following exchange took place:

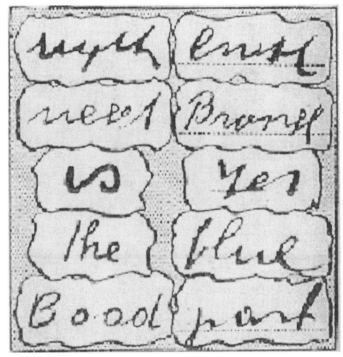

FIGURE 4.7.
Prosecution handwriting exhibit. (Ransom note writing sample on
left; Hauptmann handwriting sample on right)
Federal Bureau of Investigation.

Q. Did you ever attend any school or college or institution of learning for the purpose of qualifying yourself to examine disputed handwritings?

A. No. My college was the experience—

Q. There is no such school or institution of learning that teaches the art of examining disputed handwritings, is there?

A. Not that I know of.

Then defense presented its own expert, John M. Trendley, and argued that his qualifications were sufficient to render an opinion:

Mr. Reilly [defense attorney]: I submit his experience of 387 cases covering a period of 49 years—and the Court will recall we didn't have the opportunity to send all over the world and examine into the records of the $150,000 case prepared by the State of New Jersey and the experts

FIGURE 4.8.
Bruno Hauptmann.
Federal Bureau of Investigation.

brought in here. They brought men in here that we did not know five minutes before they took the stand they were going to be called.

When we did get by wire instances of where Mr. Osborn corrected
himself or was mistaken, and we asked him, he admitted it. . . . I say that
a man who has testified in 387 cases, as Mr. Trendley has, and admits that

in three or four cases he may have been mistaken, is honest in his opinion, but it doesn't destroy his value as an expert.

This is not a science, *this is the opinion of those who have devoted their lives to examining disputed writings* and, while it is true he may have offered papers for the purpose of confusing the experts on the other side, that is no disrespect to him, nor does it lessen his ability as an expert. I ask the Court to pass on his qualifications.

The judge agreed and then Hendley testified:

> Q. As a result of your study, are you in a position to render an opinion as to whether or not Hauptmann wrote the ransom notes?
> A. In my opinion he did not.

The judge allowed all of the handwriting witnesses to testify and later instructed the jury:

> A very important question in the case is, did the defendant, Hauptmann, write the original ransom note found on the window sill, and the other ransom notes which followed? Numerous experts in handwriting have testified, after exhaustive examination of the ransom letters, and comparison with genuine writings of the defendant, that the defendant, Hauptmann, wrote every one of the ransom notes, and Mr. Osborne, Senior, said that that conclusion was irresistible, unanswerable and overwhelming. On the other hand, the defendant denies that he wrote them, and a handwriting expert, called by him, so testified. And so the fact becomes one for your determination. The weight of the evidence to prove the genuineness of handwriting is wholly for the jury.

The jury found Bruno Richard Hauptmann guilty of first-degree murder and sentenced him to death. The conviction was upheld on appeal and Hauptmann was executed on April 3, 1936. His last statement was written in German and translated as:

> I am glad that my life in a world which has not understood me has ended. Soon I will be at home with my Lord, so I am dying an innocent man. Should, however, my death serve for the purpose of abolishing capital punishment—such a punishment being arrived at only by circumstantial evidence—I feel that my death has not been in vain. I am at peace with God. I repeat, I protest my innocence of the crime for which I was convicted. However, I die with no malice or hatred in my heart. The love of Christ has filled my soul and I am happy in Him.

CASE STUDY

Handwriting Comparison Reconsidered: *U.S. v. Fujii,*
152 F.Supp.2d 939 (2000)

Masao Fujii, a Japanese man, was charged with participating in a
scheme to arrange the fraudulent entry of two Chinese nationals into
the United States in 1999. The government claimed that, as part of the
scheme, Fujii had filled out immigration forms that were used at Kennedy Airport in New York City. The entries on the forms had been made
by handprinting, rather than in cursive writing, and the government
obtained exemplars of handprinting by Fujii. The prosecution sought to
present expert opinion testimony from a document examiner at the Immigration and Naturalization Service (INS) that the entries on the form
were made by Fujii. The defense moved to exclude her testimony based
on *Daubert* and offered its own expert claiming that handwriting analysis in general, and the particular conclusion in this case, were not reliable scientific evidence. Federal District Judge Joan Gottschall agreed:

> *Ruling on Defendant's Motion to Exclude the Testimony of the Govern-*
> *ment's Handwriting Expert*
>   Handwriting analysis does not stand up well under the *Daubert* stan-
> dards. Despite its long history of use and acceptance, validation studies
> supporting its reliability are few, and the few that exist have been criticized
> for methodological flaws. . . . [T]here has been no peer review by an unbi-
> ased and financially disinterested community of practitioners and academ-
> ics; the acceptance of handwriting identification expertise has largely been
> driven by handwriting experts. Its potential rate of error is almost entirely
> unknown. . . . [T]here are few if any other studies in existence that tend to
> validate the reliability of handwriting analysis. The defense expert in this
> case testified to studies that have undermined some of handwriting analy-
> sis' key principles, such as its principle that no two people write exactly
> alike. . . . Of course, on the fourth test, general acceptance, handwriting
> analysis scores high.
>   This court need not weigh in on this question, however, for whether
> handwriting analysis per se meets the *Daubert* standards, its application to
> this case poses more significant problems. The questioned writing in this
> case was handprinting. Typical handwriting analysis involves cursive writ-
> ing, and the record is devoid of evidence that there is even a recognized
> field of expertise in the identification of handprinting. While Ms. Cox testi-

fied that many of the documents she examines at the INS involve hand-printing, and while she testified that in her prior employment with ATF, she was tested in identifying handprinting, "erred," studied, was retested and passed, the court has no idea whether there is a recognized and accepted expertise in identifying handprinted documents, let alone whether Ms. Cox is an expert in this putative field. Michael Saks, who testified for the defense, testified that he was aware of only one study of the reliability of handprinting identification, and in that study, only 13% of the handwriting experts tested got the right answer; 45% identified the wrong person. . . .

The reliability of handprinting identification, however, is only part of the problem. The government has offered no evidence that Ms. Cox's expertise extends to making an identification of handprinting when the handprinter[s] in question are native Japanese writers. Neither the government's expert, Ms. Cox, nor the defendant's witness, Mr. Saks, is aware of any studies attempting to validate handprinting (or even handwriting) identification of the writings of foreign-trained writers. . . .

Considering the questions about handwriting analysis generally under *Daubert,* the lack of any evidence that the identification of handprinting is an expertise that meets the *Daubert* standards and the questions that have been raised—which the government has not attempted to answer—about its expert's ability to opine reliably on handprinting identification in dealing with native Japanese writers taught English printing in Japan, the court grants the defendant's motion.

Mr. Fujii's handwriting evidence victory, however, was not the end of the story. He was convicted of a similar scheme when he attempted to smuggle three other Chinese nationals into Chicago's O'Hare Airport in 2000. He was convicted of attempting to smuggle aliens into the United States for private financial gain, of encouraging and inducing aliens to come to, enter, or reside in the United States, knowing that it was in violation of law, and of knowingly using a counterfeit passport. In that case, Judge Gottschall sentenced Fujii to thirty-six months in prison. His conviction and sentence were affirmed on appeal in *U.S. v. Fujii,* 301 F.3d 535 (7th Cir. 2002).

5

More "Who" Questions

Hair Analysis

Hair analysis can be a forensic tool because human hairs are routinely shed and can be discovered at a crime scene. Examination of hair found at the scene and compared with hair from a known source may be helpful to the extent that it reflects similarities. The extent of the similarity in those samples and the examiner's ability to discover and compare those similarities is the principal issue when hair analysis is offered in a criminal case. Microscopic hair examination and analysis has been undertaken for over a century but has limited capability to identify individuals. Recent developments in DNA testing have greatly expanded the ability of hair sample examination to make individual identifications.

Microscopic Hair Analysis

Traditionally, forensic evidence comparing human hair was based on a microscopic comparison of the evidentiary sample with a known sample from the defendant.[1] To make a microscopic hair comparison, a control group of hairs from a known source must be properly collected by pulling or combing hairs from a subject.[2] That requires a total of fifty hairs from different areas of the scalp or a total of twenty-five hairs from a pubic region.[3] The samples are then examined macroscopically for gross feature comparison, such as color, form, and thickness. In the microscopic stage, hairs are mounted on slides using a mounting medium that has the same refractive index as the hair. The hair analyst then attempts to identify the part of the body from which the hair might have come, based on certain area characteristics.

Features of the hair are divided into "major and secondary characteristics." Major characteristics include color, treatment, pigment aggregation, shaft form, pigment distribution, medulla appearance, hair diameter, medullary index, and the presence or absence of a root or shaft. Secondary characteristics include cuticular margin, pigment density, pigment size, tip shape, and shaft diameter.[4] The examiner then formulates an opinion as to exclusion or consistency.

Although used by investigative agencies, including the FBI,[5] it is uniformly recognized that microscopic hair comparisons do not constitute a basis for an absolute identification.[6] It can be useful, however, as exclusionary evidence, but for identification the most that it can show is a "class" identification, that a hair is consistent with having originated from a particular person but would also be consistent with many others.[7] Prosecutorial and expert claims of a "match" based on hair analysis are gross overstatements of the capabilities of microscopic hair analysis.[8] And it is clear that substantial errors have occurred using microscopic hair analysis.[9] In one recent case, a man

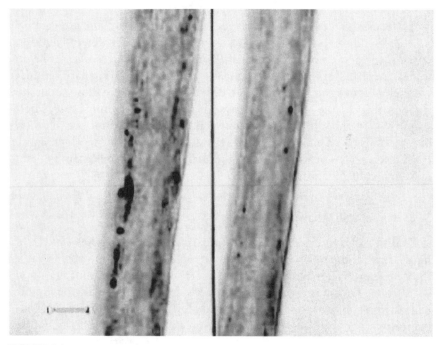

FIGURE 5.1.
Microscopic hair comparison.
Missouri State Highway Patrol.

served sixteen years in prison after he was convicted of rape based in part on the testimony of a police forensic analyst that "she believed each person's hair was unique and that she could identify the unique characteristics" of the hair, and that hairs found near the victim matched the defendant's hair. The defendant was eventually exonerated by postconviction DNA testing.[10] In a subsequent portion of a civil action, the Tenth Circuit characterized her testimony as "bogus."[11] In another case, a defendant was sentenced to serve over 3,000 years in prison after his conviction for rape, sodomy, and other charges based in part on an analyst testimony that he compared hairs from the crime scene with the defendant's hair and found similar characteristics that he had seen in "less than 5 percent" of hair samples he had examined. The defendant was exonerated by DNA testing after serving over three years of his sentence.[12]

Nevertheless, courts have even recently allowed hair analysis testimony as generally accepted evidence.[13] Many other courts have begun to exclude such testimony, at least when the analyst attempts to suggest that there is an individual identification by comparison.[14] The National Academy of Sciences (NAS) report assessed the state of microscopic hair analysis:

> No scientifically accepted statistics exist about the frequency with which particular characteristics of hair are distributed in the population. There appear to be no uniform standards on the number of features on which hairs must agree before an examiner may declare a "match." . . .
>
> The committee found no scientific support for the use of hair comparisons for individualization in the absence of nuclear DNA.[15]

DNA Analysis of Hair Samples

The advent of DNA, and particularly the mitochondrial (mtDNA) method, has changed the field of forensic hair analysis completely. If the evidence sample has a root, typical and much more definitive nuclear DNA can, of course, be used.[16] The mtDNA method, on the other hand, is not nearly as discriminating as the usual nuclear DNA method, since it is based on mitochondria in human cells, which are shared by maternal relatives.[17] Thus siblings will be indistinguishable based on mtDNA comparison.[18] In spite of that limitation, its value lies in the fact that mitochondria are found outside the nuclei of human cells and exist in shafts of hair that have no roots attached.[19] Where there is no root, as is often the case, mtDNA is very effectively used to supplant, or at least support, a microscopic hair analysis.[20] There are significant limitations on the accuracy of microscopic comparisons.[21] Analysis of mtDNA can give the court a much more substantial basis for admitting hair analysis as a significant part of a prosecution.

In *State v. Pappas*, the Supreme Court of Connecticut conducted an exhaustive review of the status of mtDNA sequencing for hair analysis comparison.[22] In language that would satisfy either *Frye* or *Daubert*, the court concluded that "the procedures used to extract and chart the chemical bases of mtDNA—extraction, PCR [polymerase chain reaction] amplification, capillary electrophoresis, and the use of an automated sequencing machine to generate a chromatograph—are scientifically valid and generally accepted in the scientific community."[23]

The use of mtDNA sequencing evidence, for hair and other sample analysis, is becoming widespread and has been accepted by many courts.[24] The trend is clearly that mtDNA evidence has become the standard for hair analysis testimony and that microscopic analysis alone may no longer be sufficiently reliable for admission, regardless of the qualifiers placed on the testimony by the analyst.

CASE STUDY

Faulty Hair Comparison Evidence: Kenneth Adams and the "Ford Heights Four"

In the early morning hours of May 11, 1978, a gas station in the mostly white Chicago suburb of Homewood was looted and the overnight attendant and his fiancée were kidnapped. The white man and woman were taken to an abandoned townhouse in the predominantly black community later known as *Ford Heights*. The attendant's body was found the next day by two children on the bank of Deer Creek near the townhouse. He had been shot twice in the head and once in the back with a .38-caliber pistol. The woman's half-naked body was discovered by police in a bedroom in the townhouse. She had been shot twice in the head with the same pistol and had been raped.

Based on a tip from a witness placing them at the scene of the crime, police arrested Kenneth Adams and three of his friends, Dennis Williams, Willie Rainge, and Verneal Jimerson. The group would later be dubbed the "Ford Heights Four" by the media. All four came from devoutly religious families. Twenty-one-year-old Adams had no criminal record and was a high school graduate with a steady work history as a maintenance worker.

FIGURE 5.2.
Kenneth Adams.
Photograph courtesy of the Center on Wrongful Convictions.

The tip from the witness eventually led to testimony before a grand jury from a woman, Paula Gray, who claimed to have been with the four men when the killing occurred. She later recanted her testimony and the police charged her both with being an accomplice and with perjury.

In addition to the eyewitness supposedly placing the four men at the townhouse, the prosecutor presented forensic evidence, the most significant of which was from Michael Podlecki, a criminalist with the Illinois State Police, regarding blood and hair evidence. He testified that several white head hairs recovered from the trunk and back seat of the car in which the four men were riding that night "matched" the hair of the victims. He testified, "Just like if you drop two dollar bills and you see dollar bills on the floor. You see two one dollar bills. It's obvious."

All four men and Paula Gray were convicted. Adams was sentenced to seventy-five years in prison, Jimerson and Williams to death, and Rainge to life without parole. Paula Gray was sentenced to fifty years in prison. On appeal, Williams and Rainge won new trials but Paula Gray

FIGURE 5.3.
Paula Gray.
Photograph courtesy of the Center on Wrongful Convictions.

then reverted to her original story and testified to gain her own release from prison.

Kenneth Adams's appeals were denied and he remained in prison for the next eighteen years with the other three members of the "Ford Heights Four."

Several years after the convictions, a group of journalism students from Northwestern University began working on the case and found a police file showing that, within a week of the crime, a witness told the police that they had arrested the wrong men. The witness said he knew who committed the crime because he heard shots, saw four men run away from the scene, and the next day saw them selling items taken from the robbery of the victims. Based on this and other information, DNA testing, which was unavailable in 1987, was conducted comparing semen found in the victim with the four defendants. All four were exonerated, pardoned by the Illinois governor, and released in 1996.

The DNA testing also implicated the four men identified by the witness whose statement the police had suppressed. One of the men identified by that witness was by then dead, but the other three ultimately confessed. Paula Gray later recanted her story again, saying she made it up because she felt pressured and threatened by the police. In 1999, the "Ford Heights Four" brought a civil suit against the Chicago Police and Cook County paid them a total settlement of $36 million.

Further Reading

Protess, David, and Rob Warden. *A Promise of Justice: The Eighteen-Year Fight to Save Four Innocent Men.* New York: Hyperion Books, 1998.

The Innocence Project. "Kenneth Adams." Retrieved April 12, 2010, from http://www.innocenceproject.org/Content/46.php.

Bite-Mark Analysis

Bite-mark testimony seeks to identify a perpetrator by comparing a cast or image of teeth from a bite mark left on a victim or otherwise at a crime scene with a sample of the defendant's teeth. A forensic odontologist offers testimony in which the bite marks are analyzed and compared. The basic premise underlying bite mark forensic evidence is that human dentition is unique and that, when compared within a reasonable time, an expert opinion identifying the person who made both impressions can be made.[25]

Obtaining and Analyzing Odontology Evidence

The American Board of Forensic Odontology has established methods to be used in obtaining and preserving bite-mark evidence.[26] Bite marks on human skin can be recorded with a number of accepted techniques, including various forms of photography. Casting three-dimensional impressions of bite marks is also suggested when feasible. Since the bite marks are a potentially valuable source of suspect DNA, a bite mark is usually swabbed for later DNA analysis as well. The dentition from a suspect to be compared is obtained through dental records, x-rays, or actual physical examination if possible. At least two casts are made and, if possible, a suspect's bite mark into a comparable substance is obtained and casted. Odontologists will make exemplars of the suspect's teeth by anything from a hand-traced outline to xerographic copying to computer imaging.

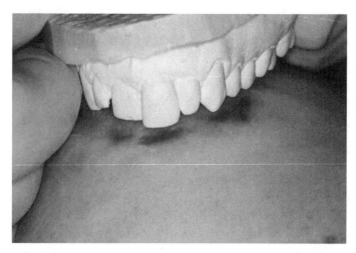

FIGURE 5.4.
Bite-mark comparison in *State v. Krone*, 182 Ariz 319 (1995).
Courtesy of Alan Simpson. Used by permission.

While there is little dispute about the validity of these techniques, there are significant problems associated with the deterioration of bite marks with the passage of time or contamination from other sources or deformation through the natural healing process. Additionally, problems can arise with the normal changes in a suspect's dentition as well. The eventual comparison is made visually, microscopically, and, in some cases, with digital photography.

The Scientific Validity of Bite-Mark Testimony

The basic concept of dental uniqueness has been accepted by many courts.[27] Indeed, bite-mark evidence in general has received widespread acceptance. In *State v. Timmendequas*,[28] when admitting bite mark evidence, the Supreme Court of New Jersey stated that "[j]udicial opinions from other jurisdictions establish that bite-mark analysis has gained general acceptance and therefore is reliable. . . . Over thirty states considering such evidence have found it admissible and no state has rejected bite-mark evidence as unreliable." Nevertheless, significant questions remain about the scientific validity of bite-mark comparison testimony.[29]

First, despite its acceptance in various cases, there is significant disagreement among odontologists and other scientists about the basic premise of dental uniqueness. The American Society of Forensic Odontology asserts that the uniqueness premise has been established by at least two studies.[30] And odontologists are convinced that human dentition is unique to each living person.[31] However, the National Academy of Sciences report states that "the uniqueness of the human dentition has not been scientifically established."[32] That claim is supported by the studies of several other scholars.[33] If human dentition is not unique, there may be very little proper use for bite-mark testimony in criminal proceedings.

Beyond the basic question of uniqueness, a number of factors in a particular case may affect the accuracy of bite mark identification.[34] These include such things as the "freshness" of the bite-mark impression and its changes over time, temperature or contamination effects at the crime scene, damage to soft tissue around the bite mark, and dental similarities among individuals.[35] A primary concern is often that the impression includes only a limited number of teeth.[36] When experts rely, as they often do, on photographic images of bite marks made at the scene or during an autopsy, the quality of the photography and the enhancement techniques used for comparison can clearly affect the reliability of the odontologist's conclusions.[37] Guidelines have been suggested by the American Board of Forensic Odontology that specifically address many of these factors.[38]

Perhaps the biggest technical evidentiary issues relating to these factors are questions of whether a reliable pattern of bite marks is transferred to human skin when a bite occurs and, if so, whether the skin can retain that pattern for any period of time without undergoing a distortion caused by the biological reaction of the skin to being punctured. The NAS report was specific and very critical in its findings on these points:

> The ability of the dentition, if unique, to transfer a unique pattern to human skin and the ability of the skin to maintain that uniqueness has not been scientifically established.
>
> i. The ability to analyze and interpret the scope or extent of distortion of bite mark patterns on human skin has not been demonstrated.
>
> ii. The effect of distortion on different comparison techniques is not fully understood and therefore has not been quantified.[39]

As to the first point, "[c]entral to bitemark analysis are the characteristics of the skin receiving the mark, because in cases of physical assault having skin injuries, the anatomy and physiology of the skin, and the position of the victim, affect the detail and shape of the bitemark."[40] There is one recent study that attempted to measure the accuracy of human skin as a "substrate," or recording recipient, of bite marks by using the same dentition to make bites on cadavers. The authors found that no two bites were measurably identical and that there was distortion between the bites of as much as 80 percent.[41] In a subsequent study of the cadavers, several selected dentition models were used and the investigators found that up to 86 percent of the models could not be excluded by examination and that, indeed, some of the nonbiter dentitions appear to "fit" better than the actual biter's dentition.[42] The odontologists concluded that "this study suggests that an open population postmortem bitemark should be carefully and cautiously evaluated." That assessment has been called "understated."[43]

As to the issue of distortion, from bruising, healing, or other biological skin reactions to injury, the scientific research indicates that there is a significant degree of distortion that takes place in a bite-mark impression on the skin with any passage of time.[44] The longer the time interval, the greater the distortion, and it appears that even preservation of the skin where possible does not necessarily lessen the distortion.[45]

In spite of its general admissibility, expert testimony has varied to such a degree that some courts have excluded the testimony altogether. The conclusions that an expert can draw from the evaluation are necessarily limited by the number and quality of corresponding points in the evidentiary sample. Testifying odontologist experts have expressed opinions ranging from stating that the bite mark was "consistent" with the defendant's teeth, to stating that the defendant's teeth "probably" made the bite mark, to conclusively claiming that there was a "match" that was a positive identification of the defendant.[46]

The error rate for odontologist experts appears to be high. An interpretation of results of the latest study by the American Board of Forensic Odontology indicated an error rate of 12.5 percent out of a possible 27 percent, meaning that participating diplomates were almost half as wrong as they could be in that study.[47] Of particular concern in criminal cases, the bulk of that error rate was from false positives.

As with all scientific testimony, the qualifications and bias of a particular proffered expert is always an issue. In *Ege v. Yukins*,[48] for example, the District Court for the Eastern District of Michigan found constitutional error in a state court case in which testimony about bite marks was a critical factor in the conviction. The court found that testimony of the government's bite-mark expert comparing a photograph of a disputed bite mark on the victim's cheek with a mold of the defendant's teeth made some nine years prior was unreliable, grossly misleading, and "so extremely unfair that its admission violates fundamental concepts of justice." Specifically, the court ruled that the expert's testimony that out of the 3.5 million people residing in the Detroit metropolitan area, the defendant was the only one whose dentition could match the individual who left the possible bite mark on the victim's cheek "was unreliable and not worthy of consideration by a jury." The court specifically noted that "[t]he opinion apparently was based on the mathematical product theory, a proposition that long has been condemned." Other bite-mark experts have also been the subject of blistering reviews by the courts.[49]

As in other types of long-accepted forensic scientific evidence, postconviction DNA exonerations have called the validity of bite-mark evidence into question. In a case that received a great deal of publicity, bite-mark evidence from two experts convicted a defendant of capital murder, who was later exonerated by DNA while on death row.[50] Publicity surrounding other DNA exonerations of murder convictions based on bite-mark evidence has led to serious public and professional doubts about its validity.[51] The extent to which bite-mark evidence will survive *Daubert* scrutiny, especially in light of both these significant and public reversals and the lack of empirical studies on the subject, remains to be seen.

CASE STUDY

A Bite Mark as Evidence of Murder:
Ege v. Yukins, 380 F.Supp.2d 852 (E.D. Mich. 2005)

Cindy Thompson was seven months' pregnant when she was found bludgeoned and stabbed to death in her bedroom in Pontiac, Michigan, in February of 1984. Her body was found by her boyfriend, Mark Davis, around 5:00 a.m. on February 22, 1984. Davis claimed to be the father of the child Thompson was carrying. There was no sign of forced entry at Thompson's home. The back door was unlocked and the telephone cords had been cut.

An unproductive police investigation lasted only a couple of months. It was reopened in 1992, when persons approached the police and implicated Carol Ege, a woman with whom Thompson had also had a sexual relationship at the time of the murder. In June 1992, evidence collected at the murder scene in February 1984 was submitted to the state police lab for the first time and none of it connected Ege to the crime. The medical examiner was asked to review Thompson's autopsy records and he suggested to the prosecutor's office that the body be exhumed for further examination. Photographs taken at the crime scene in 1984 showed a mark on the victim's cheek and her body was exhumed in 1993, apparently to investigate it. In April of 1993, Ege was charged with the Thompson murder.

Figure 5.5.
Carol Ege.
Michigan Department of Corrections.

The prosecution had found an expert who claimed that the mark on the victim's cheek was a bite mark and that it was made by the teeth of Carol Ege. The prosecution theory was that the defendant was obsessed with Cindy Thompson and was enraged about Mark Davis and the child Thompson was carrying. The prosecutor claimed that Ege had plotted to kill Thompson.

At a fifteen-day trial in December 1993 and January 1994, a principal witness for the prosecution was Dr. Alan Warnick, who testified that the injury was a bite mark. Dr. Warnick compared the defendant's dental impressions and concluded that the bite mark was made by the defendant. Dr. Warnick testified to the probability that Ege made the alleged bite mark found on the victim's cheek:

> Q: Now, Doctor, with regard to your testimony, you indicated that it's highly consistent with the dentition of Defendant Carol Ege; is that correct?

A: Yes.

Q: Okay. With regard to—let me ask you a question. Let's say you have the Detroit Metropolitan Area, three, three and a half million people. Would anybody else within that kind of number match like she did?

A: No, in my expert opinion, nobody else would match up.

Dr. Warnick also testified that his comparisons of the nondental forensic photo of the possible bite mark and dental molds taken from other potential suspects excluded them as having made the bite mark.

The jury found Ege guilty of first-degree murder and she was sentenced to life imprisonment without the possibility of parole. The Michigan Court of Appeals affirmed the conviction and the Michigan Supreme Court denied leave to appeal to that court. On a further motion in the trial court, Ege maintained that the Warnick testimony was not properly admitted. The trial judge agreed but nevertheless said she was "not prejudiced" by the testimony and denied her request for a new trial. Eventually, she filed a petition for habeas corpus in the federal court, claiming that she was denied a fundamentally fair trial in violation of due process of law through the admission of Warnick's bite-mark testimony.

The federal district judge agreed:

There is no question that the evidence in the case was unreliable and not worthy of consideration by a jury. Other state courts have held that bite mark evidence of this nature is not sufficient to establish guilt. See *Jackson v. State*, 511 So.2d 1047 (Fla.2d DCA 1987); *People v. Queen*, 130 Ill. App.3d 523, 85 Ill. Dec. 826, 474 N.E.2d786 (1985). . . .

The flaw in Dr. Warnick's statistical opinion should have been obvious and its admissibility readily assailable. The opinion apparently was based on the mathematical product theory, a proposition that long has been condemned and was discredited over thirty-five years ago. . . .

There are several reasons that Dr. Warnick's improperly admitted (occasioned by defense counsel's failure to object) testimony prejudiced the petitioner. Although the defense attempted to rebut Dr. Warnick's testimony with the testimony of other experts who opined that the mark on the victim's cheek was the result of livor mortis and was not a bite mark at all, the defense experts were not questioned about Dr. Warnick's probability testimony. In addition, Dr. Warnick examined the victim's corpse, which had been exhumed about nine years after her murder, but the body was too decomposed to examine the cheek tissues at that time. Dr. Warnick acknowledged that his opinion was formed solely from carefully examining an autopsy photograph of the victim, which had not been taken for the purpose of a bite mark examination and that, therefore, his opinion was less reliable that an opinion formed on the basis of a direct examination of the body soon after death, or from a photograph taken expressly for forensic dental purposes. However, defense counsel did not cross-examine Dr. Warnick directly about his opinion in statistical or probability terms. . . .

There can be no question that the bite mark evidence together with Dr. Warnick's 3.5-million-to-one odds making was powerful evidence against the petitioner. It also contradicted her claim that other logical suspects committed the crime. The evidence plainly was "material in the sense of a crucial, critical highly significant factor." . . . There was evidence presented at the trial that the petitioner harbored intense animosity against the victim and expressed a desire to see her killed. That evidence was also challenged and many of the witnesses who gave that testimony were impeached. Some even were the logical suspects themselves, as the State court of appeals observed. However, without the bite mark and opinion testimony, the nature of the State's proofs would have been altogether different and a weaker case necessarily would have resulted with no physical evidence connecting the petitioner to the crime.

Dr. Warnick's evidence was unreliable and grossly misleading. The evidence was "so extremely unfair that its admission violates fundamental concepts of justice." . . . The crime in this case was brutal, but, as the court of appeals has noted in the past, "it is in just these circumstances, when the crime itself is likely to inflame the passions of jurors, that courts must be vigilant in ensuring that the demands of due process are met." . . . The Court harbors "grave doubt" about the soundness of the verdict in this case because it is convinced that the erroneous admission of the evidence had "a substantial and injurious effect or influence in determining the jury's verdict." . . . The State court's conclusions to the contrary were an unreasonable application of federal law established by the Supreme Court . . . . For these reasons, a conditional writ of habeas corpus shall issue.

The Sixth Circuit affirmed the grant of habeas corpus in *Ege v. Yukins*, 485 F.2d 364 (6th Cir. 2007). However, Ege was tried again without the bite-mark evidence. She was convicted of first-degree murder by another jury and is serving a life sentence in a Michigan prison, but still proclaims her innocence.

6

The "How" Question

Tool Marks and Firearms

TOOL MARKS ARE THE IMPRESSIONS left when a hard tool contacts a softer object. The marks may be generated during the manufacturing process, such as when the barrel of a gun is rifled by cutting tools that leave marks on the barrel. The marks may also be generated when a manufactured item, perhaps a tool itself, is used in contact with other substances, such as when a screwdriver or crowbar is used to break into a door or window. In turn, the use of the item generates further marks on surfaces of the tool itself that were not present at the time of manufacture, such as when a gun is repeatedly fired or a screwdriver is used over time on various other items.

When a suspect tool is recovered, examiners look for distinctive features, often microscopically. They seek first to identify "class characteristics," or features that are shared by many similar objects.[1] Then they examine the item microscopically for "individual characteristics," markings which are thought to be unique to the individual tool or firearm. They may also classify some features as "subclass characteristics" when they are common only to a small group of the manufactured items. The analysis then is the comparison of two sets of marks to see if they can be identified by common individual characteristics.

The proffered basis for expert tool mark testimony is that each set of markings is somehow unique.[2] Such testimony has been almost universally accepted.[3] Testimony about a variety of tools has been admitted,[4] including screwdrivers and crowbars,[5] bolt cutters,[6] hammers,[7] pliers,[8] and a punch

FIGURE 6.1.
Comparison of pliers (left) and severed chain link fence tool marks.
FirearmsID.com. Used by permission.

tool.[9] Testimony about knives has been admitted when used as a tool.[10] A Florida court did, however, refuse to admit tool-mark testimony about a knife when used as a weapon, finding no scientific basis for proffered testimony relating a particular knife to marks made on human cartilage.[11]

In this multitude of cases, the admissibility of testimony of tool-mark witnesses seems almost presumed. However, in *United States v. Green,* the judge allowed tool-mark evidence but commented that "[t]he more courts admit this type of toolmark evidence without requiring documentation, proficiency testing, or evidence of reliability, the more sloppy practices will endure; we should require more."[12]

Weapons used in the commission of crimes are a prime source of evidence, as investigators seek to identify a particular gun as the unique source of bullets or other ammunition components. Firearms testimony is simply one branch of the larger field of tool-mark evidence. As with some other types of tool marks, firearms examiners assert that marks on firearms and ammunition bear individual characteristics that are particular to one firearm and that can be reproduced only with that firearm. The marks made by tools in the manufacture of guns or ammunition may result in particular corresponding marks on bullets, cartridge cases, and shot shells as they process through the firing mechanism.[13]

Manufacturers cut a groove in the barrel of a gun so that the bullet spins as it travels through the barrel to make it travel straighter when it leaves the barrel. This "rifling" process leaves marks and scrapes on the barrel metal. When a bullet is fired and travels through the barrel, the barrel marks are transferred to and reflected in marks, called *striae,* on the fired bullet.[14] As the gun is used repeatedly and as the barrel is cleaned, the marks in the barrel, and the resulting striae on the bullet, may develop more individual characteristics.

Other individual gun characteristics can be imparted to the brass cartridge case of the bullets as they are fired and as they are ejected from some types of guns. As the firing pin strikes the cartridge, it leaves its mark. As the cartridge case is blown back to the breech of the gun, the tool marks in that area of the gun are impressed on the exterior of the casing. If the gun ejects the casing, the tool marks of the extractor and ejector parts of the gun are imparted to the exterior of the casing as well.

To compare bullet striations or cartridge impressions, a recovered gun may be test fired so that the test bullet or casing can be compared with a found bullet or casing to see if they originated from the tested gun. As with other tool marks, a firearms examiner makes initial visual determinations of class

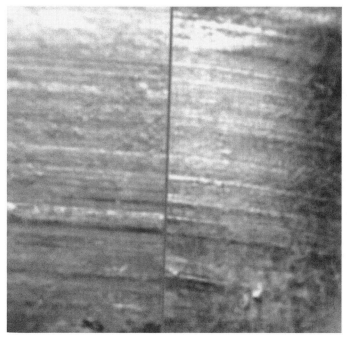

FIGURE 6.2.
Bullet striae comparison.
FirearmsID.com. Used by permission.

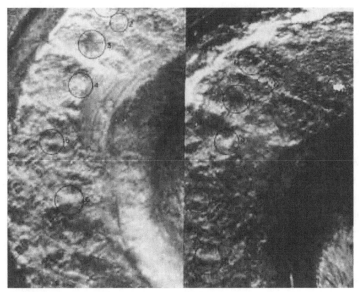

FIGURE 6.3.
Cartridge case comparison. (JFK assassination—Warren Commission).
The John F. Kennedy Assassination Information Center.

characteristics. The markings are then compared with a comparison microscope to see if the individual characteristics correspond.

American courts have admitted firearms comparison testimony routinely for over 130 years, with reported cases beginning with *Wynn v. State*.[15] Any early hesitancy about its admissibility had all but disappeared by the 1930s,[16] when the pioneer firearms scientist Calvin Goddard perfected the comparison microscope.[17] Expert testimony that a found bullet or cartridge and a test bullet or cartridge originated from the same gun has now been admitted in every U.S. jurisdiction.[18]

Tool-mark evidence may be susceptible to a viable *Daubert* challenge. The questions primarily arise in two areas: the claimed uniqueness of tool marks and the standards by which experts may testify that tool marks on two items agree or correspond sufficiently to claim a common origin.

On the uniqueness question, the National Academy of Sciences 2008 ballistics report concluded, "The validity of the fundamental assumptions of uniqueness and reproducibility of firearms-related toolmarks has not yet been fully demonstrated."[19] The report went on to state, "A significant amount of research would be needed to scientifically determine the degree to which firearms-related toolmarks are unique or even to quantitatively characterize the probability of uniqueness."

The standards, or lack thereof, for determining whether the marks on two items agree is of greater concern. Experts agree that there is no perfect match.[20] The Association of Firearms and Tool Mark Examiners states that the marks must be of "sufficient agreement," which is defined as a tool mark that "exceeds the best agreement demonstrated between tool marks known to have been produced by different tools and is consistent with the agreement demonstrated by tool marks known to have been produced by the same tool."[21] The circularity of this "standard," and the lack of more definite criteria, has been the subject of criticism.[22] And the expertise of firearms and toolmark examiners to make reliable comparisons has been steadfastly defended by its practitioners.[23]

Like fingerprint and other impression testimony, the testimony of tool mark experts is, in the final analysis, subjective. The 2009 National Academy of Sciences (NAS) report is critical of the scientific basis for the type of toolmark and ballistics evidence that has been routinely accepted by the courts because "not enough is known about the variabilities among individual tools and guns" and because "[s]ufficient studies have not been done to understand the reliability and repeatability of the methods."[24] The report found that "[a] fundamental problem with toolmark and firearms analysis is the lack of a precisely defined scientific process" and noted the "heavy reliance on the subjective findings of examiners rather than on the rigorous quantification and analysis of sources of variability."

Recent *Daubert* hearings have not resulted in a successful attack on classic firearms expert testimony. Of course, such testimony remains subject to attacks on the propriety and reliability of the laboratory procedures utilized or the qualifications of a proposed expert witness in a particular case and may require the trial judge to hold preliminary hearings into those matters to determine if they pose admissibility questions or only go to the weight of the government's evidence. In two recent Massachusetts cases, the courts conducted lengthy *Daubert* hearings to determine the admissibility of firearms expert testimony.[25] In *United States v. Montiero,* the court reviewed the *Daubert* requirements at length and found that firearms testimony was generally admissible but that the government's proffered witness was not qualified. Moreover, the judge held that even a qualified government expert "may testify that the cartridge cases were fired from a particular firearm to a reasonable degree of ballistic certainty. However, the expert may not testify that there is a match to an exact statistical certainty." Even with this limitation, there are no reported cases that reject the fundamental assumptions of firearm or other toolmark testimony based on a *Daubert* analysis.

Bullet Lead Comparison

Bullet lead comparison is of very questionable validity. Analysis of bullet lead for identification purposes is premised on the theory that batches of lead in bullets have unique combinations of arsenic, antimony, tin, copper, bismuth, silver, and cadmium.[26] The theory is that when two bullets have the same ratios of these elements, they came from the same source.[27] However, one batch of lead in the bullet making process produces a large number of bullets, and those bullets may in turn go to a variety of distribution routes.[28]

Several courts initially admitted bullet lead analysis comparison testimony for identification.[29] Subsequently, however, metallurgists and statisticians demonstrated that it is not reliable. An early *Daubert* evaluation in *United States v. Mikos*[30] found that source conclusions based on bullet lead analysis were based on faulty science and were inadmissible. The court allowed the FBI agent in that case to testify as to the chemical similarities in the bullets but not as to any probability that they came from the same source.

The National Academy of Sciences conducted a study funded by the FBI in 2004 and found that, while the methods for identifying and measuring the elements were sound, the assumptions based on those measurements were simply unsupportable.[31] Initially, the FBI rejected the results of its own funded study,[32] but shortly thereafter, the FBI announced that it had ceased to use bullet lead comparison in its investigations.[33] And no state laboratories do such analysis.[34] Since then, analysis of bullet lead comparison testimony under *Daubert* standards has been rejected by courts.[35] And even *Frye* courts have since rejected bullet lead comparisons.[36]

 CASE STUDY

Science or Politics: The Sacco and Vanzetti Trial

After the end of World War I and the Russian Revolution, a "Red Scare" took hold in the United States. A series of bombings by anarchists created an overwhelming fear of communists, socialists, and anarchists. In the midst of this fervor, on April 15, 1920, two security guards were carrying a factory payroll of $16,000 in South Braintree, Massachusetts, near Boston. Suddenly, two men standing by a fence pulled out guns and fired. One man shot both guards, and the other pumped several more bullets into them. The gunmen grabbed the money, jumped into a waiting black Buick with three other men, and sped away. An eyewitness said the men were "Italian-looking" and that one of them had a "handlebar" mustache. Police found six shell casings around the dead men and identified them as from three manufacturers: Remington, Winchester, and Peters.

Police found the abandoned Buick and linked it with an earlier robbery. They believed that the mastermind of both robberies was an Italian man named Mike Boda, but Boda fled to Italy before police could arrest him. However, police laid a trap for some of Boda's known associates. Two Italians, Nicola Sacco and Bartolomeo Vanzetti, fell into the trap and were arrested. They were ordinary Italian laborers who fit the general descriptions of the murderers. They denied owning guns, but they both were carrying guns. Sacco had a .32-caliber Colt automatic, the same type of gun believed to be the murder weapon, and two dozen bullets made by the three identified manufacturers. Sacco also had a "handlebar" mustache. Both men were members of a radical anarchist group that supported violence to resolve perceived injustices.

Sacco was also charged in the earlier robbery and was tried in that case first. He was found guilty and sentenced to twelve to fifteen years in prison. He and Vanzetti were then tried for the murder of one of the security guards in the Braintree robbery.

FIGURE 6.4.
Vanzetti and Sacco.
University of Missouri–Kansas City School of Law.

The trial included 61 prosecution witnesses and 107 defense witnesses. The eyewitness testimony was weak and contradictory in identifying the defendants. The evidence against Sacco and Vanzetti was primarily based on the testimony of firearms witnesses. Four bullets had been removed from the murdered payroll guards. Only two prosecution firearms experts testified that they could link one of the bullets, "number 3," to Sacco's .32-caliber automatic. One was a state police captain, William H. Proctor, who was an amateur at firearms identification. He testified:

> Q. Captain Proctor, have you an opinion as to whether bullets Nos. 1, 2, 5 and 6 were fired from the same weapon?
> A. I have not. . . .
> Q. Have you an opinion as to whether bullet 3 was fired from the Colt Automatic which is in evidence?
> A. I have.
> Q. And what is your opinion?
> A. My opinion is that it is consistent with being fired by that pistol.

The other firearms witness was Charles Van Amburgh, who was a Remington employee. He agreed with Proctor's conclusions but also hedged his testimony and stated that "I am inclined to believe that number III bullet was fired . . . from this automatic Colt pistol." Van Amburgh also said that there was a rough rust track at the bottom of the pistol barrel, and that corresponding marks could be traced on the bullet. Under cross-examination he admitted that it was common for Colts to rust at that particular place.

The experts for the defense were more confident in their opinion, although not one had based what they offered on scientific techniques. All were self-taught. During deliberations, the jury asked for and received a magnifying glass to examine the bullets for themselves. Sacco and Vanzetti were both convicted on July 14, 1921, and sentenced to death.

In much of the world, Sacco and Vanzetti were portrayed as innocent victims to a capitalist, xenophobic American system. An anarchist defense committee financed an effort to obtain a new trial. The judge denied two motions for new trial. In February 1923 the defense brought a new firearms expert into the case. It turned out that Captain Proctor had serious doubts about his testimony all along. Proctor signed an affidavit stating:

> Bullet Number III, in my judgment, passed through some Colt automatic pistol, but I do not intend to imply that I had found any evidence that the so-called mortal bullet had passed through this particular Colt automatic pistol and the District Attorney well knew that I did not so intend and framed his question accordingly. Had I been asked the direct question: whether I had found any affirmative evidence whatever that this so-called

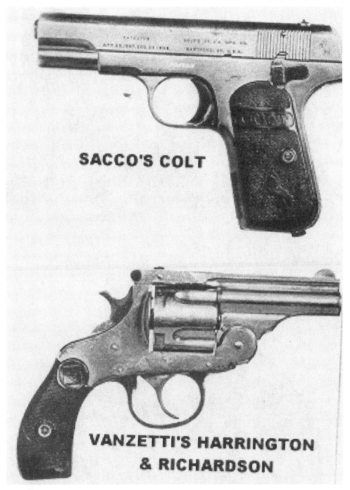

FIGURE 6.5.
Sacco's and Vanzetti's weapons.
University of Missouri–Kansas City School of Law.

mortal bullet had passed through this particular Sacco's pistol, I should have answered then, as I do now without hesitation, in the negative.

However, the prosecution's other expert, Van Amburgh, reexamined the evidence and again insisted that the bullet had been fired from Sacco's gun.

The defense, however, had retained as its new "expert" a man of doubtful integrity, Dr. Albert Hamilton, whose faulty testimony in an earlier case had almost sent an innocent man to his death. It turned out

FIGURE 6.6.
The Sacco and Vanzetti jury with three sheriffs.
University of Missouri–Kansas City School of Law.

FIGURE 6.7.
Cartridge case from Sacco and Vanzetti murder scene.
University of Missouri–Kansas City School of Law.

that Hamilton's doctorate was fraudulent. At the hearing on the last motion for a new trial, Hamilton brought in Sacco's .32 and two new Colt revolvers. He disassembled them and then attempted to switch one of the new barrels with the Sacco barrel. The attempted sleight of hand was exposed. All motions for a new trial were denied early in 1934.

The case was so controversial that a committee was appointed by the Massachusetts governor to review the case in 1927 as part of a clemency request. The committee retained the renowned Calvin Goddard who used a newly invented comparison microscope to examine the gun barrels in the presence of a defense expert. His test firing concluded that bullet 3 had been fired from Sacco's gun. Later the same year, the two men went to the electric chair, still proclaiming their innocence.

Many still claim that Sacco and Vanzetti were wrongfully convicted solely because of their political views. Felix Frankfurter later wrote a book claiming to identify the "real" perpetrators. In 1977, the governor of Massachusetts issued a proclamation asserting the innocence of Sacco and Vanzetti, and the case still remains controversial.

Further Reading

Frankfurter, Felix. *The Case of Sacco and Vanzetti: A Critical Analysis for Lawyers and Laymen.* New York: Universal Library, 1962.

Fire, Explosion, and Arson Evidence

The primary use of forensic science evidence relating to fires and explosions is to attempt to identify the source of the fire and to determine whether an accelerant was used to start or spread a fire or cause an explosion, and, if so, to determine the type of accelerant. It is an unusual forensic science because the fire or explosion being investigated by its nature tends to destroy the physical evidence that could be used to trace its origin. One result of that difference is that the number of criminal arson cases actually pursued by the government, especially in the absence of a homicide, is relatively small.[37]

The field is also unusual in that most of the experts who offer fire origin testimony, known as *cause and origin investigators,* are not scientists, have little or no scientific training, and attempt to testify primarily based on their technical knowledge in the field. Perhaps for that reason, many of the cases in this area that followed early on the heels of *Daubert* reflected an attempt by these practitioners to avoid the applicability of *Daubert* criteria on the ground that their testimony was "technical" rather than "scientific." That argument was supported, at least in part, by the decision of the Eleventh Circuit in *Michigan Millers Mut. Ins. Corp. v. Benfield*,[38] holding that the "experienced-based" testimony of a local fire investigator was not subject to *Daubert* scrutiny and could be presented to the jury. That same court had authored a similar opinion in *Carmichael v. Samyang Tire, Inc.*,[39] which was then subsequently reversed by the Supreme Court in *Kumho Tire Co., Ltd. v. Carmichael*.[40] The Supreme Court in the *Kumho* case unanimously held that the substantive basis for testimony of "technical" experts was subject to the same constraints as to validity as "scientific" experts. Since then, *Daubert* objections to fire cause and origin testimony have dramatically increased and the admission of such testimony, at least in civil cases, has been curtailed.

Fire Cause and Origin Investigation

The preferred methodology for fire investigations is set forth in a code adopted by the National Fire Protection Association.[41] That guide has been accepted as the proper standard both by investigators[42] and by many courts when determining *Daubert* challenges to fire cause and origin testimony.[43] Origins of fires are of course difficult to determine since practitioners in the field recognize that no two fires will burn alike. So-called test burns have been used to try to document common characteristics of fires in a structure before the fire engulfs the entire area, called *flashover*. But such information is primarily used for safety and prevention purposes and is of little or no value in the reconstruction of an actual fire.[44] However, those studies of test burns have served to confirm many of the investigative procedures in the National Fire Protection Association guide and to dispel many of the myths preciously used by investigators. The field investigations initially focus on observations about how and where the fire appears to have spread. All investigators agree that fire behaves based on the "fire triangle" of heat, fuel, and oxygen. Heat rises and many investigators' observations are targeted toward finding a V-shaped pattern in the remains that will lead them to the origin of the fire at the bottom of the V. Where, however, a fire has spread to the point where other ignitions occur, there may be additional V patterns and there is significant disagreement about the ability of fire investigators to determine the first origin in such circumstances.[45]

Cause determinations, especially for accelerants, proceed on a much stronger scientific footing. The presence of an accelerant is often detected by smell. Some agencies use dogs to direct an investigator to a location for further investigation.[46] Others use commercially available electronic sniffers to detect areas for possible investigation, similar to devices that have been used to detect combustible gases in mines. Gasoline or other petroleum-based products,

FIGURE 6.8.
V pattern observed in fire analysis.
Courtesy of C. Roberts, PhD, PE. Used by permission.

of course, are the dominant form of accelerants used in intentionally set fires. Once an accelerant is detected, the task then is to attempt to individualize the particular accelerant. Fire debris is examined in the laboratory to identify common petroleum-based products. The industry standard is to use gas chromatography.[47] Based on the results of the gas chromatography, petroleum products may be identified generally by classification, such as gasoline, according to a recognized petroleum distillate classification system.[48] Further individualization within any particular class is difficult, if not impossible.[49] Thus, although fire investigators may be able to locate the origin of a fire, and can probably determine the general type or class of any accelerant that was present in fire debris, they are not able to individualize cause or origin with any more particularity.

The National Academy of Sciences report expressed its findings and doubts about the validity of fire cause and origin testimony:

[M]uch more research is needed on the natural variability of burn patterns and damage characteristics and how they are affected by the presence of various accelerants. Despite the paucity of research, some arson investigators continue to make determinations about whether or not a particular fire was set. However, according to testimony presented to the committee, many of the rules of thumb that are typically assumed to indicate that an accelerant was used . . . have been shown not to be true. Experiments should be designed to put arson investigations on a more solid scientific footing.[50]

The Validity of Fire Cause and Origin Testimony under *Daubert* Standards

Since the *Kumho* case made it clear that *Daubert* standards were to be applied to fire cause and origin testimony, a number of courts have refused to admit such testimony. For example, in *Weisgram v. Marley,* the Eighth Circuit found error in the admission of a fire investigator's testimony because it lacked sufficient scientific foundation and because no testing had been performed to substantiate his conclusions or theory.[51] Other courts reached similar results after conducting a *Daubert* analysis.[52]

On the other hand, some proffered fire cause and origin testimony has been admitted after the court applied similar *Daubert* scrutiny. For example, in *Allstate Insurance Company v. Hugh Cole Builder, Inc.,* the court reviewed the scientific and factual basis for an expert to testify as to the location and cause of a house fire and determined that the testimony was based on reliable principles and that he had appropriately applied those principles to the observable facts from the scene.[53] And other courts have similarly admitted fire cause and origin testimony, although some without rigorous application of *Daubert* criteria.[54]

Fire Cause and Origin Testimony in Criminal Arson Cases

Reputable scholars have asserted that *Daubert* criteria are being applied by the courts primarily to exclude expert testimony offered by plaintiffs in civil cases and that courts rarely, if ever, rigorously apply *Daubert* standards to expert testimony proffered by prosecutors in criminal cases.[55] Perhaps no area of forensic evidence more clearly demonstrates what some believe to be the discriminatory application of *Daubert* to criminal cases than fire cause and origin testimony.

There appear to be no reported criminal cases where courts have completely excluded fire cause and origin testimony from prosecution experts on the basis of its scientific invalidity under *Daubert.* On the other hand, several courts in criminal cases have specifically allowed such testimony. In *United States v. Norris,* the Fifth Circuit upheld a trial court decision to allow a government expert videotape of a reproduced burn and held that *Daubert* only applied to the expert's qualifications, which were found to be appropriate.[56] In *United States v. Gardner,* the Seventh Circuit approved prosecution fire cause and origin testimony with virtually no real discussion of *Daubert* standards.[57] In *United States v. Diaz*, the First Circuit found no clear error in the admission of government expert testimony as to the cause of the fire in an arson case.[58]

State courts, where most arson cases are tried, appear to have similarly routinely held that fire cause and origin testimony is generally admissible under *Daubert*. In *Commonwealth v. Goodman*, the court upheld the admission of prosecution fire cause and origin testimony even though the National Fire Protection Association's investigation protocol was not followed.[59] In *State v. Interest of W.T.B.*, the Louisiana Court of Appeals affirmed a juvenile conviction based on testimony from an investigator, following a lead from his canine accelerant sniffer, that the fire patterns indicated an accelerant was used. The only reported case where a state court has even limited government fire cause and origin testimony in a criminal prosecution is *State v. Campbell*, where the court found that such testimony was admissible but that the investigator's statement that the defendant started the fire was improperly admitted.[60]

CASE STUDY

Money to Burn?: *United States v. Norris*, 217 F.3d 262 (5th Cir. 2000)

In 1989, James A. Norris, Jr., was the district attorney for Ouachita and Morehouse Parishes in Louisiana. He was also a partner in the law firm of Johnson & Placke. Norris had a dispute with his partners over money and in June of 1989 he withdrew $500,000 from the law firm's accounts. His law partners filed a lawsuit against him to get the money back. That suit was still pending in February of 1994, but apparently Norris sensed that he was going to lose. He withdrew $500,000 in cash from his personal bank accounts and placed the five thousand $100 bills in a safe deposit box. Later that year, Johnson & Placke got a judgment against him in the civil suit, awarding them $540,000 plus prejudgment interest, totaling almost $800,000. The next day, Norris took all of the cash out of the safe deposit box.

The law firm attempted to collect on its judgment against the former partner, who claimed that he had no money to pay them. The firm eventually forced him into an involuntary bankruptcy proceeding. On March 30, 1995, Norris was questioned about the missing $500,000 in bankruptcy court. He claimed that, apparently in a fit of anger, he had burned 4,900 of the 5,000 $100 bills from the bank safe deposit box. He testified in detail that he had poured gasoline on the money and burned it all in a metal trash barrel at his home. In three succeeding bankruptcy hearings, Norris repeated his story, under oath, about burning the cash. The bankruptcy judge did not believe Norris's testimony and ordered him to turn over the cash. On January 31, 1996, the federal district court held Norris in civil contempt and ordered him incarcerated until he produced the money. Every month during his incarceration, he was brought before the bankruptcy court and each time he again claimed that he had burned the money.

The federal prosecutor then charged Norris with four counts of perjury for lying to the bankruptcy court about burning the money. At the trial the prosecutor proffered an expert witness from the Department of Alcohol, Tobacco, and Firearms (ATF) to testify that he had reenacted the alleged burning as described by Norris and that Norris could not have burned the money as he had described under oath. The government witness also presented a videotape of his attempt to re-create the Norris description of the burning. Before trial, Norris filed a motion to exclude the videotape and testimony on the ground that this evidence was not reliable under *Daubert*. The trial judge held a hearing at which he found the government's proffered evidence was "reliable and relevant." He ruled that *Daubert* did not apply and that the evidence was admissible.

At trial, the ATF agent testified as an expert in fire investigation. He testified that he had attempted to burn 4,950 uncirculated $5 bills in the manner Norris claimed to have burned the 4,900 $100 bills. He placed them in a five-gallon plastic container, poured one and three-fourths gallons of gasoline into the container, waited fifteen minutes, and then tossed the contents into a new fifty-five gallon steel trash barrel. He lit the contents on fire with an electric match, and the currency and gasoline burned for five minutes, after which he extinguished the fire by dumping the contents of a fifty-pound bag of corn feed into the barrel, all as Norris had claimed. The agent testified that only about 10 percent of the bills had been either damaged or destroyed. He testified to his "conclusion" that Norris's "recipe" could not have burned more than a small portion of the cash.

On cross-examination, the agent admitted to some differences in the method he used from the Norris description. The re-creation was done in February in Maryland as opposed to October in Louisiana; a slight rain led him to perform the burning portion of the experiment under cover; the $5 bills he used weighed approximately 8 to 9 percent more than $100 bills; he used newly minted, uncirculated currency; the barrel used was new rather than used; ignition was with an electric match rather than a kitchen match as Norris claimed; the bills were stacked as opposed to fanned out in the container; and the agent used one and three-fourths gallons of gasoline while in Norris's statements the amount of gasoline ranges from one-half to one-and-three-fourths gallons. Nevertheless, the agent testified that in all of the differences he erred in the direction of a "hotter" burn and that any variations in the re-creation resulted in only a "minimal" difference.

The jury convicted Norris on all four counts. He was sentenced to thirty-three months' imprisonment, followed by three years' probation, and was ordered to pay $490,000 in restitution to Johnson & Placke.

On appeal, Norris argued that the trial judge had wrongfully ruled that *Daubert* did not apply to the fire expert's testimony. The Fifth Circuit Court of Appeals agreed, but still ruled against Norris and upheld his conviction:

> We conclude that, although the district court erroneously determined that the principles of *Daubert* did not apply to the re-creation and Agent Constantino's testimony, the district court did not err in admitting the evidence. . . .
>
> As the Supreme Court explained in Kumho, *Daubert*'s gate-keeping obligation applies to all expert testimony, and the district court erred in concluding that the videotape re-creation and [the ATF agent's] testimony about the re-creation did not trigger a *Daubert* inquiry. . . . We find, however, that this error was substantially only in form or nomenclature, as the district court analyzed the reliability of the government's evidence, thus in substance essentially performing its gate-keeping role under *Daubert and Kumho.*
>
> Norris argues that the re-creation and [the agent's] deductions from it should have been excluded, because there was no protocol followed during the re-creation, no theory or manuals were relied upon, no error rate was known, there was no independent validation of the re-creation, and the re-creation was only performed once. In the absence of these factors, Norris concludes that the re-creation cannot meet *Daubert*'s requirement · for reliability. However, "[t]he test of reliability is flexible and bends according to the particular circumstances of the testimony at issue." . . . The relevant issue is whether [the agent] could reliably draw a conclusion as to whether Norris's "recipe" would in fact cause all or substantially all the bills to burn up. . . . Therefore, we conclude that the district court did not abuse its discretion in determining that the re-creation was "substantially similar," as the conditions need not be precisely reproduced, but they must only be so nearly the same as to provide a fair comparison.
>
> By making a finding of "substantial similarity," the district court effectively conducted a *Daubert* inquiry by ensuring that the evidence

was relevant and reliable, despite not expressly addressing the four non-exclusive factors listed in *Daubert* or those suggested by Norris. *Daubert's* list of factors "neither necessarily nor exclusively applies to all experts or in every case." . . .

Although the district court erroneously stated that *Daubert's* teachings did not apply to the videotape re-creation and [the agent's] testimony, under the circumstances of this case the district court did not abuse its discretion in admitting the evidence, because it in substance conducted an inquiry into the relevancy and reliability of the evidence. Therefore, Norris's challenge fails.

Norris apparently completed his thirty-three month sentence without disclosing the whereabouts of the money, but his troubles did not end with his release. In 2004, the local Louisiana court ordered him to be incarcerated for continued contempt in refusing to produce the money, although that decision was overturned by a Louisiana Court of Appeals. In 2006, the Louisiana Supreme Court disbarred him and ordered that he be "permanently prohibited from being readmitted to the practice of law in this state."

Bloodstain Pattern Evidence

Bloodstains and bloodstain patterns are often the subject of forensic science testimony in assault or homicide cases. It is important for investigators to understand how a particular stain and pattern occurred. Initially, the investigative question can simply be whether a particular stain is blood or not. More complex is the question of what can be learned from a pattern of blood stains or spattering. It is used to form the basis for testimony about such issues as the sequence of events, the distance from which a victim was shot, claims of self-defense, and any number of other homicide or assault dynamics. It may include determination of whether a stain resulted from arterial spurting, blood dripping, expirated (coughed) blood, back spatter, angular deposits, flight paths, or many other characteristics of the blood path that led to the recorded bloodstain pattern.

Bloodstains

Investigators often view, record, and collect blood from a crime scene. The question sometimes is whether the particular substance is indeed a bloodstain

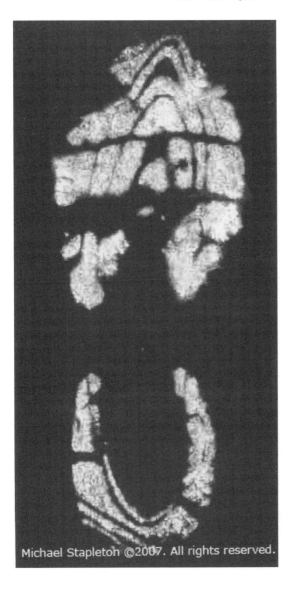

FIGURE 6.9.
Bloodstain reaction
to luminol.
Courtesy of M. Stapleton.
Used by permission.

or some other substance. The presence or absence of blood can be an important piece of evidence. Investigators may want to make presumptive tests at
the scene to see if a stain is indeed blood. Several chemicals may be used to
make such field determinations,[61] the most common of which is luminol.[62]
Luminol is the same chemical used to create the glow of popular light sticks.

Criminal investigators use the same reaction to detect traces of blood at crime scenes. Luminol powder is mixed with hydrogen peroxide and a hydroxide. When the solution is sprayed on blood, the iron from the hemoglobin in the blood acts as a catalyst for the reaction that produces a blue glow.

Unfortunately, luminol is also known to produce false positives, indicating that the stain is blood when it is actually some other substance.[63] Notwithstanding that significant problem, some courts have admitted evidence that field tests with luminol revealed the presence of blood.[64] However, a more appropriate ruling is one reflected in *Ayers v. State*, in which the court ruled that evidence about a luminol reaction is not admissible unless additional tests confirmed that the stain was human blood.[65] Further refinements to the forensic use of luminol are being studied.[66] In the meantime, however, luminol should be regarded as a field test, which is only presumptive for disclosing the presence of blood, and whenever possible the sample should be recovered and preserved for more definitive serology or DNA testing.

Blood Spattering Patterns

The most common bloodstain testimony relates to conclusions drawn from the pattern of blood spattering at a crime scene. The role of blood pattern analysis has been defined by its practitioners as follows:

> BPA [blood pattern analysis] focuses on the analysis of the size, shape and distribution of bloodstains resulting from bloodshed events as a means of determining the types of activities and mechanisms that produced them. . . .
>   BPA is a discipline that uses the fields of biology, physics and mathematics. BPA may be accomplished by direct scene evaluation, and/or careful study of scene photographs (preferably color photographs with a measuring device in view) in conjunction with detailed examination of clothing, weapons, and other objects regarded as physical evidence. Details of hospital records, postmortem examination, and autopsy photographs also provide useful information and should be included for evaluations and study.[67]

The basic mechanical premise of blood pattern analysis has been stated as follows:

> Acts of extreme violence often create a dispersion of blood volumes forced from a wound site. Gunshot and other high energy impacts, such as blunt force beatings, may disperse blood volumes along relatively flat trajectories.
>   Molecular cohesion creates surface tension at the boundaries of these blood volumes. Surface tension causes the drop volumes to assume nearly spherical shapes in free flight. These drops result in bloodstain evidence being deposited

FIGURE 6.10.
Bloodstain pattern field measurements.
Courtesy of J. Slemko Consulting. Used by permission.

on the floor, walls, ceiling or other surfaces or objects within a crime scene. Interpretation of the resulting stain patterns may permit an analyst to approximate
the three-dimensional point of origin.[68]

Forms of blood pattern analysis have been part of criminal investigations for
over a century.[69]

Notwithstanding the claimed basis of the practice in "biology, physics
and mathematics," there are no formal educational requirements for persons claiming to be experts in blood pattern analysis. Some professional
organizations, such as the International Association for Identification
(IAI) and the Scientific Working Group on Bloodstain Pattern Analysis
(SWGSTAIN), recommend training and workshops, but those requirements are minimal. For certification, the IAI requires as little as 240 hours
of workshop training.[70] SWGSTAIN's guidelines for minimum training
would recognize an analyst who had a "[h]igh school diploma or equivalent and four years of job-related experience."[71] The National Academy

of Sciences report was critical of these seemingly minimalist qualification requirements and the subjective nature of blood pattern analysts in general:

> This emphasis on experience over scientific foundations seems misguided, given the importance of rigorous and objective hypothesis testing and the complex nature of fluid dynamics. In general, the opinions of bloodstain pattern analysts are more subjective than scientific. In addition, many bloodstain pattern analysis cases are prosecution or defense driven, with targeted requests that can lead to context bias.[72]

The report summarized its highly critical assessment regarding bloodstain pattern analysis:

> Scientific studies support some aspects of bloodstain pattern analysis. One can tell, for example, if the blood spattered quickly or slowly, but some experts extrapolate far beyond what can be supported. Although the trajectories of bullets are linear, the damage that they cause in soft tissue and the complex patterns that fluids make when exiting wounds are highly variable. For such situations, many experiments must be conducted to determine what characteristics of a bloodstain pattern are caused by particular actions during a crime and to inform the interpretation of those causal links and their variabilities. For these same reasons, extra care must be given to the way in which the analyses are presented in court. The uncertainties associated with bloodstain pattern analysis are enormous.[73]

Nevertheless, the legal history of bloodstain pattern testimony from such experts has been characterized by almost routine acceptance of qualifications and findings of admissibility. Courts are willing to qualify experts on minimal credentials, even after *Daubert*.[74]

The case of *Holmes v. State* demonstrates the courts' reluctance to disallow blood pattern analysis evidence and to allow a witness with minimal credentials to be qualified as an expert.[75] There the Court considered the Texas rule that "evidence derived from a scientific theory, to be considered reliable, must satisfy three criteria in any particular case: (a) the underlying scientific theory must be valid; (b) the technique applying the theory must be valid; and (c) the technique must have been properly applied on the occasion in question." The appellate court found, however, that the prosecution was not required to produce any evidence of the theory or technique of blood pattern analysis because they decided that, after a review of other mostly pre-*Daubert* legal opinions, "we take judicial notice of the validity of blood spatter analysis and hold that the State was not required, and will not be required in the future, to produce evidence on the first two criteria." They also approved the trial court's qualification of a local police officer who had "45–50 hours" of instruction at a conference as an expert in blood pattern analysis.

CASE STUDY

Blood Spatter Evidence: *State v. Davolt*, 207 Ariz. 191, 84 P.3d 456, 475 (2004)

On November 23, 1998, James Davolt was a sixteen-year-old eleventh grader at Lake Havasu High School in Arizona. He left home as usual that Monday morning on his bicycle, carrying his book bag. On the way to school he saw Nicholas Zimmer, an elderly resident in his neighborhood. Davolt knew Mr. Zimmer and the two began to talk. Zimmer took Davolt with him to a local hardware store and the two returned to the Zimmer residence, where they went into the garage.

The police claim that in the garage, Davolt picked up a hatchet and hit Mr. Zimmer in the head three times. According to the police, Mr. Zimmer nevertheless was able to run into the house. Davolt broke into the house, found Mr. Zimmer, and shot him three times in the chest. Davolt then found the elderly Mrs. Zimmer and forced her to go to a bank and write him a check for $1,500, which he cashed. They returned to the house and, according to police, Davolt strangled Mrs. Zimmer to death. The two victims' bodies were then placed in the kitchen of their home, covered with paper, and set on fire.

Davolt took the Zimmers' car and drove to California, where police ultimately apprehended him at a motel room. In his motel room they seized a toy remote-control vehicle, a Green Bay Packers shirt, jacket and cap, red duct tape, a black duffel bag containing clothing belonging to Mr. Zimmer, cut-off jean shorts stained with Davolt's own blood, and a crossword puzzle book and files belonging to the Zimmers. The passenger compartment of the car contained Davolt's school books, food wrappers, packs of Marlboro cigarettes, the book *Masters of Deceit* by J. Edgar Hoover, and a lunch ticket from Lake Havasu High School. A partially dismantled mountain bike was found in the trunk.

James Davolt's trial on charges of murder and robbery included a large amount of forensic evidence. Defense attorneys objected to much of the prosecution's forensic expert testimony, including the testimony of an investigating detective about blood spatters found in the garage. In addition to his observations of blood at the scene, the trial judge allowed the detective to testify to his conclusion that "there appeared to be spots of blood around the perimeter—inside the perimeter of the garage, and

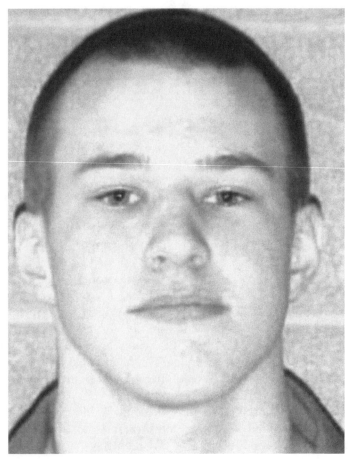

FIGURE 6.11.
Sixteen-year-old James Davolt.
Arizona Department of Corrections.

it was in such a fashion as to suggest that somebody had walked around something there. Presumably, walked around a car in the garage." In reality the detective was simply one of the investigating officers on the case and had never worked as a forensic science technician.

On April 20, 2000, the jury convicted Davolt of two counts of first-degree murder, one count of first-degree burglary, one count of theft of property valued at $1,000 or more, one count of arson of an occupied structure, and one count of auto theft. Following a sentencing hearing, the trial judge sentenced the teenager to death for each of the murder counts and to consecutive sentences of twenty-one years for the burglary, two years for the theft, ten years for the arson of an occupied structure, and seven years for the auto theft. While Davolt's appeal was pending, he proclaimed his innocence but wrote a letter to the trial judge firing his lawyers and asking for an immediate execution. It was not carried out.

Part of Davolt's appeal to the Arizona Supreme Court involved the detective's "expert" testimony concerning the blood spots in the garage. The Arizona Supreme Court gave short shrift to that part of the appeal:

> Rule 702 of the Arizona Rules of Evidence provides: "If scientific, technical, or other specialized knowledge will assist the trier of fact to understand the evidence or to determine a fact in issue, a witness qualified as an expert by knowledge, skill, experience, training, or education, may testify thereto in the form of an opinion or otherwise." The test of whether a person is an expert is whether a jury can receive help on a particular subject from the witness. . . . The degree of qualification goes to the weight given the testimony, not its admissibility. . . .
>
> Detective Harry's training in blood splatter analysis consisted of attending classes on crime scene management, a class on homicide investigation, and watching two training videos on blood splatter analysis as part of his advanced officer training at the Lake Havasu Police Department. While this training is not extensive, it is significantly more extensive than the average person has received and is sufficient to allow the testimony to be heard by the jury.

Davolt's convictions were affirmed. As to sentence, the Arizona Supreme Court remanded the case to the trial judge "to determine whether, at the time of the offense, Davolt possessed moral responsibility and culpability sufficient to render him eligible for the death penalty."

Before Davolt could be resentenced, however, the Supreme Court of the United States held in *Roper v. Simmons*, 543 U.S. 551 (2005), that it is unconstitutional to impose capital punishment for crimes committed when younger than the age of eighteen. Ultimately he was resentenced to two consecutive life terms and that sentence was upheld on appeal in 2010.

7

The "Whether" Question: Social Science Evidence in Criminal Cases

THE SO-CALLED SOFT SCIENCES HAVE BOTH been developed and called into serious question by modern scientific examination. On the one hand, eyewitness testimony, long considered by jurors to be the most important evidence they hear, is itself being challenged as unreliable and courts are being asked to admit expert testimony as to its fallibility.[1] On the other, scientists are challenging the lack of a scientific foundation for such behavioral science claims of "battered woman syndrome" or "rape trauma syndrome."[2]

There is an underlying question of whether *Daubert*, or even *Frye*, applies to the behavioral sciences at all. It is an interesting conundrum for many behavioral scientists. Many have fought the stigma of the sobriquet *soft sciences* for many years and insisted that behavioral science is based upon the same demanding standards reflected in the scientific method used by the physical sciences.[3] Now, however, some behavioral scientists are fighting equally hard to escape the gatekeeping standards of *Frye* or *Daubert* by arguing that the same principles of general acceptance or scientific validity and reliability should not apply to them.[4] They insist that behavioral sciences are "different" and should be treated differently by the courts.

After *Daubert*, there was some dispute about whether its gatekeeping requirements applied to what the Court of Appeals for the Eleventh Circuit, for example, characterized as "nonscientific," technical expert testimony.[5] In *Carmichael v. Samyang Tire, Inc.,* that court held that *Daubert* should not apply to expert testimony based on experience, as opposed to scientific theory.[6] The Supreme Court of the United States rejected the notion and reversed the Eleventh Circuit in that case in *Kumho Tire Co. v. Carmichael.*[7] Similar distinctions used by other federal courts were also presumably invalidated by the broader requirements of *Kumho*.[8]

Obviously, neither *Daubert* nor *Kumho* are controlling in the state courts where most criminal cases are tried. Some states that still use the *Frye*-type test have held that it simply does not apply to testimony from behavioral science experts. In *People v. Beckley*,[9] the Supreme Court of Michigan held that the Michigan version of *Frye*, known as *Davis/Frye*, simply did not apply to behavioral science testimony. It is unclear whether other *Frye* states will follow the *Beckley* line of reasoning. Michigan more recently became a *Daubert* state,[10] and it remains to be seen if the Supreme Court of Michigan will exempt the behavioral sciences from its requirements as well. The state also amended its rules of evidence to correspond with *Daubert*, and it may therefore be more difficult to carve out such an exemption.[11]

In *Daubert* states, presumably, there should have been little doubt after *Kumho* and *Joiner* that its prescription applied to social science evidence. In the *Daubert* opinion itself, Justice Blackmun cited with approval, several times, the decision in *United States v. Downing*, where the issue was the admissibility of testimony from a psychologist regarding the reliability of eyewitness testimony.[12] Nevertheless, some social scientists argued that the scientific analysis of *Daubert* should not be applied, or at least not very strictly applied, to the testimony of social science experts.[13] On the other hand, many believe that the issue was already resolved in *Daubert* itself. Clearly aware of the use and attempted use of social science evidence in criminal courts, the Supreme Court chose to deal with the "junk science" issue by establishing precisely the admissibility criteria that some behavioralists claim that they do not utilize. Several social scientists have embraced, or at least accepted the judgment of the Supreme Court and have suggested that the behavioralists need to adapt their processes if they expect them to form the basis of admissible expert testimony, especially when that testimony may be a factor in a criminal case.[14]

Predictably, behavioral science experts have not fared well in states that have applied *Daubert* or even *Frye* to them.[15] Sound scientific theory is testable if its rate of error can be calculated and subjected to peer review and the test of general acceptance. Human behavior, on the other hand, is more difficult to duplicate and is often apparently incapable of providing appropriate testing and review. Several states have applied *Frye* and *Daubert* to behavioral science testimony and found it wanting.[16]

Eyewitness Identification Experts

Unlike much forensic science evidence, eyewitness identification experts are typically proffered by the defense in criminal cases to raise a reasonable doubt about the reliability of a government witness claiming to identify the defendant as a perpetrator. The defense may seek to present expert testimony based on the scientific research that eyewitness testimony in general is not very reliable, and may also want to elicit testimony that the particular conditions present at the particular identification in the case is scientifically suspect. The necessity for such testimony from the defense perspective is strong. Jurors appear to give great weight to the testimony of eyewitnesses, even at the expense of other forensic evidence in the case.[17]

There is a significant body of scientific research to support the defense position. Studies going back over twenty-five years have demonstrated the unreliability of eyewitness testimony generally.[18] These psychological studies have shown that humans are just not very good (some achieving less than 50-percent accuracy) at identifying people they saw briefly during a traumatic incident. They also indicate that identifications of persons of a different race than the witness are especially unreliable.[19] In the wake of DNA exonerations of persons convicted on the basis of eyewitness testimony, the Department of Justice convened a working group that studied the issue of eyewitness identifications.[20] The report stated that recent cases in which DNA evidence has been used to exonerate individuals convicted primarily on the basis of eyewitness testimony have shown that eyewitness evidence is not infallible.

Notwithstanding this research, some courts have been very reluctant to admit expert testimony about eyewitness identification. A few jurisdictions even have adopted a *per se* rule excluding it, most notably the Eleventh Circuit in *United States v. Holloway*.[21] A few states have also employed a *per se* exclusion.[22] The Eleventh Circuit revisited its *per se* exclusion after *Daubert* in *United States v. Fred Smith,* but did not change its position and relied on the trial judge's finding that such testimony "would not assist the jury."[23] The Eleventh Circuit Court appears to be the only federal circuit to have a rule that such testimony is not admissible *per se.*

More generally, however, courts have held that the admissibility of expert testimony about eyewitness identification is to be decided by the same factors used in evaluating other proffered scientific testimony, whether under *Frye, Daubert,* or general relevancy considerations. Courts have always focused on whether the accuracy of eyewitness identifications is a matter in which jurors need assistance. Even before *Daubert,* trial judges were required to consider many traditional admissibility factors in deciding the admissibility of such testimony, including how it might "fit" the facts of a particular case. Several courts held that, contrary to the Eleventh Circuit position, the failure to make such an analysis and the blanket exclusion of eyewitness identification expert testimony was an error.[24]

Using these parameters, many courts, however, still exclude expert testimony about eyewitness identification in particular cases on the grounds that it is not a proper subject because it will not assist the jury. The rationale is that jurors are able to evaluate the credibility of an eyewitness using their common knowledge and experience after hearing competent cross-examination, and that expert testimony is simply not useful in making the credibility decision.[25] Others, especially in more recent cases, have rejected this "common knowledge" approach in favor of scientific research casting doubt on such "myths."[26]

While some judges still insist that jurors are fully capable of understanding the dangers of eyewitness identification without the necessity of expert assistance, the trend appears to be in the opposite direction. The spate of recent exonerations after postconviction DNA testing has some lessons that appear not to be lost on judges when considering whether to admit expert testimony about eyewitness identification. The Innocence Project analysis of such cases led them to conclude that "[m]istaken eyewitness identifications contributed to over 75% of the more than 248 wrongful convictions in the United States overturned by post-conviction DNA evidence."[27] When eyewitness identification is a principal part of the government's prosecution in a particular case, courts are increasingly recognizing the need to allow expert testimony about the limitations of human perception and recall and about how situational factors affect the accuracy of such identification.

Forensic Abuse Syndromes

Much of the debate about the application of legal standards of admissibility has arisen in the context of proffered expert testimony of psychiatrists and psychologists. Even before *Daubert,* some maintained that testimony from clinical psychologists and psychiatrists could rarely, if ever, meet the legal standard of reasonable certainty that would aid the trier of fact. Indeed, such clinicians may be no more accurate than laypersons.[28] Nevertheless, over the last twenty years, prosecutors have sought to present expert testimony concerning various "syndromes" of symptoms or characteristics that the government claims are typical of, or at least consistent with, the behavior of victims of certain crimes. Various syndromes have been offered, including child sexual abuse accommodation syndrome, battered child syndrome, battered woman syndrome, battering parent syndrome, separation trauma, and rape trauma syndrome.[29] The testimony is usually offered to corroborate the testimony of the complainant or to rebut certain claims of the defendant. Some preliminary legal issues that arise in these cases are common to the behavioral concept of a "syndrome." Initially, as noted earlier, some courts have held that the *Frye* or *Daubert* admissibility analysis may not be applicable at all to testimony from experts in the behavioral sciences, and many of those cases arose in the context of proffered "syndrome" testimony.[30] The idea that social and political pressure to redress gender imbalance, and not good science, is the basis for forensic syndrome evidence is not shared by all, but many agree that such social pressures are at least one of the factors leading to the production of such testimonial evidence and even to the willingness of the courts to accept it. As one group of scholars concluded:

> Media attention to social issues (e.g., battering), or specific high profile cases, may facilitate the readiness of a legal culture to adopt evidence that addresses the social issue. Increased media attention to the problem of battering in each country has undoubtedly contributed to the education of the public regarding the prevalence of domestic violence, as well as to demands that domestic violence be taken into account in legal actions related to such evidence.[31]

The syndrome concept has a theoretical basis within the psychiatric parlance. The current *American Psychiatric Association Diagnostic & Statistical Manual of Mental Disorders* offers a general definition of syndrome as "a grouping of signs and symptoms, based on their frequent co-occurrence, that may suggest a common underlying pathogenesis, course, familial pattern, or treatment selection."[32] A syndrome is not necessarily a medical diagnosis but rather a collection of related symptoms.[33] A diagnosis depends on whether the pattern of symptoms is the result of an underlying pathological process that is recognized as a "disorder."[34]

The "battered woman syndrome" is a psychological and behavioral phenomenon that describes characteristics of women living in battering relationships.[35] Although expert testimony on the syndrome originated in self-defense cases, it has been proffered by prosecutors for a variety of reasons and by defendants claiming duress short of self-defense.[36] The syndrome has been discussed for over thirty years. It is regarded as a subcategory of posttraumatic stress disorder and has four principle elements: (1) the woman believes that the violence was her fault; (2) the woman has an inability to place the responsibility for the violence elsewhere; (3) the woman fears for her life or her children's lives; and (4) the woman has an irrational belief that the abuser is omnipresent and omniscient.[37]

Prosecutors often offer evidence of the syndrome in prosecutions of alleged batterers to explain to the jury why the complainant may have changed her testimony to favor the defendant.[38] Yet prosecutorial use of the syndrome raises substantial questions and some courts have held that it constitutes impermissible bad character or "bad acts" evidence.[39]

The battered woman syndrome has received more attention from the legal system, and greater acceptance by the courts, than perhaps any other area of psychological research or testimony.[40] Courts applying *Frye* have admitted it.[41] Nevertheless, its underlying scientific basis has been the subject of criticism, finding that neither the legal nor empirical bases for the syndrome are sound.[42] At least one court has reviewed battered woman syndrome under a *Daubert*-type standard and found that it was not based on a valid underlying scientific theory.[43]

"Rape trauma syndrome" is "used to describe common responses to a sexual assault."[44] The term was coined by Burgess and Holmstrom to describe two stages of recovery from rape.[45] Rape trauma syndrome evidence is usually offered to prove lack of consent. Courts are fairly clear about the purposes for which the evidence cannot be used. As with other syndrome evidence, it is not probative that a rape occurred[46] and cannot be used simply to bolster the credibility of the alleged witness that the rape occurred.[47] The most accepted use of rape trauma syndrome is as evidence when the defense is consent and the prosecutor wishes to show that the complainant's behavior is consistent with that of a rape victim.[48] It usually speaks to postrape behavior. It has specifically been allowed to explain postincident behavior of minor victims where the defendant denies any misconduct.[49]

Many activists have promoted the introduction of rape trauma syndrome testimony in rape trials for social or political reasons. Rape trauma syndrome clearly has primarily social and political origins. Shirley Dobbin and Sophia Gatowski examined those origins and attempted to place the resulting forensic syndrome in evidentiary context:

> After examining the sociopolitical emergence and production of RTS [rape trauma syndrome] testimony and the development of the evidence industry that surrounds that production, the question remains one of whether or not RTS testimony has a place in court. Feminists, activists and others advocated for the introduction of RTS testimony in rape trials to give voice to women, to empower them and to combat negative myths and stereotypes about women and rape. However, while RTS was introduced into the court with the best of intentions, it has not had the intended consequences. Any perceived benefits of its introduction must be weighed against its negative impact. In deciding what place RTS evidence should have in court, we must recognize its social and political history and the social and political consequences of its use in court. We must question the legitimacy of a type of evidence that medicalizes and pathologizes women, that removes rape from its political and social context and potentially opens the door for the revictimization of women by the legal system.[50]

They urge that social science is "science" and that the application of *Daubert* to rape trauma syndrome evidence is appropriate, at least to the extent of determining if it really is "good science."

"Child sexual abuse syndrome" is the phrase often used to describe the profile of characteristics experienced by children after being sexually abused.[51] Originally, it was described as the "child sexual abuse accommodation syndrome" by Dr. Roland Summit. His theory described five coping mechanisms commonly observed in sexually abused children: "(1) [s]ecrecy; (2) [h]elplessness; (3) [e]ntrapment and accommodation; (4) [d]elayed, conflicted, and unconvincing disclosure; and (5) [r]etraction."[52]

The shorter phrase, child sexual abuse syndrome, is a broader term than Dr. Summit's original theory and includes a longer list of observed characteristics.[53] The American Medical Association has many more characteristics on its list, including overt or subtle and indirect disclosures to a "relative, friend, or teacher"; highly sexualized play; withdrawal and excessive daydreaming; low self-esteem and "feelings of shame or guilt"; falling grades; pseudomature personality development; sexual promiscuity; poor peer relationships; suicide attempt; positive relations exhibited toward the offender; and frightened or phobic reactions, especially toward adults.[54]

Many courts have admitted expert testimony regarding child sexual abuse syndrome in light of the significant problems associated with the testimony of children in general and especially the testimony of children relating to sexual abuse. There are significant challenges presented by such testimony. In light of these difficulties, expert testimony has been allowed for a variety of purposes.[55] Among the courts that allow child sexual abuse syndrome testimony, a typical approach is that (1) an expert may not testify that the sexual abuse occurred, (2) an expert may not vouch for the veracity of a victim, and (3) an expert may not testify whether the defendant is guilty. But an expert may testify regarding typical and relevant symptoms of child sexual abuse for the sole purpose of explaining a victim's specific behavior that might be incorrectly construed by the jury as inconsistent with that of an actual abuse victim, and with regard to the consistencies between the behavior of the particular victim and other victims of child sexual abuse to rebut an attack on the victim's credibility.[56] On the other hand, a few courts have taken a very rigid stand against any child sexual abuse syndrome testimony and find that it does not meet the scientific requirements of *Frye* or *Daubert*.[57]

Conclusions about Social Science Evidence

The development of new forms of scientific evidence and the use of DNA makes us reexamine the types and purposes of evidence considered admissible in criminal proceedings. The trial court is firmly established as the gatekeeper for making that examination to ensure that only "good science" and not "junk science" is presented to the jury as reliable. The *Daubert* standards for determining admissibility based on a scientific analysis by judges are well established in the federal courts and in many of the state courts as well. The implementation of those standards in criminal proceedings is not so clear and some courts apply *Daubert* in a manner that appears to be biased in favor of prosecution evidence.

The implementation of *Daubert*, or even *Frye*, in the evaluation of proffered social science testimony is at best unpredictable and at least irregular across the many criminal jurisdictions. Some courts have held that neither form of scientific analysis is applicable to the social sciences and the only question is whether the evidence will "aid the jury." Courts that apply a *Daubert* analysis are troubled by the deficiencies of social science evidence, especially in the important *Daubert* criteria of falsifiability and error rates. Two contrasting examples demonstrate these difficulties. There is a demonstrable scientific basis for the testimony of social scientists as to the reliability of eyewitness evidence and yet some courts, before and after *Daubert*, have been reluctant to allow the jury to hear such testimony. On the other hand, expert evidence about forensic abuse syndromes has little demonstrable scientific basis but often continues to be admitted, perhaps because of the social and political origins and impetus for the production and use of such testimony.

8

Jurors and Forensic Science Evidence

The "*CSI*" Myth

DECISIONS ABOUT THE ADMISSIBILITY of forensic science evidence assume even larger importance to the extent that jurors consider such evidence to be especially critical to their ultimate decision about guilt. It is widely perceived, especially by prosecutors and other law enforcement agencies, that modern juries give a great deal of weight to scientific evidence. They complain that jurors today demand more from the prosecution in the way of scientific evidence and that they will wrongfully acquit defendants when such evidence is not presented. Most of the blame for these expectations is heaped on a single television show, *CSI* (and its spin-offs), to the degree that it has become known, both in the popular media and in legal circles, as the "*CSI* effect."[1] However, while jurors clearly do have increased expectations and even demands for scientific evidence, it is far too simplistic to attribute those expectations and demands to a particular television show—or even to the a particular medium of television—and doing so distracts judges and lawyers from the important adjustments that need to be made in criminal trial practice to accommodate these new jurors.

Some commentators have speculated that there was no increase in juror expectations or demands about scientific evidence. They argue that the claimed *CSI* effect could be nothing more than "sour grapes" by prosecutors who were rationalizing losses[2] or attorneys for both sides just trying to influence jurors during voir dire.[3]

Empirical studies of jurors were conducted in 2006 and 2009 to determine whether current juries expect and demand scientific evidence and, if so, whether it is related to their television watching habits.[4] The studies found that jurors do indeed expect prosecutors to present scientific evidence and that, especially in cases where the rest of the evidence is circumstantial, they will demand scientific evidence before they will return a verdict of guilty. However, the studies also found that, contrary to the common media characterizations, these increased expectations and demands for scientific evidence were *not* related to watching *CSI* or similar television programs. Subsequent and other researchers have come to a similar conclusion.[5]

The "Tech" Effect

If it is not watching *CSI*, then what is causing these increased expectations and demands? It has long been understood by social scientists that juror perceptions of our criminal justice system are influenced by characterizations of that system in television and other media. An early theory for that influence was the *cultivation theory,* posited over thirty years ago by George Gerbner.[6] He theorized that television programs develop or "cultivate" the public's perceptions of societal reality.[7] Indeed, he regarded television as such a strong force in our society that it was the source of our perceptions of reality. Gerbner found that one strong message that television communicated to the public was about crime and an overestimated likelihood of becoming a victim of crime in a "mean world."

The problem with the cultivation theory as a means of explaining the impact of popular culture on individual perceptions of reality, especially as it relates to a claimed *CSI* effect, is that it is seriously technologically outdated. Television no longer has the overwhelming media impact on our culture today that it did when Gerbner made his observations. Thirty years has turned out to be an enormous amount of time technologically. Even within television, the media has changed dramatically. Since Gerbner's time, television offerings have increased dramatically.

It certainly remains true that portrayals of crime and criminal justice on television impact the perception of law and, in particular, criminal justice in our popular culture.[8] However, today the medium of television conveys only a few of the many messages about crime and criminal justice that potential jurors receive. Perhaps more importantly, television itself is no longer the overpowering media influence in our society that it once was, and to some extent messages from other media have displaced television and certainly newspapers.[9] Postmodern society is globalized and interconnected, not only by goods and commerce, but by "changing, swirling, and colliding" media messages and other cultural forces that frame our perceptions of crime and criminal justice in a myriad of different messages and media.[10] The 2006 study concluded that "[r]ather than any direct '*CSI* effect' from watching certain types of television programs, . . . juror expectations of and demands for scientific evidence are the result of broader changes in popular culture related to advancements in both technology and information distribution . . . that could be more accurately referred to as the 'tech effect.'"[11]

A unique feature of the rapid development of new scientific technology is that it has led to applications that have almost immediately become part of popular culture. Ordinary citizens know about and use their own personal and business applications of this technology. They may use a personal laptop, a high-powered business computer, or perhaps a brightly colored cellular phone with some of the capabilities of both types of computers. They may have a satellite-driven global positioning system on the dash of their car, or perhaps it is incorporated into that satellite-driven cellular phone as well. They may even use a mail-in or portable DNA kit to determine the parentage of their child. They also know that it can be used in criminal courts. They have learned from the media about the now hundreds of wrongly convicted defendants who have had their innocence proven with DNA. They have watched countless television shows and films with news or fictional depictions of police solving crimes with some new technology, whether that technology is real or imagined. The 2009 juror study found that there was a connection between the sophistication of the technology equipment jurors used and their demands for scientific evidence. This supports the idea of a "tech effect" as opposed to a "*CSI* effect."

The sources of this tech effect, and the various sociological theories that might explain it, are relevant to criminal justice professionals only to the extent that we might tailor our reactions to it in court. If we appreciate the complexity of the tech effect, then law enforcement personnel and defense lawyers must tailor the investigations, the evidence, and the arguments either to provide the evidence the jury seeks or to explain to them why that evidence is not forthcoming in a particular case. If, on the other hand, juror expectations arise simply from watching a television show, as the *CSI* effect label suggests, then lawyers can simply ask jurors whether they watch those shows and whether they understand the differences between fiction and reality as applied to criminal proceedings. Indeed, the latter approach is significantly easier and, probably predictably, is the approach most often used. In their report of the 2009 study, Shelton, Barak, and Kim suggested a more complicated "indirect" model for understanding juror reactions to various forensic science messages.

Prosecutors argue that heightened jury expectations, regardless of their source, have improperly increased their burden of proof.[12] Prosecutors who do so violate the admonition of Judge Margaret Hinkle that "an effective advocate cannot ignore or talk down to jurors, whatever the composition of the jury" and that, especially in the area of forensic science evidence, they should "[n]ever underestimate jurors' intelligence, wisdom and common sense."[13] The constitutional commitment to a jury system is a judgment that justice in individual cases *should* reflect the values of popular culture. The jury system dictates that those trends, regardless of their source, will be reflected in individual cases.

Jurors think that DNA and other modern scientific techniques are extremely accurate—and they are right. DNA evidence is viewed by jurors as being qualitatively different from other traditional forms of evidence with a "special aura of credibility."[14] One recent study found that jurors rated DNA evidence as 95 percent accurate.[15] One reason why *CSI* is so popular, and perhaps so threatening to prosecutors, is that "although *CSI* depicts unrealistic crimes in a melodramatic fashion, this crime drama does so in a manner that suggests that its science is valid, that the audience understands science and can use it to solve crimes."[16] As Edward Imwinkelried put it, "Common sense suggests that a rational trier of fact would treat testimony about a random-match probability of one in 7.87 trillion as highly probative, if not dispositive."[17] The trends by jurors to expect and demand scientific evidence, exemplified by the tech effect, will undoubtedly continue. It is the government and the judicial system that must respond and adapt to those trends.

"Negative" Evidence

One prosecutor response to the increasing tech effect demand for scientific evidence by jurors is to introduce evidence about tests that were not done or tests that did not incriminate the defendant. It is a technique designed to anticipate questions that jurors may have about the thoroughness of the government investigation so they will not speculate about the possible exculpatory results of tests left undone.

A good example of this technique was presented in the recent Delaware case of *State v. Cooke*,[18] in which the defendant was charged with murder, rape, burglary, and arson.[19] The prosecutor attempted to introduce several test results that were either inconclusive or exculpatory, and the defense filed a motion *in limine* to exclude that evidence as irrelevant. The government's offer of proof read like a recitation of many modern forensic science testing procedures, including DNA prediction analysis, video enhancement, trace (hair) analysis, tool-mark analysis, hair comparison, fingerprint analysis, voice identification analysis, footwear analysis, fabric impression analysis, and handwriting comparison. The prosecution claimed that the *CSI* effect can encourage improper speculation by jurors and that it needed to show all of the tests that were done, even if they had negative results.

In his extensive opinion, Judge Herlihy reviewed several studies and opinions regarding the so-called *CSI* effect, and the debate over whether it exists. In the end, he did not conclude that there actually is an effect attributable to *CSI*, but observed that jurors appear to have expectations for scientific evidence and that those expectations are influencing trials that would justify the prosecution's desire to present such "negative" evidence.

Increased juror demands for scientific evidence may in fact justify the introduction of evidence that might otherwise be considered more prejudicial than probative. In *United States v. Fields*,[20] a death penalty case, the defendant argued that admitting nineteen photos of the body at the crime scene and thirteen autopsy photos was an abuse of discretion by the trial judge. Although the United States Court of Appeals for the Fifth Circuit found many of the pictures shocking and gruesome, including photos of the victim's decomposing body, it found them nevertheless to be highly probative based on the defense's position that there was no reliable DNA evidence and little crime scene evidence regarding the body itself. The court held that "[i]n this age of the supposed 'CSI effect,' explaining to the jury why the Government had little in the way of physical or scientific evidence was arguably critical to the Government's case" and found no error in the admission of the photographs.

Voir Dire, Argument, and Jury Instructions

A second method of coping with the tech effect expectations of jurors is to address those expectations directly with the jurors at the trial. Attorneys have begun to do so using voir dire and opening and closing statements, and requesting jury instructions that pose the issue. Voir dire about *CSI* watching habits has been a typical prosecutorial approach.

Prosecutors' questions about whether potential jurors watch the program are certainly proper, and comments about the program or attempts to distinguish the investigations depicted on the program from reality have generally been upheld. For example, in *People v. Marquez* the court approved a prosecutor's voir dire, which asserted: "All of you have watched one kind of show, whether it's 'Law and Order,' 'CSI,' any of those shows. How many of you do that? How many of you have a certain expectation that both Mr. Mack and

I, and the judge, will perform in a similar manner as in those shows? Those are shows and that's not real life, and this is real life." [21] *People v. Smith* held that the prosecutor's remarks during voir dire that "real life is not akin to CSI television shows and that he was not trying to 'pull the wool' over the juror's eyes" were "merely" attempts to ensure that the jury not hold the prosecution to a higher burden of proof than was required. [22] Yet another example, *State v. Latham,* held that there was no prejudice in prosecutor's statements during voir dire that:

> [C]ertain types of forensic evidence were not technologically possible. . . . CSI is a bunch of you know what. . . . It doesn't happen that way. . . . The guy on CSI who's now a heart throb and everything else, this William Peterson, that might be—make for a good TV show, but that's not reality, okay. . . . That would be great if we could do that. That would be fabulous. But you can't. Okay. In all the years I been doing this, I've never had—that's just not something that—technologically is not there yet. [23]

Failing to object to a long prosecutor voir dire statement about *CSI* was held not to be a sign of ineffective counsel by the Ohio Court of Appeals of Ohio in *State v. Taylor,* in which the prosecutor had stated:

> This is kind of an interesting story. I tell it in every one of my Voir Dires. I had a rape case a few years back when I was a fairly new Prosecutor. They found a pubic hair on the victim's underwear. Now, the victim knew the perpetrator, the alleged perpetrator, so I said, let's test it and see if it is his pubic hair. So, I call the Attorney General's Office, who does our genetic testing, and they tell me that is not good science. No, no. I just saw it on CSI. Of course it is good science. Just to double-check I called the county Coroner's Office, and they tell me the same thing. So, a lot of those TV shows are fictional, or the science is no good. It is fictional for purposes of solving their fictional crimes. [24]

In *United States v. Harrington,* [25] the trial judge took it upon himself to state to the jury venire during voir dire that "CSI evidence" was not required to convict the defendant. The Court of Appeals for the Eleventh Circuit found that the trial judge "did not err by questioning jurors about whether they would be able to separate television shows from the facts of the case and stating that there may not be 'CSI' evidence presented to them."

Many of the reported cases involving *CSI* voir dire have arisen in the context of a *Batson* challenge, [26] in which the prosecutor attempted to prove that it was the juror's answers to *CSI* questions, rather than race, that motivated a peremptory challenge. In *United States v. Hendrix,* [27] the prosecution claimed that it had excused the only two black jurors on race-neutral grounds: as to one of the black jurors, the prosecutor explained that the exclusion was because he was "one of those CSI guys," and the prosecutor had "great concern about the jurors who watch a lot of CSI." The United States Court of Appeals for the Seventh Circuit held that, coupled with other factors, the *CSI* explanation was not pretextual and defeated the *Batson* challenge. In *State v. Carson,*[28] a juror's response to the defense during defense voir dire about *CSI* was offered as the basis for the prosecution's peremptory challenge of a minority juror, and the court found that to be a race-neutral reason. Other cases have similarly found answers to *CSI* voir dire to be a race-neutral basis for excusing minority jurors.[29]

Opening statements and closing arguments about the *CSI* effect have caused more difficulty for prosecutors. In *Boatswain v. State,*[30] the prosecutor's closing argument included the following:

> The one issue left in this case is: Was it him? The defense would say, well—and you know they will—there's [*sic*] no fingerprints of him [*sic*]. They didn't print the money. They didn't find his prints on the note. In today's day and age, unfortunately, the police and the State isn't [*sic*] put to the same test that they wrote 200 years ago in the Constitution [in] which they said the proof must be beyond a reasonable doubt. Unfortunately, the test, of course, of criminal defendants now is, can they meet the TV expectation that they hope folks like you want. Can they meet CSI?
> [Objection overruled]
> [I]f they don't have fingerprints, he can't be guilty. On TV, they would have found fingerprints. But this isn't TV, this is real life.

Although the Supreme Court of Delaware did not find that the argument required reversal, it did find clear error in allowing such an argument because statements that trivialize the actual constitutional standard of the burden of proof are improper.

In the subsequent case of *Mathis v. State,*[31] the Supreme Court of Delaware distinguished *Boatswain* in a situation in which it found that the prosecutor's opening statement did not disparage the burden of proof. Later, in *Morgan v. State,*[32] the Supreme Court of Delaware reaffirmed *Boatswain* and found that it was improper for the prosecutor to argue that "[t]his is not CSI Las Vegas or CSI New York where police do all sorts of different tests all the time. It's fact specific. In this case it wouldn't have worked. So why do it?" The court held that the argument was improper because there was no evidentiary basis for the statement that the tests were unavailable or would have been to no avail.[33] Other courts have followed the *Boatswain* reasoning and found *CSI* statements or arguments to be improper.[34] In *People v. Compean,* the court found it to be error, although corrected by a jury instruction, when a prosecutor stated:

> Nobody is going to fingerprint a little baggie like you see there. This is not "CSI." These are the economic realities and times of Contra Costa County. . . . All of ya'll lives [*sic*] in this county, I think you know the economic realities of it.[35]

On the other hand, some courts have approved arguments or statements that urge the jury to consider the *CSI* effect in a way that reinforces rather than disparages the burden of proof. For example, in *State v. Pittman*,[36] the prosecutor's opening statement included the following comments:

> Do not hold the State of New Jersey to a standard that is not given to you by the Court. Do not hold the State of New Jersey to what I call the Hollywood standard. This is not TV. This is not CSI New York. This is not CSI New Brunswick, okay. What you see on TV is not real. This is what happens. Not what you see on Law & Order. Not what you see on Court TV. Not what you see on the Grammys that come from a Hollywood producer with writers and producers that, to sell commercials. It is not real. Do not hold the State of New Jersey to the Hollywood standard. Hold it to the standard of what reality is. You're going to hear reality in this courtroom. That is how it's done. It is what happens on the streets. . . . .
>
> Do not hold the State of New Jersey to that Hollywood standard. Hold it to the standard of reality and what the Court gives you. Keep that in mind when you are hearing the testimony.

The Appellate Division of the New Jersey Superior Court found no error and held that the prosecutor was just "trying to dispel any illusion jurors may have had that a trial in the real world is like a trial in the world of fiction."

Objections that comments about *CSI* are based on facts outside the record have been rejected on the basis that "the prosecutor was merely referring to the jurors' common knowledge that, unlike in the real world, investigations on television typically wrap up in less than an hour."[37] Similar *CSI* arguments have been allowed by trial judges and approved on appeal.[38] On the other hand, the Supreme Court of Montana brought up *CSI* in an interesting context dealing with a motion to suppress a search of a drug dealer, saying in *State v. Goetz:*

> Truly, it is a different world today, not only in terms of technological advances, but also in the expectation of the use of technology. I would submit, as the questioning italicized above likewise indicates, that our citizens, especially young people in today's society who have been raised in the age of *Law and Order* and *CSI*, would think it unusual that a drug dealer would have a *reasonable* expectation that his conversations during a drug sale to a non-confidant were not being consensually monitored. The drug dealer may have a *subjective* expectation, but it is not an expectation that our society would deem reasonable.[39]

Prosecutors and even defense attorneys have also elicited testimony referring to *CSI*, or the *CSI* effect, that has been the subject of appeals. For example, in *State v. McKinney*,[40] the prosecutor questioned witnesses about whether the defendant watched *CSI* and the defendant objected that the questioning was improper character evidence. On appeal, the Ohio court ruled that it was "not willing to hold that watching network crime series such as *CSI* or in previous decades *Perry Mason, Dragnet,* and others constitutes evidence of bad character."[41] Other courts have also allowed testimony referring to *CSI.*[42]

To address the tech effect, some courts have given jury instructions about how the jury should consider issues concerning the lack of scientific evidence. In *United States v. Saldarriaga*,[43] the defense had questioned government witnesses in a drug-delivery trial about the failure of the government to record, photograph, or videotape the undercover transaction or to test the bag containing the drugs for fingerprints. Apparently *sua sponte,* the trial judge gave the following instructions to the jury:

The law is clear that the government has no obligation to use any particular techniques. The government's techniques [are] not on trial here. The government has no obligation to use all the possible techniques that are available to it. The government's function is to give enough evidence to satisfy you beyond a reasonable doubt that the charges are true, and the fact that there are a thousand other things they could have done is wholly irrelevant.

However, if suggesting things that they could have done leads you to think, well, maybe I have a reasonable doubt because I didn't have any evidence on that subject, if that happens, why, then, of course, that is a reasonable doubt like anything else. . . .

If evidence is such that without the picture you would have a reasonable doubt as to whether the government established the defendant[']s identity as the person who did these things, then you have a reasonable doubt and it doesn't make any difference whether the government could have or could not have. Maybe the government could establish beyond peradventure that it would be impossible to have that picture, it doesn't make any difference. If you have a reasonable doubt because you didn't get the picture, then you [have] a reasonable doubt.

It is wholly immaterial whether the government could have done it or couldn't have done it or how many people the government had available that would do it.

The United States Court of Appeals for the Second Circuit, *per curiam,* held:

[T]he jury correctly was instructed that the government has no duty to employ in the course of a single investigation all of the many weapons at its disposal, and that the failure to utilize some particular technique or techniques does not tend to show that a defendant is not guilty of the crime with which he has been charged.

A similar instruction about the failure to conduct fingerprint tests was approved by the United States Court of Appeals for the Fourth Circuit earlier in *United States v. Mason*.[44]

In *Evans v. State*,[45] the defense attacked the government's heroin delivery case because no video record had been made of the alleged undercover drug purchase. In its instructions to the jury, the court addressed the claimed testing deficiency:

> During this trial, you have heard testimony of witnesses and may hear argument of counsel that the State did not utilize a specific investigative technique or scientific test. You may consider these facts in deciding whether the State has met its burden of proof. You should consider all of the evidence or lack of evidence in deciding whether a defendant is guilty.
>
> However, I instruct you that there is no legal requirement that the State utilize any specific investigative technique or scientific test to prove its case. Your responsibility as jurors is to determine whether the State has proven, based on the evidence, the defendants' guilt beyond a reasonable doubt.[46]

The appeals court noted that such arguments are commonly used by the defense to raise a reasonable doubt. Relying on *Saldarriaga,* the court found that the instruction did not undermine the prosecution's duty to prove guilt beyond a reasonable doubt and affirmed the conviction. However, the court offered some advice as to a better way of giving such an instruction:

> [W]e stress that the salutary effect of the instruction is found in the advisement that the absence of such evidence should be factored into the juror's determination of whether the State has shouldered its burden if, *and only if,* the absence of such evidence, itself, creates reasonable doubt. The absence of evidence, available to the State, may not, *ipso facto,* constitute reasonable doubt. The risk is greatest that such an instruction will run afoul of the prohibition against relieving the State of its burden where the instruction is predominant in the overall instructions and its relation to the reasonable doubt standard unclear. Consequently, the preferable practice is for the court's instruction to be promulgated in conjunction with the explication of the State's burden to prove the defendant guilty beyond a reasonable doubt.[47]

The advice in *Evans* is worth heeding. If the trial judge gives an instruction regarding the lack of scientific evidence, whether requested or *sua sponte,* it should be cast in terms of reasonable doubt to make sure that the jury understands that while a lack of scientific evidence alone does not mean there is reasonable doubt, they must never nevertheless determine whether the government has proven, without such scientific evidence, the defendant's guilt beyond a reasonable doubt.

9

Conclusions:
Where Do We Go from Here?

The Last Twenty Years: An Era of Doubt

THE STATUS OF FORENSIC SCIENCE EVIDENCE began to change in the 1990s. As
Professor Michael J. Saks put it recently:

> Whatever tests of admissibility of expert testimony might formally have existed
> in various jurisdictions at various periods over the past century or so, they were
> applied infrequently to government proffers of forensic science. . . . The casual
> acceptance by courts over the past century of whatever the government prof-
> fered in the name of scientific expert testimony is beginning to catch up with
> the law.[1]

It is important to understand that the questioning of the rather routine
admission of forensic science evidence in criminal prosecutions began during
an era when science and technology, including information technology, was
experiencing a surge of development. It was, and still is, an amazing technological age of discovery and information exchange. A 2006 Rand research
study stated:

> Based on our technical foresights . . . , we see no indication that the accelerated
> pace of technology development is abating, and neither is the trend toward mul-
> tidisciplinarity nor the increasingly integrated nature of technology applications.
> . . . Underlying all of this is the continuing trend toward globally integrated
> publications media, Internet connectivity, and scientific conferences, as well

as the development and crossfertilization of ever more sensitive and selective instrumentation.[2]

The development and miniaturization of computers and the application of computer technology to almost every human endeavor has been a primary force in scientific and technological developments, and of our awareness of those developments.[3]

Perhaps no other development exemplifies this age as poignantly as the discovery of the ability to understand the complexity of DNA that is at the source of our being, and then to begin to effectively "map" the entire human genome. DNA mapping also illustrates another feature of modern technology that is relevant to developments in forensic science. This modern technology made it possible to gather and systematically analyze enormous amounts of empirical data. Specifically as it affects forensic science, this hyperextension of the abilities of quantitative analysis presents a much more scientific model in some areas where we had been content to rely on anecdotal or experiential, or perhaps more generously called *qualitative analysis,* conclusions.

Against this technological backdrop, changes in the legal, scientific, and cultural landscape have cast some significant doubts on our continued use of several types of previously admitted forensic science evidence in criminal cases. Professor Saks recently posited three such events:

> First, the Supreme Court's decision in *Daubert v. Merrell Dow Pharmaceuticals* changed the inquiry for admissibility to essentially the question scientists ask: What empirical evidence supports the validity of the expert's claims? . . .
>
> Second, the advent of DNA typing provided a general model of how forensic identification could be accomplished: basing it on a sound theoretical foundation, borrowed from normal science, developing an acceptable probabilistic model, and building a database of empirical data on which to base case-by-case probabilistic conclusions.
>
> Third, the use of DNA typing to exonerate innocent individuals who had been erroneously convicted led to analysis of the underlying cases in search of understanding what went wrong in those trials. Forensic science emerged as a surprisingly large part of the problem.[4]

Those events are certainly three of the developments that have helped create the current view that existing forensic science may not always be properly admitted in criminal cases. In the context of the larger changes in science and technology, two other specific forces should be added: the recent report of the National Academy of Sciences[5] and the impact that technology changes are having on the expectations and demands of jurors.

Daubert's Change in the Legal Standard for Admissibility

As to *Daubert,* it is ironic, and perhaps significant, that the issue of the admissibility of forensic science evidence was decided by the Supreme Court in a civil rather than criminal case. Indeed, the three cases involved in the *Daubert* trilogy were all civil cases in which the plaintiff was offering scientific evidence that the corporate defendant wanted to exclude. One can only speculate as to whether the Court would have reached the same conclusions had the issue been presented in the context of a prosecutor attempting to use an expert to prove the guilt of an accused, rather than in the context of a civil plaintiff trying to use an expert to prove liability for damages against a large corporation. The speculation is especially intense in the *Kumho* case, in which the Court applied *Daubert* to "technical" as well as "scientific" testimony, since much of the prosecution evidence proffered in criminal cases is more technical than scientific at its foundation.

Whatever the motivation, *Daubert* significantly changed the legal landscape for the admission of forensic science evidence in criminal cases, as well as civil, in two important ways. First, the *Daubert* trilogy changed the basic question of admissibility from simply "general acceptance" to a requirement that the proponent of the evidence establish the scientific validity of the evidence being offered, by demonstrating that its foundations are empirically sound and that its application to the particular case is appropriate. In addition to general acceptance, the new criteria required proof of testability, error rate, and peer review. Second, the Court firmly established the trial judge as the "gatekeeper" of forensic science evidence, who must make the scientific reliability and applicability assessment of the proffered evidence before it is allowed to be presented to the jury. On the criminal side, while the bulk of criminal cases are in state court and several of those states still adhere to some version of the *Frye* test, the *Daubert* criteria have resulted in new challenges to prosecution proffers that have forced trial judges in *Daubert* courts to at least reexamine the basis for their admissibility. Even in some state versions of *Frye,* courts have begun to address the fundamental questions posed by a *Daubert* analysis.

The Emergence of DNA as a New Model for Forensic Scientific Evidence

The impact of DNA testing and typing developments on forensic evidence in criminal cases has been dramatic. The prosecution use of DNA in criminal cases has become the new "gold standard" of criminal identification techniques. This is due not to the claimed expertise of a technical examiner based on anecdotal or experiential comparisons, as was the case of the former "gold standard" of fingerprint comparison, but rather on the basis of a firm scientific foundation established outside of the context of criminal litigation. This feature of DNA, when compared with other forms of prosecution proffered scientific evidence, is significant.

After the Supreme Court remanded the *Daubert* case to the Ninth Circuit, that court again declined to allow the plaintiff's evidence, even without an additional evidentiary hearing, and added a significant amplification to the *Daubert* requirement for peer review. Writing for a panel of the Ninth Circuit, Judge Kozinski stated:

> One very significant fact to be considered is whether the experts are proposing to testify about matters growing naturally and directly out of research they have conducted independent of the litigation, or whether they have developed their opinions expressly for purposes of testifying. That an expert testifies for money does not necessarily cast doubt on the reliability of his testimony, as few experts appear in court merely as an eleemosynary gesture. But in determining whether proposed expert testimony amounts to good science, we may not ignore the fact that a scientist's normal workplace is the lab or the field, not the courtroom or the lawyer's office.
>
> That an expert testifies based on research he has conducted independent of the litigation provides important, objective proof that the research comports with the dictates of good science. . . . For one thing, experts whose findings flow from existing research are less likely to have been biased toward a particular conclusion by the promise of remuneration; when an expert prepares reports and findings before being hired as a witness, that record will limit the degree to which he can tailor his testimony to serve a party's interests. Then, too, independent research carries its own *indicia* of reliability, as it is conducted, so to speak, in the usual course of business and must normally satisfy a variety of standards to attract funding and institutional support. Finally, there is usually a limited number of scientists actively conducting research on the very subject that is germane to a particular case, which provides a natural constraint on parties' ability to shop for experts who will come to the desired conclusion. That the testimony proffered by an expert is based directly on legitimate, pre-existing research unrelated to the litigation provides the most persuasive basis for concluding that the opinions he expresses were "derived by the scientific method." . . .
>
> If the proffered expert testimony is not based on independent research, the party proffering it must come forward with other objective, verifiable evidence that the testimony is based on "scientifically valid principles." One means of showing this is by proof that the research and analysis supporting the proffered conclusions have been subjected to normal scientific scrutiny through peer review and publication.[6]

In the criminal forensic science field, most of the testimony has no origin or basis outside of the context of criminal investigation and litigation and it was developed strictly for use by the government to aid in the prosecution of alleged criminal activity in court. Whether Judge Kozinski would have applied the same standard had *Daubert* been a criminal case is open to debate, but, on the other hand, DNA is clearly the model for scientific evidence admissibility that Judge Kozinski and others presumably prefer. It was developed entirely outside the courtroom context and rests upon a foundation of empirical data that forms the database for identification testimony that is probabilistic to an almost astronomical degree of certainty.

The Impact of DNA Exonerations

Beyond its new status as the scientific model for admissible evidence, DNA typing and testing has had another dramatic effect on the reexamination of other forensic science evidence that was certainly never intended by prosecutors when they embraced the use of DNA in criminal proceedings. DNA typing in closed cases has led to the exoneration of persons who were erroneously convicted, often by the use of other supposedly reliable forms of forensic science evidence. A recent study was conducted of 137 of the persons who have been exonerated by later DNA testing:

> In conducting a review of these 137 exonerees' trial transcripts, this study found invalid forensic science testimony was not just common but prevalent. This study found that 82 cases—60% of the 137 in the study set—involved invalid forensic science testimony. . . .
>
> The testimony at these 137 exonerees' criminal trials chiefly involved serological analysis (100 cases) and microscopic hair comparison (65), because most of these cases involved sexual assaults for which such evidence was commonly available at the time. Indeed, in many cases, where both hair and semen were recovered from the crime scene, both disciplines were utilized. Some cases also involved testimony concerning: fingerprint comparison (13 cases), DNA analysis (11), forensic geology (soil comparison) (6), forensic odontology (bite mark comparison) (6), shoe print comparison (4), fiber comparison (2), voice comparison (1), and fingernail comparison (1).
>
> In the two main categories of evidence present in the study set, serology and hair comparison testimony, this study found the following: Of the 100 cases involving serology in which transcripts were located, 57 cases, or 57%, had invalid forensic science testimony. Of the 65 cases involving microscopic hair comparison in which transcripts were located, 25 cases, or 38%, had invalid forensic science testimony.[7]

These exonerations, and the apparent association of their underlying convictions with many forms of routinely admitted prosecution forensic science evidence, are clearly a factor in causing the public, defense lawyers and the courts to doubt or at least reexamine the scientific validity of such evidence.

The Impact of the National Academy of Sciences Report

The DNA exonerations, at least in part, led to what should now be another factor in the current questioning of criminal scientific evidence: the results of the National Academy of Sciences study commissioned by Congress. The Congressional charge to the committee was to:

(1) assess the present and future resource needs of the forensic science community, to include State and local crime labs, medical examiners, and coroners;

(2) make recommendations for maximizing the use of forensic technologies and techniques to solve crimes, investigate deaths, and protect the public;

(3) identify potential scientific advances that may assist law enforcement in using forensic technologies and techniques to protect the public;

(4) make recommendations for programs that will increase the number of qualified forensic scientists and medical examiners available to work in public crime laboratories;

(5) disseminate best practices and guidelines concerning the collection and analysis of forensic evidence to help ensure quality and consistency in the use of forensic technologies and techniques to solve crimes, investigate deaths, and protect the public;

(6) examine the role of the forensic community in the homeland security mission;

(7) [examine] interoperability of Automated Fingerprint Information Systems; and

(8) examine additional issues pertaining to forensic science as determined by the Committee.[8]

The NAS conducted a two-year study of the use of forensic science in criminal cases and made specific findings both generally and as to several specific areas of commonly admitted evidence. Those findings were relayed to Congress in 2009 in a report of over three hundred pages.

The summary of the NAS report includes this caustic analysis of the use of forensic science in criminal cases:

The bottom line is simple: In a number of forensic science disciplines, forensic science professionals have yet to establish either the validity of their approach or the accuracy of their conclusions, and the courts have been utterly ineffective in addressing this problem. For a variety of reasons—including the rules governing the admissibility of forensic evidence, the applicable standards governing appellate review of trial court decisions, the limitations of the adversary process, and the common lack of scientific expertise among judges and lawyers who must try to comprehend and evaluate forensic evidence—the legal system is ill-equipped to correct the problems of the forensic science community.[9]

The specific analyses of each of the separate areas of forensic evidence were, for the most part, damning. The committee researched the alleged scientific basis for each specialty, the training requirements for persons holding themselves out as experts in that field, and the nature of the substantive testimony proffered in court by those persons. With the exception of nuclear DNA typing and testing, in most areas of forensic science the NAS report found a distinct failure to provide the type of criteria mandated by a *Daubert* analysis.

The Council made thirteen recommendations for improving the system,[10] beginning with the creation of a new National Institute of Forensic Science to oversee improvements in the system. The recommendations also include the following:

Research is needed to address issues of accuracy, reliability, and validity in the forensic science disciplines. The National Institute of Forensic Science (NIFS) should competitively fund peer-reviewed research in the following areas:

(a) Studies establishing the scientific bases demonstrating the validity of forensic methods.

(b) The development and establishment of quantifiable measures of the reliability and accuracy of forensic analyses. Studies of the reliability and accuracy of forensic techniques should reflect actual practice on realistic case scenarios, averaged across a representative sample of forensic scientists and laboratories. Studies also should establish the limits of reliability and accuracy that analytic methods can be expected to achieve as the conditions of forensic evidence vary. The research by which measures of reliability and accuracy are determined should be peer reviewed and published in respected scientific journals.

(c) The development of quantifiable measures of uncertainty in the conclusions of forensic analyses.

(d) Automated techniques capable of enhancing forensic technologies.[11]

Congress has not yet acted on the recommendations, but the findings in the NAS report have quickly reverberated throughout the forensic science community and parts of the legal community. The response of the forensic science community has been mixed. Formally, the scientific organizations have supported the general recommendations of the NAS report, while continuing to believe that future scientific research will validate most of the bases for forensic science disciplines. The American Academy of Forensic Sciences (AAFS) made an official "Position Statement" in response to the report:

> The American Academy of Forensic Sciences supports the recommendations of the National Academy of Sciences report *Strengthening Forensic Science in the United States: A Path Forward* (NAS Report). From among the various views and recommendations espoused, we particularly emphasize, endorse and promote the following principles:
>   1. All forensic science disciplines must have a strong scientific foundation.
>   2. All forensic science laboratories should be accredited.
>   3. All forensic scientists should be certified.
>   4. Forensic science terminology should be standardized.
>   5. Forensic scientists should be assiduously held to Codes of Ethics.
>   6. Existing forensic science professional entities should participate in governmental oversight of the field.
>   7. Attorneys and judges who work with forensic scientists and forensic science evidence should have a strong awareness and knowledge of the scientific method and forensic science disciplines.[12]

The organization added that it would undertake its own validation studies, beginning with latent fingerprint identification and handwriting comparison analysis.[13] This prominent organization is apparently taking the challenge of the NAS report seriously, even titling its 2010 convention "Putting Our Forensic House in Order: Examining Validation and Expelling Incompetence."[14] Notwithstanding this positive formal response, the organization president acknowledged that some of the practitioners in various disciplines have taken a more hostile or evasive tack:

> [I]t certainly is inappropriate to attack the person or entity that questions whether the needed validation has been done. I have been dismayed to see and hear attacks on the NAS Report, not because what it says is untrue but rather because it "gives aid to the enemy" (by which is meant the defense bar) or because it puts "forensic science" in a bad light, in short because it "gives scandal." . . .
>
> After *Daubert* came down, requiring scientific evidence to be shown to be reliable before it could be introduced in court, a shameful period followed in which various practitioners, in spite of having long claimed to engage in scientific investigation, began to deny that they were scientists. These word games played by some experts, sometimes in response to advice from their professional organizations, were undertaken in the mistaken belief that somehow they would remove these experts' testimony from having to be shown to be reliable, that by denying science in their work they could continue to justify their testimony on no more than "my years and years of experience in the field." The Supreme Court of the United States put reasonably short shrift to this maneuver in *Kumho Tire*, ruling that the reliability requirement applied to all expert testimony in federal

court. In the wake of the NAS Report, and in advance of the legislative Juggernaut feared by some to be coming down the track, history is repeating itself. There are attempts to define forensic science so narrowly that (1) no injustices have ever occurred as the result of flawed forensic science testimony and (2) expected certification and other requirements for forensic practitioners will not apply to huge sectors of practitioners. Attempts to downgrade to "investigative science" or "police science" work that clearly constitutes forensic science under the Academy's definition must be combated by our broad-based and diverse scientific organization.[15]

Some parts of the practitioner communities have been more subtle in their defensive posture, including their repeated contention that such things as "error rates" cannot be properly applied to their discipline.[16] Regardless of the positions taken, the forensic science community has taken notice of the contents of the NAS report and is at least beginning to alter, or at least reevaluate, the basis premises of some of its disciplines.

In the meantime, practitioners are being told to expect new challenges in court. Barry A. Fisher testified before Congress and later advised his AAFS testifiers that they should expect courtroom challenges and perhaps consider modifying their proffered testimony:

> While Congress and the Administration consider their responses to the NAS report, forensic scientists may be confronted with fresh attacks by the defense bar on the reliability of pattern evidence. . . . Challenges on the question of adequate research to support statements of single source uniqueness can most certainly be anticipated. . . . It may be that absolute statements of uniqueness are not possible to support statistically. [Nonetheless], strong statements can still be made to convey to juries the idea that there is a close relationship between the known sample and the questioned sample. Expressing that kind of opinion will be a challenge to articulate.[17]

In spite of the expected challenges, the legal community has been, perhaps predictably, slower and more muted in its response to the NAS report. Appellate decisions take time to materialize and there is no way to measure whether *Daubert* motions have increased in the short time since the NAS report. There are few reported trial court rulings on the issue. And at least one or two of them indicate that the courts may not give the NAS report a great deal of weight in making an admissibility threshold determination. As discussed later in this chapter, the judge in *United States v. Rose*[18] had the benefit of the NAS findings regarding fingerprint testimony but also noted the fingerprint examiner's opposition to those findings. The judge relied on a statement by the NAS committee chair, Judge Harry T. Edwards, to support his conclusion that "nothing in the Report was intended to answer the 'question whether forensic evidence in a particular case is admissible under applicable law.'"[19] That citation seems to be a rather selective excerpt of Judge Edwards's more complete remarks in which he indicates that he fully expects that the findings of the report will be considered by trial judges in making admissibility determinations:

> It will be no surprise if the report is cited authoritatively for its findings about the current status of the scientific foundation of particular areas of forensic science. And it is certainly possible that the courts will take the findings of the committee regarding the scientific foundation of particular types of forensic science evidence into account when considering the admissibility of such evidence in a particular case. However, each case in the criminal justice system must be decided on the record before the court pursuant to the applicable law, controlling precedent, and governing rules of evidence. The question whether forensic evidence in a particular case is admissible under applicable law is not coterminous with the question whether there are studies confirming the scientific validity and reliability of a forensic science discipline.[20]

In other cases, a federal magistrate considered the NAS report at great length in a hearing involving the admissibility of tool-mark firearms comparison testimony and eventually recommended that the proffered government testimony be severely limited.[21] On the other hand, a federal district court judge has recently upheld a magistrate's refusal to admit the NAS report at a hearing regarding the reliability of drug sniffing dogs, finding that the balance of the evidence was overwhelming and that "the Court finds little value in" the report.[22]

The Impact of New Technology Awareness by Jurors

A final factor needs to be added to understand the doubt that is emerging about the reliability of certain forensic evidence in criminal cases. As is apparent from recent studies, jurors know a great deal about modern scientific developments, and about how they intersect with the criminal justice system.[23] They know about DNA and its tremendous identification powers to both convict and exonerate. In fact, many jurors expect the prosecution to present DNA evidence in virtually every case, even in property offenses or relatively minor assault cases.[24] As a result, jurors have come to demand scientific evidence from the government in many types of cases as a prerequisite to conviction.[25] And the scientific evidence they demand from the prosecution may need to have the same degree of both reliability and certainty that jurors know DNA can provide. When an expert witness is forced to limit identification or other comparisons to a statement that the crime scene evidence is "consistent with" the evidence from the defendant, as opposed to "matching" the defendant, jurors may well find that testimony to be so pale in comparison with what they know about DNA's capabilities that it will simply not be enough to satisfy their demands. The jury becomes a factor in the suspicions about non-DNA forensic science evidence when they begin to conclude that proof beyond a reasonable doubt means that it is reasonable to demand that the prosecutor present scientific evidence—and scientific evidence that is reliable and convincing.

The pressure to either produce very convincing scientific evidence or to attempt to exclude jurors who have such demands is already showing on prosecutors in their courtroom conduct. It seems rational that it is also influencing the investigative and charging decisions that prosecutors are making. Judges are also responding with instructions, sometimes *sua sponte*.

The Current State of Forensic Science Evidence in Criminal Cases

Whatever doubts have arisen about the continued validity of forensic science evidence in the last twenty years, most criminal courts seem to have continued business as usual and routinely admit almost all expert testimony offered by prosecutors. Even though there are serious questions about the scientific validity of most non-DNA forms of forensic science evidence, this study also shows that criminal court judges, both at the trial and appellate level, continue to admit virtually all prosecution proffered expert testimony. Only when the government itself decides that a particular type of supposedly scientific evidence is not reliable, as in the case of bullet lead analysis, do the courts stop routinely admitting it.

Studies by scholars have substantiated this form of pro-prosecution pattern in the admissibility of scientific evidence in criminal cases. Professor Risinger's 2000 study found that while the rate of challenges to scientific evidence increased markedly after *Daubert,* most of that increase was in civil cases in which the defendant was attempting to preclude expert testimony proffered by the civil plaintiff.[26] And they were significantly more successful after *Daubert.*[27] The opposite was true in criminal cases.[28] The Risinger study found that criminal defense *Daubert* challenges to government evidence were successful less than 10 percent of the time in federal trial courts and 25 percent of the time in state trial courts.[29] An experienced attorney for the Innocence Project concluded that "despite the frequency with which scientific and expert testimony is proffered in criminal cases, there is a dearth of *Daubert* challenges and hearings. When the issue *is* raised in criminal proceedings, the outcome is vastly different than what occurs in civil cases."[30] In a study of appellate decisions before and after *Daubert*, Groscup and colleagues concluded that "the basic rates of admission at the trial and the appellate court levels did not change significantly after *Daubert* in criminal cases on appeal" and that:

> One explanation for the lack of any changes in the observed rates of admission before versus after *Daubert* is that admissibility depends on the party offering the testimony. The party for whom the key expert testified was significantly related to admission at both the trial court, . . . and the appellate court levels. . . . At both adjudicative levels, experts proffered by the prosecution were more likely to be admitted than experts proffered by defendants. At the trial court level, prosecution experts were admitted 95.8% . . . of the time, and defendant–appellant experts were admitted only 7.8% . . . of the total number of times they were offered. This pattern was slightly less pronounced at the appellate level, with prosecution experts admitted 85.1% . . . of the time and defense experts admitted 18.8% . . . of the total number of times they were offered.[31]

What accounts for the current relative lack of defense challenges to government expert testimony and the overwhelming court rejection of those challenges that are made? As to the lack of challenges, some have suggested that it is "poorly funded, unskilled counsel" and "inadequate pool of experts" available to the defense, especially when compared with resources available to civil plaintiffs.[32] As to the overwhelming judicial rejection of criminal defense challenges that are made, there are several possibilities.

One possibility is that the science being proffered by the government in criminal cases is simply of higher quality than that being offered by civil plaintiffs. The results of this study, and more particularly the findings in the NAS report, indicating that many non-DNA forms of expert testimony used by prosecutors is of questionable validity should dispel that notion. Moreover, the judicial decisions reviewed in this study, for the most part, do not indicate that the judges, trial or appellate, weighed the scientific validity of the proffered evidence in any meaningful way.[33] Rather, most of the decisions simply rationalized admissibility based on the prior admission of such evidence by other judges. In other words, the typical analysis was one of *stare decisis,* rather than the scientific inquiry required by *Daubert*.

More likely is the suggestion that there is a systemic pro-prosecution bias on the part of judges and that such a bias is reflected in admissibility decisions, regardless of what the standard of admissibility is under *Frye* or *Daubert*. As Groscup and colleagues found, "the *Daubert* decision did not impact on the admission rates of expert testimony at either the trial or the appellate court levels."[34] To put the bias question another way, "as a general proposition, judges disfavor civil plaintiffs and criminal defendants and are more likely to rule against them than against their opposites even when presenting equivalent evidence or arguments."[35]

Systemic pro-prosecution bias is a function of fairly obvious psychological concepts. Dean Chris Guthrie described judicial bias as a reflection of an "attitudinal blinder," relying on significant empirical studies of judicial attitudes and actions:

> Whether elected or appointed, judges come to the bench with political views. This is not to say that they have pre-committed to positions in particular cases, but it strains credulity to claim, as, for example, Justice Alito claimed during his Supreme Court confirmation hearings, that a judge "can't have any preferred outcome in any particular case." Rather, judges do have opinions, and these opinions or attitudes can predispose them to rule in ways that are consistent with those opinions or attitudes.
>
> To establish the presence of attitudinal blinders among judges, political scientists have developed, and provided empirical evidence to support, the so-called attitudinal theory or model. Most of this work has focused on the Supreme Court, but political scientists and legal scholars have also explored whether judicial attitudes influence judges on the courts of appeals and on the trial bench. The evidence suggests that attitudinal blinders are an issue not only at the highest court in the land but also in these lower courts.[36]

These "attitudinal blinders" are especially prevalent in criminal cases and especially in the state courts where most criminal cases are tried. As Professor Rodney Uphoff put it, "In the end, state court judges are, for the most part, rational actors whose attitudinal biases reflect their self-interest and their backgrounds. Most are answerable to a tough-on-crime electorate and are often reluctant, therefore, to make risky political decisions upholding the constitutional rights of criminal defendants."[37] Specifically, Uphoff comments on how this attitudinal bias manifests itself in criminal cases:

> Most judges, especially those with prosecutorial experience, presume that most defendants are, in fact, guilty, even though some are, in fact, innocent. This presumption of guilt, pro-prosecution perspective not only affects the manner in which many judges rule on motions, evaluate witnesses, and exercise their discretion, but it also adversely affects the willingness of many judges to police law enforcement agents and prosecutors. Judges tolerate sloppy police work because they do not want to be viewed as micro-managing the police. Judicial reluctance to let the guilty go free has meant a decreased use of the exclusionary rule. Similarly, courts are hesitant to dismiss cases because of Brady violations or take other steps to reign [*sic*] in prosecutorial misconduct. Finally, even when courts find error, too many errors are deemed harmless. The expanded use of harmless error not only allows questionable verdicts to stand, it does little to discourage misconduct and sloppy practices in the administration of justice.

As the result of what appears to be a distinct pro-prosecution bias in trial and appellate judges, the current legal state of forensic science evidence in criminal cases is somewhat schizophrenic. While many scientists, scholars, and even a congressionally mandated national study seriously question whether there is validity to non-DNA forensic evidence, trial judges simply continue to admit such evidence and appellate judges continue to affirm those decisions.

Thoughts about the Future of Criminal Forensic Science

How, and even whether, significant improvements are made in the quality of either criminal forensic science or the rulings of trial and appellate courts on its admissibility is not a single-faceted issue. The problem is not single faceted. As Professor Saks has said:

> To view the problems identified by the NRC Committee as problems owned exclusively by the forensic science community would be a mistake. There is no lack of blame to go around. In addition to the forensic science community, we find an academic community that has taken little interest in building the scientific foundations of forensic science; lawyers on both sides of the courtroom who have not informed themselves adequately about the state of the art and science; an absence of any institutional forensic science resources for the defense, preventing the adversary process from working to keep prosecution witnesses honest; a federal government that has offered few resources for building the basic science needed in many areas of forensic science; state governments that never fully accepted their responsibility for ensuring that the many things the NRC found lacking were done and done well; and courts whose judges lacked the information they needed, or the courage or desire to apply the law as stringently to government proffers in criminal cases as they did to private parties' proffers in civil cases.[38]

Responses may come from all, or none, of these sources.

Implementation of the recommendations contained in the NAS report by legislation could create a new federal organization that could mandate the research and testing to validate or finally discredit many forms of non-DNA forensic evidence. Meaningful legislative action by Congress, however, seems unlikely. After over two years of study by the National Academy of Sciences, and within just a few months of presentation of the report to Congress, major proposals in the report appear to be "all but dead" in Congress.[39] Given the reality that they currently can get almost any type of evidence they want admitted, prosecutors have quite predictably lined up against the proposals.[40] In Congress, as in the courts, prosecutors generally get what they want, and what they clearly want is the status quo. With that opposition, the current economic condition of the nation, and the pressures to spend federal monies on the prevention and prosecution of terrorism, the prospect for any action in Congress that might benefit accused defendants, and cost a considerable sum doing so, is very dim.

The scientific and academic communities may make progress on their own, given the spotlight created by the NAS report. Practitioners in forensic science may be led by true science leaders, like the AAFS, to conduct meaningful research into the alleged bases for their claimed expertise. Some beginning steps have been taken in that direction. More likely, and more importantly, purely academic scientists may undertake independent research, perhaps even without the lure of federal grant money, to establish or dispel claimed scientific foundations for non-DNA forensic evidence. On the other hand, there is a strong temptation, as Dr. Bohan of the AAFS has stated, for practitioners to try to avoid such studies, or even disregard their potential results, by claiming to base their testimony on "experience and judgment" rather than quantitative or empirical analysis. That tack has been successful in court for much social science expert testimony so it has some attraction, in spite of the holding in *Kumho*.

The best prospect for improving or eliminating questionable forms of non-DNA forensic criminal evidence may lie in the courtroom, but probably not with trial or appellate judges. The systemic pro-prosecution bias of trial judges is one of the reasons for the current state of affairs and is not likely to change. As for appellate judges, Professor Uphoff puts it well:

> Given electoral politics and the pro-prosecution perspective of a significant numbers of appellate judges, it is hard to be particularly optimistic about criminal justice reform. Certainly some judges do change dramatically during their tenure on the bench. Nonetheless, unless and until more judges recognize the effects of their attitudinal blinders and acknowledge the significant flaws in our criminal justice system, it is unlikely that we shall see many appellate courts taking a more active role in policing the system.[41]

There is always hope that trial and appellate judges, hopefully in the same case, will begin to recognize and overcome any such bias and rule fairly and intelligently on forensic evidence admissibility motions. It will take courage to do so. Those who do will remember the admonition of Justice William Brennan about judges who are tempted to make decisions based on the natural tendency to want to help put away a dangerous criminal:

> Yet the judge's job is not to yield to the visceral temptation to help prosecute the criminal, but to preserve the values and guarantees of our system of criminal justice, whatever the implications in an individual case.[42]

Collective breaths will not be held awaiting that day.

Perhaps the most promising impetus for change lies in another part of the courtroom—the jury box. Given the reluctance of judges to prohibit prosecutors from presenting questionable scientific evidence to the jury, defense lawyers who lose motions *in limine* could take up judges on their often used cliché that such issues are to be weighed by the jury. Defense counsel can present all of the now well-documented frailties of the particular claimed expertise to the jury. For indigent defendants, counsel can request, and constitutionally insist on, public funds to retain expert witnesses to attack the foundation of the government expert's testimony. Even without such an expert, at least the findings of the NAS report should be admissible themselves as a learned treatise under the Federal Rules of Evidence or its state counterpart.[43]

Jurors are becoming very technologically savvy, regardless of their formal education. Jurors may well be skeptical of prosecution experts who are impeached with evidence that their so-called science has been characterized by a government study as faulty, or "of questionable validity." To bolster that impeachment, defense counsel may want to use the growing number of examples of DNA exonerations where a particular form of government scientific evidence was used to obtain the original conviction.

Jurors are well aware that DNA can identify perpetrators with certainty. Using the NAS report, attorneys who are unable to convince judges to exclude prosecution testimony at a *Daubert* hearing may nevertheless be able to limit the testimony of a particular expert to such terms as "consistent with" rather than declaring a "match" to the defendant. As the NAS report states, "With the exception of nuclear DNA analysis, however, no forensic method has been rigorously shown to have the capacity to consistently, and with a high degree of certainty, demonstrate a connection between evidence and a specific individual or source."[44]

The point is that this era of doubt about the validity of non-DNA forensic science may not yet have persuaded judges to refuse to admit such evidence, but it has provided evidence that may be effectively used to impeach some prosecution experts. In the end, what may cause legal reform in this area is acquittals. Jurors, not judges, may be the source of the strongest message to the government about the vulnerability of some evidence prosecutors try to use to gain convictions. When prosecutors begin to lose cases they have built around such non-DNA experts, they will stop using them until their validity can be scientifically proven.

Appendix

Recommendations of the National Academy of Sciences: *Strengthening Forensic Science in the United States: A Path Forward (2009)*

Recommendation 1:

To PROMOTE THE DEVELOPMENT of forensic science into a mature field of multidisciplinary research and practice, founded on the systematic collection and analysis of relevant data, Congress should establish and appropriate funds for an independent federal entity, the National Institute of Forensic Science (NIFS). NIFS should have a full-time administrator and an advisory board with expertise in research and education, the forensic science disciplines, physical and life sciences, forensic pathology, engineering, information technology, measurements and standards, testing and evaluation, law, national security, and public policy. NIFS should focus on:

(a) establishing and enforcing best practices for forensic science professionals and laboratories;

(b) establishing standards for the mandatory accreditation of forensic science laboratories and the mandatory certification of forensic scientists and medical examiners/forensic pathologists—and identifying the entity/entities that will develop and implement accreditation and certification;

(c) promoting scholarly, competitive peer-reviewed research and technical development in the forensic science disciplines and forensic medicine;

(d) developing a strategy to improve forensic science research and educational programs, including forensic pathology;

(e) establishing a strategy, based on accurate data on the forensic science community, for the efficient allocation of available funds to give strong support to forensic methodologies and practices in addition to DNA analysis;

(f) funding state and local forensic science agencies, independent research projects, and educational programs as recommended in this report, with conditions that aim to advance the credibility and reliability of the forensic science disciplines;

(g) overseeing education standards and the accreditation of forensic science programs in colleges and universities;

(h) developing programs to improve understanding of the forensic science disciplines and their limitations within legal systems; and

(i) assessing the development and introduction of new technologies in forensic investigations, including a comparison of new technologies with former ones.

Recommendation 2:

The National Institute of Forensic Science (NIFS), after reviewing established standards such as ISO 17025, and in consultation with its advisory board, should establish standard terminology to be used in reporting on and testifying about the results of forensic science investigations. Similarly, it should establish model laboratory reports for different forensic science disciplines and specify the minimum information that should be included. As part of the accreditation and certification processes, laboratories and forensic scientists should be required to utilize model laboratory reports when summarizing the results of their analyses.

Recommendation 3:

Research is needed to address issues of accuracy, reliability, and validity in the forensic science disciplines. The National Institute of Forensic Science (NIFS) should competitively fund peer-reviewed research in the following areas:

(a) Studies establishing the scientific bases demonstrating the validity of forensic methods.

(b The development and establishment of quantifiable measures of the reliability and accuracy of forensic analyses. Studies of the reliability and accuracy of forensic techniques should reflect actual practice on realistic case scenarios, averaged across a representative sample of forensic scientists and laboratories. Studies also should establish the limits of reliability and accuracy that analytic methods can be expected to achieve as the conditions of forensic evidence vary. The research by which measures of reliability and accuracy are determined should be peer reviewed and published in respected scientific journals.

(c) The development of quantifiable measures of uncertainty in the conclusions of forensic analyses.

(d) Automated techniques capable of enhancing forensic technologies.

Recommendation 4:

To improve the scientific bases of forensic science examinations and to maximize independence from or autonomy within the law enforcement community, Congress should authorize and appropriate incentive funds to the National Institute of Forensic Science (NIFS) for allocation to state and local jurisdictions for the purpose of removing all public forensic laboratories and facilities from the administrative control of law enforcement agencies or prosecutors' offices.

Recommendation 5:

The National Institute of Forensic Science (NIFS) should encourage research programs on human observer bias and sources of human error in forensic examinations. Such programs might include studies to determine the effects of contextual bias in forensic practice (e.g., studies to determine whether and to what extent the results of forensic analyses are influenced by knowledge regarding the background of the suspect and the investigator's theory of the case). In addition, research on sources of human error should be closely linked with research conducted to quantify and characterize the amount of error. Based on the results of these studies, and in consultation with its advisory board, NIFS should develop standard cooperating procedures (that will lay the foundation for model protocols) to minimize, to the greatest extent reasonably possible, potential bias and sources of human error in forensic practice. These standard operating procedures should apply to all forensic analyses that may be used in litigation.

Recommendation 6:

To facilitate the work of the National Institute of Forensic Science (NIFS), Congress should authorize and appropriate funds to NIFS to work with the National Institute of Standards and Technology (NIST), in conjunction with government laboratories, universities, and private laboratories, and in consultation with Scientific Working Groups, to develop tools for advancing measurement, validation, reliability, information sharing, and proficiency testing in forensic science and to establish protocols for forensic examinations, methods, and practices. Standards should reflect best practices and serve as accreditation tools for laboratories and as guides for the education, training, and certification of professionals. Upon completion of its work, NIST and its partners should report findings and recommendations to NIFS for further dissemination and implementation.

Recommendation 7:

Laboratory accreditation and individual certification of forensic science professionals should be mandatory, and all forensic science professionals should have access to a certification process. In determining appropriate standards for accreditation and certification, the National Institute of Forensic Science (NIFS) should take into account established and recognized international standards, such as those published by the International Organization for Standardization (ISO). No person (public or private) should be allowed to practice in a forensic science discipline or testify as a forensic science professional without certification. Certification requirements should include, at a minimum, written examinations, supervised practice, proficiency testing, continuing education, recertification procedures, adherence to a code of ethics, and effective disciplinary procedures. All laboratories and facilities (public or private) should be accredited, and all forensic science professionals should be certified, when eligible, within a time period established by NIFS.

Recommendation 8:

Forensic laboratories should establish routine quality assurance and quality control procedures to ensure the accuracy of forensic analyses and the work of forensic practitioners. Quality control procedures should be designed to identify mistakes, fraud, and bias; confirm the continued validity and reliability of standard operating procedures and protocols; ensure that best practices are being followed; and correct procedures and protocols that are found to need improvement.

Recommendation 9:

The National Institute of Forensic Science (NIFS), in consultation with its advisory board, should establish a national code of ethics for all forensic science disciplines and encourage individual societies to incorporate this national code as part of their professional code of ethics. Additionally, NIFS should explore mechanisms of enforcement for those forensic scientists who commit serious ethical violations. Such a code could be enforced through a certification process for forensic scientists.

Recommendation 10:

To attract students in the physical and life sciences to pursue graduate studies in multidisciplinary fields critical to forensic science practice, Congress should authorize and appropriate funds to the National Institute of Forensic Science (NIFS) to work with appropriate organizations and educational institutions to improve and develop graduate education programs designed to cut across organizational, programmatic, and disciplinary boundaries. To make these programs appealing to potential students, they must include attractive scholarship and fellowship offerings. Emphasis should be placed on developing and improving research methods and methodologies applicable to forensic science practice and on funding research programs to attract research universities and students in fields relevant to forensic science. NIFS should also support law school administrators and judicial education organizations in establishing continuing legal education programs for law students, practitioners, and judges.

Recommendation 11:

To improve medicolegal death investigation:

(a) Congress should authorize and appropriate incentive funds to the National Institute of Forensic Science (NIFS) for allocation to states and jurisdictions to establish medical examiner systems, with the goal of replacing and eventually eliminating existing coroner systems. Funds are needed to build regional medical examiner offices, secure necessary equipment, improve administration, and ensure the education, training, and staffing of medical examiner offices. Funding could also be used to help current medical examiner systems modernize their facilities to meet current Centers for Disease Control and Prevention-recommended autopsy safety requirements.

(b) Congress should appropriate resources to the National Institutes of Health (NIH) and NIFS, jointly, to support research, education, and training in forensic pathology. NIH, with NIFS participation, or NIFS in collaboration with content experts, should establish a study section to establish goals, to review and evaluate proposals in these areas, and to allocate funding for collaborative research to be conducted by medical examiner offices and medical universities. In addition, funding, in the form of medical student loan forgiveness and/or fellowship support, should be made available to pathology residents who choose forensic pathology as their specialty.

(c) NIFS, in collaboration with NIH, the National Association of Medical Examiners, the American Board of Medicolegal Death Investigators, and other appropriate professional organizations, should establish a Scientific Working Group (SWG) for forensic pathology and medicolegal death investigation. The SWG should develop and promote standards for best practices, administration, staffing, education, training, and continuing education for competent death scene investigation and postmortem examinations. Best practices should include the utilization of new technologies such as laboratory testing for the molecular basis of diseases and the implementation of specialized imaging techniques.

(d) All medical examiner offices should be accredited pursuant to NIFS-endorsed standards within a time frame to be established by NIFS.

(e) All federal funding should be restricted to accredited offices that meet NIFS-endorsed standards or that demonstrate significant and measurable progress in achieving accreditation within prescribed deadlines.

(f) All medicolegal autopsies should be performed or supervised by a board certified forensic pathologist. This requirement should take effect within a time frame to be established by NIFS, following consultation with governing state institutions.

Recommendation 12:

Congress should authorize and appropriate funds for the National Institute of Forensic Science (NIFS) to launch a new broad-based effort to achieve nationwide fingerprint data interoperability. To that end, NIFS should convene a task force comprising relevant experts from the National Institute of Standards and Technology and the major law enforcement agencies (including representatives from the local, state, federal, and, perhaps, international levels) and industry, as appropriate, to develop:

(a) standards for representing and communicating image and minutiae data among Automated Fingerprint Identification Systems. Common data standards would facilitate the sharing of fingerprint data among law enforcement agencies at the local, state, federal, and even international levels, which could result in more solved crimes, fewer wrongful identifications, and greater efficiency with respect to fingerprint searches; and

(b) baseline standards—to be used with computer algorithms—to map, record, and recognize features in fingerprint images, and a research agenda for the continued improvement, refinement, and characterization of the accuracy of these algorithms (including quantification of error rates).

Recommendation 13:

Congress should provide funding to the National Institute of Forensic Science (NIFS) to prepare, in conjunction with the Centers for Disease Control and Prevention and the Federal Bureau of Investigation, forensic scientists and crime scene investigators for their potential roles in managing and analyzing evidence from events that affect homeland security, so that maximum evidentiary value is preserved from these unusual circumstances and the safety of these personnel is guarded. This preparation also should include planning and preparedness (to include exercises) for the interoperability of local forensic personnel with federal counterterrorism organizations.

Notes

Chapter 1: The History and Development of Forensic Scientific Evidence

1. Generally, see William Tilstone, *Forensic Science: An Encyclopedia of History, Methods, and Techniques* (Santa Barbara, Calif.: ABC-CLIO, 2006).

2. *State v. Hauptmann*, 180 A. 809 (N.J. 1935).

3. *Andrews v. State*, 533 So.2d 841(Fla. Dist. Ct. App. 1988).

4. *State v. Woodall*, 385 S.E.2d 253 (W. Va. 1989).

5. The Innocence Project, available online at http://www.innocenceproject.org.

6. Keith A. Findley, *Innocents at Risk: Adversary Imbalance, Forensic Science, and the Search for Truth*, 38 Seton Hall L Rev 893 (2008). Retrieved January 2, 2010, from http://ssrn.com/abstract=1144886.

7. Brandon L. Garrett, *Judging Innocence*, 108 Colum L Rev 55, 81–83 (2008).

Chapter 2: The Problem of Junk Science

1. *Frye v. United States*, 293 F. 1013 (D.C. App. 1923). Despite *Frye's* limitations and the subsequent federal cases, it remains the standard by which science is evaluated for courtroom use in several states. See Joseph R. Meaney, *From Frye to Daubert: Is a Pattern Unfolding?* 35 Jurimetrics J. 191, 193–194 (1995).

2. *Frye, supra* 293 F. at 1014.

3. *Daubert v. Merrell Dow Pharm., Inc.,* 509 U.S. 579 (1993). The standards governing expert testimony in the various states are described in Jane Campbell Moriarty, *Psychological and Scientific Evidence in Criminal Trials* (Eagen, Minn.: Thomson/West, 2009). See generally Kenneth R. Foster & Peter W. Huber, *Judging Science: Scientific Knowledge and the Federal Courts* (Cambridge, Mass.: MIT Press, 1997).

4. *Gen. Elec. Co. v. Joiner*, 522 U.S. 136 (1997).

5. *Kumho Tire Co. v. Carmichael*, 526 U.S. 137 (1999).

6. *Daubert v. Merrell Dow Pharm., Inc.*, 509 U.S. 579 (1993), at 589–592.

7. *Gen. Elec. Co. v. Joiner*, 522 U.S. 136, 140 (1997).

8. Ibid. (emphasis added).

9. *Kumho Tire Co. v. Carmichael*, 526 U.S. 137, 145–146 (1999).

10. Ibid., 141.

11. For an overview of how *Daubert* has changed the way judges evaluate expert evidence, see generally Lloyd Dixon and Brian Gill, *Changes in the Standards for Admitting Expert Evidence in Federal Civil Cases Since the Daubert Decision* (Santa Monica, Calif.: Rand, 2001); Margaret A. Berger, *Expert Testimony in Criminal Proceedings: Questions Daubert Does Not Answer*, 33 Seton Hall L Rev 1125 (2003); Keith A. Findley, *Innocents at Risk: Adversary Imbalance, Forensic Science, and the Search for Truth*, 38 Seton Hall L Rev 893, 929–950 (2008), retrieved January 2, 2010, from http://ssrn.com/abstract=1144886; Jennifer L. Groscup et al., *The Effects of* Daubert *on the Admissibility of Expert Testimony in State and Federal Criminal Cases*, 8 Psychol Pub Pol'y & L 339 (2002); Peter J. Neufeld, *The (Near) Irrelevance of* Daubert *to Criminal Justice and Some Suggestions for Reform*, 95 Am J Pub Health 107 (2005); D. Michael Risinger, *Navigating Expert Reliability: Are Criminal Standards of Certainty Being Left on the Dock?* 64 Alb L Rev 99 (2000).

12. National Research Council of the National Academy of Sciences, *Strengthening Forensic Science in the United States: A Path Forward*, Executive Summary, S-1–S-24 (2009).

13. Ibid., 3-1.

14. From Andrew B. Flake, Eric R. Harlan, and James A. King, *50 State Survey of the Applicability of Daubert*, American Bar Association Section of Litigation. Retrieved February 9, 2009, from http://www.abanet.org/litigation/committees/trialevidence/daubert-frye-survey.html.

Chapter 3: DNA: The New Gold Standard

1. Lisa R. Kreeger and Danielle M. Weiss, *Forensic DNA Fundamentals for the Prosecutor: Be Not Afraid* (Alexandria, Va.: American Prosecutors Research Institute, 2003), 3. Retrieved January 3, 2010, from www.ndaa.org/pdf/forensic_dna_fundamentals.pdf.

2. Edward J. Imwinkelried, "The Relative Priority That Should Be Assigned to Trial Stage DNA Issues," in *DNA and the Criminal Justice System: The Technology of Justice*, ed. David Lazer (Cambridge, Mass.: MIT Press, 2004), 92–93.

3. For descriptions of the development of DNA testing and its use in the criminal justice system, see David L. Faigman, Michael J. Saks, Joseph Sanders, and Edward K. Cheng, eds., *Modern Scientific Evidence: The Law and Science of Expert Testimony* (Eagen, Minn.: Thomson/West, 2009), §§ 31:1 *et seq.*; Imwinkelried, 91–101; and Jane Campbell Moriarty and Michael J. Saks, "Forensic Science: Grand Goals, Tragic Flaws, and Judicial Gatekeeping," *Judges' Journal*, Fall (2005): 16, 19, 24–25.

4. Karen Cormier, Lisa Calandro, and Dennis Reeder, "Evolution of DNA Evidence for Crime Solving: A Judicial and Legislative History," *Forensic Magazine,* June–July (2005): 13. Retrieved January 3, 2010, from http://www.forensicmag.com/articles.asp?pid=45.

5. *Andrews v. State,* 533 So. 2d 841, 842 (Fla Dist Ct App 1988). For a historical review of the use of DNA evidence, see Cormier, Calandro, and Reeder, 13.

6. *Andrews v. State,* 533 So. 2d at 843 (Fla Dist Ct App 1988).

7. *State v. Woodall,* 385 S.E. 2d 253 (W Va 1989).

8. See, for example, *United States v. Yee,* 134 F.R.D. 161, 165–66 (ND Ohio 1991).

9. Cormier, Calandro, and Reeder, 13–14.

10. See Erin Murphy, *The New Forensics: Criminal Justice, False Certainty, and the Second Generation of Scientific Evidence,* 95 Cal L Rev 721, 793–794 (2007) (arguing that because of "the government's domination of forensic science, . . . rather than simply selecting and advocating for the theory that suits it best, the government should bear a burden of presenting evidence and disclosing results derived from all legitimate, competing theories").

11. Kreeger and Weiss, 3.

12. National Research Council of the National Academy of Sciences, *Strengthening Forensic Science in the United States: A Path Forward* (Washington, D.C.: National Academies Press, 2009), 3-12, 5-3.

13. See John W. Strong et al., eds., *McCormick on Evidence,* ed. 5 (Eagen, Minn.: Thomson West, 1999), § 205, 318; Edward J. Imwinkelried and D. H. Kaye, *DNA Typing: Emerging or Neglected Issues,* 76 Wash L Rev 413 (2001).

14. Moriarty and Saks, *supra* note 23, 19.

15. Moriarty and Saks, 19, 24–25. For a detailed description of the chemistry and mechanics of each method, see Kreeger and Weiss, 19.

16. Kreeger and Weiss, 19.

17. Ibid.

18. Ibid., 18.

19. See generally Jonathan J. Koehler, *Error and Exaggeration in the Presentation of DNA Evidence at Trial,* 34 Jurimetrics J. 21 (1993) (discussing how experts and attorneys may misrepresent and misinterpret estimates, resulting in overstated statements regarding the strength and implications of DNA evidence); William C. Thompson, "Guide to Forensic DNA Evidence" in *Expert Evidence: A Practitioner's Guide to Law, Science, and the FJC Manual,* ed. Bert Black and Patrick W. Lee (St. Paul, Minn.: West Group, 1997).

20. William C. Thompson, Franco Taroni, and Colin G. G. Aitken, *How the Probability of a False Positive Affects the Value of DNA Evidence,* 48 J Forensic Sci 47 (2003).

21. Joel D. Lieberman et al., *Gold Versus Platinum: Do Jurors Recognize the Superiority and Limitations of DNA Evidence Compared to Other Types of Forensic Evidence?* 14 Psychol Pub Pol'y & L 27, 31 (2008).

22. Ibid. (citing Carl W. Gilmore, *Challenging DNA in Paternity Cases: Finding Weaknesses in an Evidentiary Goliath,* 90 Ill B J 472, 474 [2002]).

23. Kamrin T. MacKnight, *The Polymerase Chain Reaction (PCR): The Second Generation of DNA Analysis Methods Takes the Stand*, 20 Santa Clara Computer & High Tech L J 95 (2003); Jennifer N. Mellon, Note, *Manufacturing Convictions: Why Defendants Are Entitled to the Data Underlying Forensic DNA Kits*, 51 Duke L J 1097 (2001).

24. William C. Thompson, "Tarnish on the 'Gold Standard': Understanding Recent Problems in Forensic DNA Testing," *Champion* Jan.–Feb. (2006): 10.

25. David Johnston, "Report Criticizes Scientific Testing at F.B.I. Crime Lab," *New York Times*, Apr. 16, 1997, A1.

26. *See* Julie Bykowicz and Justin Fenton, "City Crime Lab Director Fired: Database Update Reveals Employees' DNA Tainted Evidence, Throwing Lab's Reliability into Question," *Sun* (Baltimore, Md.), Aug. 21, 2008, 1A; James Dao, "Lab's Errors in 82 Killing Force Review of Virginia DNA Cases," *New York Times*, May 7, 2005, A1; Leslie Griffy, "Crime Lab in Spotlight: Senate Committee Hears Testimony Faulting DA's Internal Investigation," *San Jose Mercury News*, Jan. 24, 2008, 1B; Deborah Hastings, "Memo: Chemist May Have Altered Evidence," *Mobile Register*, Apr. 21, 2004, A5; George Hunter, "Detroit Shuts Down Error-Plagued Crime Lab," *Detroit News*, Sept. 26, 2008, 1A; Roma Khanna and Steve McVicker, "Police Lab Tailored Tests to Theories, Report Says: Investigators Hope to Establish Whether Mistakes Were Deliberate," *Houston Chronicle*, May 12, 2006, A1; Steve Mills and Maurice Possley, "Report Alleges Crime Lab Fraud: Scientist Is Accused of Providing False Testimony," *Chicago Tribune*, Jan. 14, 2001, A1; Ruth Teichroeb, "Rare Look Inside State Crime Labs Reveals Recurring Problems," *Seattle Post-Intelligencer*, July 22, 2004, A1; Richard Willing, "Errors Prompt States to Watch over Crime Labs," *USA Today*, Mar. 31, 2006, 3A.

27. Darren K. Carlson, "Americans Conclusive about DNA Evidence," *Gallup*, Nov. 15, 2005. Retrieved January 3, 2010, from http://www.gallup.com/poll/19915/Americans-Conclusive-About-DNA-Evidence.aspx.

28. See Brooke G. Malcom, Comment, *Convictions Predicated on DNA Evidence Alone: How Reliable Evidence Became Infallible*, 38 Cumb L Rev 313, 338 (2008) (urging consideration of the proposition that DNA evidence alone, without corroboration, is not sufficient for conviction).

29. See generally National Institute of Justice, U.S. Department of Justice, *Convicted by Juries, Exonerated By Science: Case Studies in the Use of DNA Evidence to Establish Innocence After Trial* (Washington, D.C.: U.S. Department of Justice and National Institute of Justice, 1996), retrieved January 3, 2010, from www.ncjrs.gov/pdffiles/dnaevid.pdf; National Commission on the Future of DNA Evidence, U.S. Department of Justice, *Postconviction DNA Testing: Recommendations for Handling Requests* (Washington, D.C.: U.S. Department of Justice and National Institute of Justice, 1999), retrieved January 3, 2010, from www.ncjrs.gov/pdffiles1/nij/177626.pdf.

30. Imwinkelried, 92–93, 96.

31. National Commission on the Future of DNA Evidence, iii, vi, xiii.

32. Ibid., xiii–xiv.

33. Ariz. Rev. Stat. Ann. § 13-4240 (2001); Ark. Code Ann. §§ 16-112-201 To -208 (2006); Cal. Penal Code § 1405 (West Supp. 2009); Colo. Rev. Stat. Ann. §§ 18-1-411 To -416 (West 2004 & Supp. 2008); Conn. Gen. Stat. Ann. § 54-102kk (West Supp. 2008); Del. Code Ann. Tit. 11, § 4504 (2007); Fla. Stat. Ann. §§ 925.11, 943.3251

(West Supp. 2009); Ga. Code Ann. § 5-5-41 (1995 & Supp. 2008); Idaho Code Ann. §§ 19-4901 To -4902 (2004); 725 Ill. Comp. Stat. Ann. 5/116-3 (West 2002 & Supp. 2008); Ind. Code Ann. §§ 35-38-7-1 To -19 (West 2004); Kan. Stat. Ann. § 21-2512 (2007); Ky. Rev. Stat. Ann. §§ 422.285, .287 (LexisNexis 2005 & Supp. 2008); La. Code Crim. Proc. Ann. Arts. 924, 926.1 (2008 & Supp. 2009); Me. Rev. Stat. Ann. Tit. 15, §§ 2136-2138 (2003 & Supp. 2008); Mich. Comp. Laws Ann. § 770.16 (West 2006); Minn. Stat. Ann. §§ 590.01-.04, .06 (2000); Mo. Rev. Stat. §§ 547.035, 650.055 (2008); Mont. Code Ann. §§ 46-21-110, 53-1-214 (2007); Neb. Rev. Stat. §§ 29-4119 To -4123 (2003); Nev. Rev. Stat. § 176.0918 (LexisNexis 2006); N. J. Stat. Ann. § 2A:84A-32A (West Supp. 2008); N.M. STAT. ANN. § 31-1A-2 (West Supp. 2008); N.Y. Crim. Proc. Law § 440.30 (McKinney 2005); Ohio Rev. Code Ann. §§ 2953.71 To -.83 (LexisNexis 2002); Okla. Stat. Ann. Tit. 22, §§ 1371-1371.2 (2009); Or. Rev. Stat. §§ 138.690-.698 (2007); 42 Pa. Const. Stat. § 9543.1 (2006); R.I. Gen. Laws §§ 10-9.1-11 To -12 (Supp. 2008); Tenn. Code Ann. §§ 40-30-301 To -313 (2006); Tex. Code Crim. Proc. Ann. Arts. 64.01-.05 (Vernon 2006); Utah Code Ann. §§ 78B-9-301 To -304 (2008); Va. Code Ann. § 19.2-327.1 (2008); Wash. Rev. Code Ann. § 10.73.170 (LexisNexis 2007); Va. Code Ann. § 15-2B-14 (LexisNexis 2004 & Supp. 2008); Wis. Stat. Ann. §§ 974.07 (West 2007).

34. Justice for All Act of 2004, Pub L 108-405, 118 Stat. 2260 (2004).

35. Cormier, Calandro, and Reeder, 15.

36. See, for example, *People v. Callace,* 573 N.Y.S.2d 137, 139–40 (Gen Term 1991).

37. *Brady v. Maryland,* 373 U.S. 83 (1963).

38. See, for example, *Sewell v. State,* 592 N.E.2d 705, 707 & n.4, 708 (Ind Ct App 1992); *Mebane v. State,* 902 P.2d 494, 497 (Kan Ct App 1995); *State v. Thomas,* 586 A.2d 250, 253 (NJ Super Ct App Div 1991); *Dabbs v. Vergari,* 570 N.Y.S.2d 765, 767–68 (Sup Ct 1990); *Commonwealth v. Brison,* 618 A.2d 420, 423–25 (Pa Super Ct 1992).

39. *Dist. Attorney's Office v. Osborne,* 557 U.S. ___, 129 S Ct 2308 (2009).

40. Stephen Breyer, "Furthering the Conversation about Science and Society," in *DNA and the Criminal Justice System: The Technology of Justice,* ed. David Lazer (Cambridge, Mass.: MIT Press, 2004), 13, 16.

Chapter 4: The "Who" Question

1. For a description of the evolution and history of fingerprint identification, see Simon A. Cole, "Fingerprint Identification and the Criminal Justice System: Historical Lessons for the DNA Debate," in *DNA and the Criminal Justice System: The Technology of Justice,* ed. David Lazer (Cambridge, Mass.: MIT Press, 2004).

2. See International Association for Identification, *Friction Ridge Skin Identification Training Manual,* retrieved December 23, 2009, from www.theiai.org; Scientific Working Group on Friction Ridge Analysis, *Training to Competency for Latent Print Examiner* (2002), retrieved December 23, 2009, from www.swgfast.org.

3. See generally David Maltoni, Darri Maio, Anil K. Jain, and Salil Prabbakar, *Handbook of Fingerprint Recognition* (London: Springer-Verlag, 2009); Mark R. Hawthorne,

Fingerprints: Analysis and Understanding (Boca Raton, Fla.: CRC Press, 2008); Henry C. Lee and Robert E. Gaensslen, eds., *Advances in Fingerprint Technology,* ed. 2 (Boca Raton, Fla.: CRC Press, 2001); David A. Stoney, "The Scientific Basis of Expert Testimony on Fingerprint Identification," in *Modern Scientific Evidence: The Law and Science of Expert Testimony,* ed. David L. Faigman, Michael J. Saks, Joseph Sanders, and Edward K. Cheng (Eagen, Minn.: Thomson/West, 2009), §§ 32.21 *et seq.*

4. Lee and Gaensslen, eds.

5. Ibid.; Stoney, § 33.28.

6. See G. Williams, H. McMurray, and D. Worsley, *Latent Fingerprint Detection Using a Scanning Kelvin Microprobe,* 46 J Forensic Sci 1005 (2001).

7. Christopher G. Worley, Sara S. Wiltshire, Thomasin C. Miller, George J. Havrilla, and Vahid Majidi, *Detection of Visible and Latent Fingerprints Using Micro-X-Ray Fluorescence Elemental Imaging,* 51 J Forensic Sci 57 (2005).

8. National Institute of Standards and Technology, U.S. Department of Commerce, *American National Standard for Information Systems—Data Format for the Interchange of Fingerprint, Facial, & Other Biometric Information,* NIST Special Publication No. 500-271, ANSI/NIST-ITL 1-2007 (2007), retrieved December 26, 2009, from http://fingerprint.nist.gov/standard/index.html; and see *FBI Biometric Specifications,* retrieved December 26, 2009, from http://www.fbibiospecs.org/biospecs.html.

9. FBI Criminal Justice Information Services, U.S. Department of Justice, *Taking Legible Fingerprints,* retrieved December 26, 2009, from http://www.fbi.gov/hq/cjisd/takingfps.html.

10. See Christopher M. Brislawn, *Fingerprints Go Digital,* 42 Notices of the American Mathematical Society 1278 (1995), retrieved December 26, 2009, from http://www.ams.org/notices/199511/brislawn.pdf.

11. Y. Sun, J. Paik, A. Koschan, D. L. Page, and M. A. Abidi, "Point Fingerprint: A New 3-D Object Representation Scheme," *IEEE Trans. on Systems, Man, and Cybernetics-Part B: Cybernetics* 33 (August 2003): 712–717.

12. FBI Criminal Justice Information Services, U.S. Department of Justice, *Integrated Automated Fingerprint Information System,* retrieved December 26, 2009, from http://www.fbi.gov/hq/cjisd/iafis.htm.

13. National Research Council of the National Academy of Sciences, *Strengthening Forensic Science in the United States: A Path Forward* (Washington, D.C.: National Academies Press, 2009), 136.

14. Ibid., 137–139; Lyn Haber and Ralph N. Haber, *Scientific Validation of Fingerprint Evidence under* Daubert, 7 Law, Probability and Risk 87 (2008); David R. Ashbaugh, *Quantitative-Qualitative Friction Ridge Analysis: An Introduction to Basic and Advanced Ridgeology* (Boca Raton, Fla.: CRC Press, 1999); J. Vanderkolk, *ACE-V: A Model,* 54 J Forensic Ident 45 (2002); Michele Triplett and Lauren Cooney, *Etiology of ACE-V and Its Proper Use: An Exploration of the Relationship Between ACE-V and the Scientific Method of Hypothesis Testing,* 56 J Forensic Ident 345 (2006).

15. Scientific Working Group on Friction Ridge Analysis, Study and Technology, *Friction Ridge Examination Methodology for Latent Print Examiners* (2002), retrieved May 28, 2010, from http://www.swgfast.org/documents/methodology/10056 -Methodology-Reformatted-1.01.pdf.

16. Ibid., 139–140. See also Haber and Haber, 87.

17. Ibid., 140.

18. The details of fingerprinting and fingerprinting comparison, as well as some of its limitations, are described in Stoney.

19. Faigman, Saks, Sanders, and Cheng, §§33:1 *et seq;* Robert Epstein, *Fingerprints Meet Daubert: The Myth of Fingerprint "Science,"* 75 S Cal L Rev 605 (2002); Simon A. Cole, *More Than Zero: Accounting for Error in Latent Fingerprint Identification,* 95 J Crim L & Criminology 985 (2005); Michael J. Saks and Jonathan J. Koehler, *The Coming Paradigm Shift in Forensic Identification Science,* 309 Science 892 (2005); Nathan Benedict, *Fingerprints and the Daubert Standard for Admission of Scientific Evidence: Why Fingerprints Fail and a Proposed Remedy,* 46 Ariz L Rev 519 (2004): Simon A. Cole, *Grandfathering Evidence: Fingerprint Admissibility Rulings from Jennings to Llera Plaza and Back Again,* 41 Amer Crim L Rev 1189 (2004); Simon A. Cole, *The Prevalence and Potential Causes of Wrongful Conviction by Fingerprint Evidence,* 37 Golden Gate Univ L Rev 39 (2006).

20. Brooke G. Malcom, *Convictions Predicated on DNA Evidence Alone: How Reliable Evidence Became Infallible,* 38 Cumb L Rev 313 (2008)

21. National Research Council of the National Academy of Sciences, 142–144 (footnotes omitted).

22. "[W]e report a range of existing evidence that suggests that examiners differ at each stage of the method in the conclusions they reach. To the extent that they differ, some conclusions are invalid. We have analysed the ACE-V method itself, as it is described in the literature. We found that these descriptions differ, no single protocol has been officially accepted by the profession and the standards upon which the method's conclusions rest have not been specified quantitatively. As a consequence, at this time the validity of the ACE-V method cannot be tested." Haber and Haber, 19; and see National Research Council of the National Academy of Sciences.

23. Jennifer Mnookin, *The Validity of Latent Fingerprint Identification: Confessions of a Fingerprinting Moderate,* 7 Law, Probability and Risk 111 (2008).

24. *State v. Rose,* Case No. K06-0545 (Md Balt Co Cir Oct 19, 2007), retrieved December 27, 2009, from http://www.baltimoresun.com/media/acrobat/2007-10/33446162 .pdf.

25. Ibid., 22, 24.

26. *U.S. v. Crisp,* 324 F.3d 261 (4th Cir 2003) (holding that it was not an abuse of discretion to admit expert fingerprint identification testimony in a criminal case under the *Daubert* standard).

27. *U.S. v. Rose,* No. CCB-08-0149 (D Md, December 8, 2009), retrieved December 27, 2009, from http://www.mdd.uscourts.gov/Opinions/Opinions/Brian%20 Rose%20Mem-FINAL.pdf.

28. Ibid., 5.

29. Ibid., 6.

30. "[L]atent print individualization may have survived its *Daubert* trials only to end up in the '*Fryeing* pan.' Further, it may contradict the conventional wisdom that *Daubert* is a more stringent admissibility threshold than *Frye,* especially for unpopular litigants with unpopular causes." Simon A. Cole, *Out of the Daubert Fire and into*

the Fryeing Pan? Self-Validation, Meta-Expertise and the Admissibility of Latent Print Evidence in Frye *Jurisdictions,* 9 Minn J L Sci & Tech 453, 537 (2008).

31. See, for example, *U.S. v. Crisp,* 324 F.3d 261 (4th Cir. 2003); *U.S. v. Havvard,* 117 F.Supp.2d 848 (2000).

32. *U.S. v. Frias,* 2003 WL 296740 (SD NY 2003), modified in part, 2003 WL 352502 (SD. NY 2003); *U.S. v. Sullivan,* 246 F. Supp 2d 700 (ED Ky 2003); *U.S. v. Cruz-Rivera,* 2002 WL 662128 (DPR 2002); *U.S. v. Hernandez,* 299 F 3d 984 (8th Cir 2002), cert denied, 537 U.S. 1134 (2003); *U.S. v. Navarro-Fletes,* 49 Fed. Appx 732 (9th Cir 2002); *U.S. v. Martinez-Cintron,* 136 F Supp 2d 17 (DPR 2001); *U.S. v. Cline,* 188 F Supp 2d 1287 (D Kan 2002), aff'd 349 F 3d 1276 (10th Cir 2003); *U.S. v. Rogers,* 26 Fed Appx 171 (4th Cir 2001); *U.S. v. Reaux,* 2001 WL 883221 (ED La 2001); *U.S. v. Joseph,* 2001 WL 515213 (ED La 2001).

33. See, for example, *Jacobs v. Government of Virgin Islands,* 53 Fed Appx 651 (3d Cir 2002).

34. *New Hampshire v. Langill,* 157 NH 77, 945 A 2d 1 (NH 2008).

35. *U.S. v. Llera Plaza I,* 179 F Supp 2d 492 (ED Pa 2002)

36. *U.S. v. Llera Plaza II,* 188 F Supp 2d 549 (ED Pa 2002).

37. For an analysis of these two conflicting fingerprint opinions, see Mark P. Denbeaux and D. Michael Risinger, *Kumho Tire and Expert Reliability: How the Question You Ask Gives the Answer You Get,* 34 Seton Hall L Rev 15 (2003).

38. Epstein, 650.

39. Office of the U.S. Inspector General, A *Review of the FBI's Handling of the Brandon Mayfield Case,* (March 2006), retrieved December 27, 2009, from http://www.justice.gov/oig/special/s0601/PDF_list.htm.

40. *U.S. v. Rose,* No. CCB-08-0149 (D Md, December 8, 2009), retrieved December 27, 2009, from http://www.mdd.uscourts.gov/Opinions/Opinions/Brian%20Rose%20Mem-FINAL.pdf.

41. See the reported cases of *Gene Bibbins,* retrieved December 27, 2009, from http://www.innocenceproject.org/Content/53.php; and *Stephan Cowans,* retrieved December 27, 2009, from http://www.innocenceproject.org/Content/73.php.

42. National Research Council of the National Academy of Sciences, 163

43. D. Michael Risinger, "Handwriting Identification," in *Modern Scientific Evidence: The Law and Science of Expert Testimony,* ed. David L. Faigman, Michael J. Saks, Joseph Sanders, and Edward K. Cheng (Eagen, Minn.: Thomson/West, 2009) §§34.1, *et seq,* 453; see also Ron N. Morris, *Forensic Handwriting Identification: Fundamental Concepts and Principles* (San Diego, Calif.: Academic Press, 2000), 129–142.

44. Risinger, §34:12, 569.

45. Ibid.

46. *State v. Hauptmann,* 180 A 809, 822 (NJ 1935).

47. See Risinger, §34:3, 455–459; Christine Beck Lyssitzyn, *Forensic Evidence in Court: A Case Study Approach* (Durham, N.C.: Carolina Academic Press, 2007), 247.

48. Jane Campbell Moriarty and Michael J. Saks, *Forensic Science: Grand Goals, Tragic Flaws, and Judicial Gatekeeping,* Judges' J, Fall, 16, 21 (2005); Risinger, §34:3, 455–459; D. Michael Risinger, Mark P. Denbeaux, and Michael J. Saks, *Exorcism of*

Ignorance as a Proxy for Rational Knowledge: The Lessons of Handwriting Identification "Expertise," 137 U Pa L Rev 731, 770–771 (1989).

49. National Research Council of the National Academy of Sciences, 165–166.

50. Roy A. Huber and A. M. Headrick, *Handwriting Identification: Facts and Fundamentals* (Boca Raton, Fla.: CRC Press, 1999).

51. See Risinger, §34:3, 455–459; Lyssitzyn, 249.

52. See, for example, *Standard Descriptions of Scope of Work Relating to Forensic Document Examiners,* ASTM E444-09 (2009); *Standard Terminology for Expressing Conclusions of Forensic Document Examiners,* ASTM E1658-08 (2008); *Standard Guide for Minimum Training Requirements for Forensic Document Examiners,* ASTM E2388-05 (2005).

53. American Board of Forensic Examiners, "Who Are We?" retrieved December 27, 2009, from http://www.abfde.org/Index.html.

54. Risinger, §34.10, 563–564; and David Ellen, *The Scientific Examination of Documents: Methods and Techniques* (Boca Raton, Fla.: CRC Press, 1989), 9.

55. Lyssitzyn, 251.

56. Michael J. Saks and Holly VanderHaar, *On the "General Acceptance" of Handwriting Identification Principles,* 50 J Forensic Sci 119 (2005).

57. Risinger, §34.14, 579.

58. R. J. Muehlberger et al., *A Statistical Examination of Selected Handwriting Characteristics,* 22 J Forensic Sci 206 (1977); Sargur N. Srihari, Sung-Hyuk Cha, Hina Arora, Sangjik Lee, *Individuality of Handwriting: A Validation Study,* Sixth International Conference on Document Analysis and Recognition, ICDAR'01, (2001), retrieved January 5, 2010, from http://www.cedar.buffalo.edu/papers/articles/Individuality_Handwriting_2001.pdf.

59. Risinger, Denbeaux, and Saks, 731.

60. Oliver Galbraith, Craig Galbraith, and Nanette Galbraith, *The "Principle of the Drunkard's Search" as a Proxy for Scientific Analysis: The Misuse of Handwriting Test Data in a Law Journal Article,* 1 Int'l J Forensic Document Examiners 7 (1995). For a full discussion of the ensuing debate, see Risinger, §34.14, 581–643.

61. Risinger, §34.14 *et seq.*

62. Ibid.

63. Ibid.

64. Ibid.

65. Galbraith, Galbraith, and Galbraith, 7.

66. Risinger, §34.14 *et seq.*

67. Moshe Kam, J. Wetstein, and R. Conn, *Proficiency of Professional Document Examiners in Writer Identification,* 39 J Forensic Sci 5 (1994). Abstract retrieved December 27, 2009, from http://www.ncjrs.gov/App/Publications/abstract.aspx?ID=146638.

68. Moshe Kam, Gabriel Fielding, and Robert Conn, *Writer Examination by Professional Document Examiners,* 42 J Forensic Sci 778 (1997).

69. The criticisms included the use of monetary incentives for the layperson subjects, aggregation of results, and other concerns. See Risinger, §34.29.

70. Moshe Kam, Gabriel Fielding, and Robert Conn, *Effects of Monetary Incentives on Performance in Document Examination Proficiency Tests,* 43 J Forensic Sci 1000 (1997).

71. Moshe Kam, K. Gummadidala, Gabriel Fielding, and Robert Conn, *Signature Authentication by Forensic Document Examiners,* 46 J Forensic Sci 884 (2001).

72. J. Sita, B. Found, and D. Rogers, *Forensic Handwriting Examiners' Expertise for Signature Comparison,* 47 J Forensic Sci 1117 (2002).

73. Srihari, Cha, Arora, and Lee, 871.

74. National Research Council of the National Academy of Sciences, 166–167.

75. *U.S. v. Starzecpyzel,* 880 F Supp 1027, 42 Fed R Evid Serv 247 (SD NY 1995).

76. *U.S. v. Fujii,* 152 F Supp 2d 939, *942* (ND Ill 2000). The Court held that "[c]onsidering the questions about handwriting analysis generally under *Daubert,* the lack of any evidence that the identification of handprinting is an expertise that meets the *Daubert* standards and the questions that have been raised, which the government has not attempted to answer, about its expert's ability to opine reliably on handprinting identification in dealing with native Japanese writers taught English printing in Japan, the court grants the defendant's motion."

77. *U.S. v. Saelee,* 162 F Supp 2d 1097, 1106 (D Alaska 2001). In a broader decision than *Fujii,* the *Saelee* court found that the government could not establish that handwriting identification was "the product of reliable methods."

78. *United States v. Hines,* 55 F Supp 2d 62, 67-68 (D Mass 1999) (holding that expert testimony about general similarities and differences between the evidentiary sample and defendant's exemplar was admissible but that the expert could not testify to the conclusion that the defendant was the author because it lacked empirical validation).

79. *U.S. v. Crisp,* 324 F 3d 261 (4th Cir 2003).

80. *U.S. v. Mooney,* 315 F 3d 54, 60 Fed Evid Serv 60 (1st Cir 2002).

81. For an extremely detailed description of post-*Daubert* cases dealing with handwriting comparison, see Risinger, §§34.4 –34.9.

Chapter 5: More "Who" Questions

1. See David L. Faigman, Michael J. Saks, Joseph Sanders, and Edward K. Cheng, eds., *Modern Scientific Evidence: The Law and Science of Expert Testimony* (Eagen, Minn.: Thomson/West, 2009), §30.46.

2. Scientific Working Group on Materials Analysis (SWGMAT), *Forensic Human Hair Examination Guidelines,* 7(2) Forensic Sci Comm (April 2005), retrieved December 28, 2009, from http://www.fbi.gov/hq/lab/fsc/backissu/april2005/standards/2005_04 _standards02.htm.

3. Ibid.

4. Ibid.

5. See, for example, Douglas W. Deedrick & Sandra L. Koch, *Microscopy of Hair Part 1: A Practical Guide and Manual for Human Hairs,* Forensic Sci Comm (Jan. 2004), retrieved December 28, 2009, from http://www.fbi.gov/hq/lab/fsc/backissu/ jan2004/research/2004_01_research01b.htm.

6. Ibid.

7. See Andre A. Moenssens, Carol E. Henderson, and Sharon G. Portwood, *Scientific Evidence in Civil and Criminal Cases,* ed 5 (Eagen, Minn.: Thomson/West, 2007), §11.13, 732–734; National Research Council of the National Academy of Sciences, *Strengthening Forensic Science in the United States: A Path Forward* (Washington, D.C.: National Academies Press, 2009), 155–161; Richard E. Bisbing, "The Forensic Identification and Association of Human Hair," in *Forensic Science Handbook,* ed. Richard Saferstein (New York: Prentice Hall, 2002), 420–421.

8. See, for example, *People v. Moore,* 662 NE 2d 1215, 1227 (Ill 1996); *People v. Linscott,* 566 NE 2d 1355, 1358-60 (Ill 1991).

9. At least one court has found that *Daubert* required the exclusion of microscopic hair analysis evidence and overturned a conviction based on it. *Williamson v. Reynolds,* 904 F Supp 1529, 1557-58, 1562 (ED Okla 1995), *aff'd sub nom. Williamson v. Ward,* 110 F 3d 1508, 1523 (10th Cir 1997); see Jane Campbell Moriarty and Michael J. Saks, *Forensic Science: Grand Goals, Tragic Flaws, and Judicial Gatekeeping,* Judges' J., Fall 2005, 16, 21 ("Of the first seventy-one convictions that were reversed on the basis of DNA testing, twenty-one involved erroneous microscopic identification of hair samples"). See generally Clive A. Stafford Smith and Patrick D. Goodman, *Forensic Hair Comparison Analysis: Nineteenth Century Science or Twentieth Century Snake Oil?* 27 Colum Hum Rts L Rev 227 (1996) (questioning the scientific foundation of microscopic hair analysis).

10. The Innocence Project, *David Johns Bryson,* retrieved December 28, 2009, from http://www.innocenceproject.org/Content/1701.php.

11. *Bryson v. Gonzales,* 534 F 3d 1282 (10th Cir 2008).

12. The Innocence Project, *Timothy Durham,* retrieved December 28, 2009, from http://www.innocenceproject.org/Content/90.php.

13. See *State v. West,* 877 A 2d 787 (Conn 2005); *Bookins v. State,* 922 A 2d 389 (Del Supr 2007).

14. See Paul C. Gianelli and E. West, *Hair Comparison Evidence,* 37 Crim L Bull 514 (2001).

15. National Research Council of the National Academy of Sciences, 160–161.

16. *State v. Council,* 515 SE 2d 508, 516 n 12 (SC 1999) (citing Brian Huseman, Note, *Taylor v. State, Rule 706, and the DNA Database: Future Directions in DNA Evidence,* 22 Okla City U L Rev 397 [1997]).

17. Edward K. Cheng, *Mitochondrial DNA: Emerging Legal Issues,* 13 J L & Pol'y 99 (2005).

18. Ibid., 106.

19. Ibid., 100.

20. For descriptions of the mtDNA process as applied to hair analysis, see *State v. Pappas,* 776 A 2d 1091, 1107-12 (Conn 2001). See also Frederick R. Bieber, "Science and Technology of Forensic DNA Profiling: Current Use and Future Directions," in *DNA and the Criminal Justice System,* ed. David Lazer (Cambridge, Mass.: MIT Press, 2004), *supra* note 30, 32–33; Terrence F. Kiely, *Forensic Evidence: Science and Criminal Law* (Boca Raton, Fla.: CRC Press, 2006), 79–81, 106–119; Cheng, 107–116; Marlan D. Walker, Note, *Mitochondrial DNA Evidence in* State v. Pappas, 43 Jurimetrics J 427

(2003) (describing the case of *State v. Pappas*, which admitted mitochondrial DNA identification evidence, and the case's consequences).

21. Max M. Houck and Bruce Budowle, *Correlation of Microscopic and Mitochondrial DNA Hair Comparison*, 47 J Forensic Sci 964, 966 (2002).

22. *State v. Pappas*, 776 A 2d at 1100-1113 (Conn 2001).

23. Ibid., 1108.

24. Ibid.; see also *United States v. Beverly*, 369 F 3d 516, 528–531 (6th Cir 2004); *United States v. Coleman*, 202 F Supp 2d 962, 970 (ED Mo 2002); *Wagner v. State*, 864 A 2d 1037, 1046–1047 (Md Ct Spec App 2005); *State v. Underwood*, 518 SE 2d 231, 239–240 (NC Ct App 1999); *State v. Council*, 515 SE 2d, 516–517.

25. For general information about bite mark comparisons, see Robert B. J. Dorion, ed., *Bitemark Evidence* (New York: Marcel Dekker, 2004); C. Michael Bowers, "Identification from Bitemarks: Scientific Issues," in *Modern Scientific Evidence: The Law and Science of Expert Testimony*, ed. David L. Faigman, Michael J. Saks, Joseph Sanders, and Edward K. Cheng (Eagen, Minn.: Thomson/West, 2009), §§ 37.1 *et seq.*

26. American Board of Forensic Odontology, Inc., *Diplomates Reference Manual* (June 28, 2009), retrieved December 31, 2009, from http://www.abfo.org/pdfs/ABFO%20Manual%20-%20revised%2010-28-09-B.pdf.

27. See, for example, *People v. Milone*, 356 NE 2d 1350, 1355 (Ill App Ct 1976); *People v. Smith*, 443 NYS 2d 551, 556–557 (Sup Ct 1981).

28. *State v. Timmendequas*, 737 A 2d 55 (NJ 1999).

29. See Jules A. Kieser, *Weighing Bitemark Evidence: A Postmodern Perspective*, 1 J Forensic Sci 75 (2005); J. M. Kittelson, J. A. Kieser, D. M. Buckingham, and G. P. Herbison, *Weighing Evidence: Quantitative Measures of the Importance of Bitemark Evidence*, 20 J Forensic Odonto-Stomatology 31 (2002).

30. David J. Sweet, "Human Bitemarks: Examination, Recovery, and Analysis," in *Manual of Forensic Odontology*, ed. C. Michael Bowers and Gary L. Bell (Austin, Tx.: American Society of Forensic Odontology, 1997), 148; R. D. Rawson, R. K. Ommen, and G. J. Kinard, *Statistical Evidence for the Individuality of the Human Dentition*, 29 J Forensic Sci 245 (1984); Reider F. Sognnaes, R. D. Rawson, B. M. Gratt, and N. B. Nguyen, *Computer Comparison of Bitemark Patterns in Identical Twins*, 105 J Am Dent Assoc 449 (1982).

31. Iain Pretty, *A Web-Based Survey of Odontologist's Opinions Concerning Bitemark Analysis*, 48 J Forensic Sci 117 (2003); Bowers, §37.8, *et seq.*

32. National Research Council of the National Academy of Sciences, 175.

33. See C. Michael Bowers, *Problem-Based Analysis in Bite Mark Misidentifications: The Role of DNA*, 159 Forensic Sci Int'l (Supp 1) 104 (May, 2006); Allen P. Wilkinson and Ronald M. Gerughty, *Bite Mark Evidence: Its Admissibility Is Hard to Swallow*, 12 W St U L Rev 519 (1985); Iain Pretty and M. D. Turnbull, *Lack of Dental Uniqueness Between Two Bite Mark Suspects*, 46 J Forensic Sci 1487 (2001); Paul C. Giannelli, *Bite Mark Analysis*, 43 Crim L Bull 930 (2007); Moriarty and Saks, 16, 21.

34. Bowers, §37:12; Bruce M. Rothwell, *Bitemarks in Forensic Dentistry: A Review of Legal, Scientific Issues*, 126 J Am Dent Assoc 223 (1995).

35. See Wilkinson and Gerughty, 535–537, 550–552.

36. See Giannelli, 932.

37. See Wilkinson and Gerughty, 557–559.

38. American Board of Forensic Odontology, *Guidelines for Bite Mark Analysis,* 112 J Am Dental Assn 383, 384–386 (1986); see also Michelle McClure, *Odontology: Bite Marks as Evidence in Criminal Trials,* 11 Santa Clara Comp & High Tech L J 269, 273–275 (1995) (summarizing the American Board of Forensic Odontology's guidelines).

39. National Research Council of the National Academies, 175.

40. Bowers, §37:18, 45.

41. Mary A. Bush et al., *Biomechanical Factors in Human Dermal Bitemarks in a Cadaver Model,* 54 J Forensic Sci 167 (2009).

42. Raymond G. Miller et al., *Uniqueness of the Dentition as Impressed in Human Skin: A Cadaver Model,* 54 J Forensic Sci 909 (2009).

43. Bowers, §37:18, 46.

44. J. C. Dailey and C. Michael Bowers, *Aging of Bitemarks: A Literature Review,* 42 J Forensic Sci 792 (1997).

45. Bruce R. Rothwell and A. V. Thien, *Analysis of Distortion in Preserved Bite Mark Skin,* 46 J Forensic Sci 573 (2001).

46. For a review of various reported cases using these qualifiers, see generally Paul C. Giannelli, *Forensic Science,* 33 J L Med & Ethics 535 (2005).

47. Bowers, §37:13.

48. *Ege v. Yukins,* 380 F Supp 2d 852 (ED Mich 2005).

49. See *Brooks v. State,* 748 So 2d 736, 739–740 (Miss 1999); *Banks v. State,* 725 So 2d 711, 715–716 (Miss 1997); *Harrison v. State,* 635 So 2d 894, 897–898 (Miss 1994).

50. See *State v. Krone,* 897 P 2d 621, 622 (Ariz 1995) (en banc); Mark Hansen, *The Uncertain Science of Evidence,* ABA J, (July 2005), 49, 49–50; James Randerson, *Bite-Mark Evidence Can Leave a False Impression,* New Scientist, (Mar. 13, 2004), 6, retrieved April 12, 2010, from http://www.newscientist.com/article/dn4758-bitemark -evidence-can-leave-false-impression.html.

51. See Melanie Lasoff Levs, *Bite-Mark Evidence Loses Teeth,* ABA J, May 2008, 16, retrieved April 12, 2010, from http://www.abajournal.com/magazine/bite_mark_evi- dence_loses_teeth; Fernanda Santos, "Evidence from Bite Marks, It Turns Out, Is Not So Elementary," *New York Times,* Jan. 28, 2007, WK 4.

Chapter 6: The "How" Question

1. National Research Council of the National Academy of Sciences, *Strengthening Forensic Science in the United States: A Path Forward* (Washington, D.C.: National Academies Press, 2009), 152.

2. National Research Council of the National Academy of Sciences, 150; Alfred Biasotti, John Murdock, and Bruce R. Moran, "Firearms and Toolmark Identification: Scientific Issues," in *Modern Scientific Evidence: The Law and Science of Expert Testimony,* ed. David L. Faigman, Michael J. Saks, Joseph Sanders, and Edward K. Cheng (Eagen, Minn.: Thomson/West, 2009), §§35.6 *et seq.*

3. See Biasotti, Murdock, and Moran, §§35.1–5; Jane Campbell Moriarty & Michael J. Saks, *Forensic Science: Grand Goals, Tragic Flaws, and Judicial Gatekeeping,* Judges' J., 16 (Fall 2005).

4. Biasotti, Murdock, and Moran, §§35.1–5; and see Andre A. Moenssens et al., *Scientific Evidence in Civil and Criminal Cases,* ed 5 (Eagen, Minn.: Thomson/West, 2009 Supp).

5. *State v. Brown,* 291 SW 2d 615 (Mo 1956); *State v. Wade,* 465 SW 2d 498 (Mo 1971); *State v. Eickmeier,* 187 Neb 491, 191 NW 2d 815 (1971); *Fletcher v. Lane,* 446 F Supp 729 (SD Ill 1978).

6. *Souza v. United States,* 304 F 2d 274 (9th Cir 1962).

7. *State v. Olsen,* 212 Or 191, 317 P 2d 938 (1957).

8. *People v. Genrich,* 928 P 2d 799 (Colo Ct App 1996).

9. *People v. Wilkes,* 280 P 2d 88 (Cal App 1955).

10. *State v. Clark,* 156 Wash 543, 287 P 18 (1930); but compare the earlier ruling of the same court in *State v. Fasick,* 149 Wash 92, 270 P 123 (1928), aff'd 149 Wash. 92, 174 P 712 (1929).

11. *Ramirez v. State,* 542 So 2d 352 (Fla 1989).

12. *United States v. Green,* 405 F Supp 2d 104, 107 (D Mass 2005).

13. See generally Biasotti, Murdock, and Moran; National Research Council of the National Academy of Sciences, 150–161; Gil Hocherman, Arie Zeichner, and Tzipi Kahana, *Firearms—A Review: 2001–2004,* 14th Interpol Forensic Science Symposium Report, (2004), 47, retrieved from December 31, 2009, from http://www.interpol.int/ Public/Forensic/IFSS/meeting14/ReviewPapers.pdf.

14. See *Expert Evidence to Identify Gun from Which Bullet or Cartridge Was Fired,* 26 ALR 2d 892 (1965); *Admissibility of Testimony That Bullet Could or Might Have Come from Particular Gun,* 31 ALR 4th 486 (1992); National Research Council of the National Academy of Sciences, *Ballistic Imaging* (Washington, D.C.: National Academies Press, 2008).

15. *Wynn v. State,* 56 Ga 113, 1876 WL 2941 (1876).

16. See *Evans v. Commonwealth,* 230 Ky 411, 19 SW 2d 1091 (1929) and the discussion of that opinion in Andre Moessens et al., §6.18; and see Biasotti, Murdock, and Moran, §35.3.

17. Calvin H. Goddard, *Scientific Identification of Firearms and Bullets* (Evanston, Ill.: Northwestern University, 1926); and see Fred E. Inbau, *Scientific Evidence in Criminal Cases,* 24 Am Inst Crim L & Criminology 825 (1933–1934); Tom A. Warlow, *Firearms, the Law and Forensic Ballistics,* ed. 2 (Boca Raton, Fla.: CRC Press, 2004).

18. *Expert Evidence to Identify Gun from Which Bullet or Cartridge Was Fired,* 892; *Admissibility of Testimony That Bullet Could or Might Have Come from Particular Gun,* 31 ALR 4th 486 (1992); and see Biasotti, Murdock, and Moran, §35.3.

19. National Research Council of the National Academy of Sciences, *Ballistic Imaging* (Washington, D.C.: National Academies Press, 2008), 3.

20. See Alfred A. Biasotti, *A Statistical Study of the Individual Characteristics of Fired Bullets,* 4 J Forensic Sci 34 (1959).

21. American Federation of Firearms and Tool Mark Examiners, *Theory of Identification, Range of Striae Comparison Reports and Modified Glossary Definitions—An*

AFTE Criteria for Identification Committee Report, 24 J Assoc of Firearm and Tool Mark Examiners 336 (1992). Further discussions of criteria appear in J. J. Masson, *Confidence Level Variations in Firearms Identification Through Computerized Technology,* 29 J Assoc of Firearm and Tool Mark Examiners 42 (1997); and J. Miller and M. M. McLean, *Criteria for Identification of Toolmarks,* 30 J Assoc of Firearm and Tool Mark Examiners 15 (1998).

22. Adina Schwartz, *A Systemic Challenge to the Reliability and Admissibility of Firearms and Toolmark Identification,* 6 Colum Sci & Tech L Rev 2 (2005).

23. Ronald G. Nichols, *Defending the Scientific Foundations of the Firearms and Tool Mark Identification Discipline: Responding to Recent Challenges,* 522 J Forensic Sci 586 (2007).

24. National Research Council of the National Academy of Sciences, 154.

25. *United States v. Monteiro,* 407 F Supp 351, 354–355 (D Mass 2006); *United States v. Green,* 405 F Supp 104 (D Mass 2005), at 108–109.

26. See generally "Bullet Lead Analysis," in *Modern Scientific Evidence: The Law and Science of Expert Testimony,* ed. David L. Faigman, Michael J. Saks, Joseph Sanders, and Edward K. Cheng (Eagen, Minn.: Thomson/West, 2009), §§ 36.1 *et seq;* Thomas L. Bohan, *Scientific Evidence and Forensic Science Since Daubert: Maine Decides to Sit Out the Dance,* 56 Me L Rev 101, 139 (2004).

27. See "Bullet Lead Analysis," §§36.1 *et seq.*

28. For a general description of the theory of bullet lead analysis, see Robert D. Koons and JoAnn Buscaglia, *Forensic Significance of Bullet Lead Comparisons,* 50 J Forensic Sci 1 (2005); and Terrence F. Kiely, *Forensic Evidence: Science and the Criminal Law,* ed. 2 (Boca Raton, Fla.: CRC Press, 2005), 199–212.

29. See, for example, *U. S. v. Davis,* 103 F 3rd 660, 46 Fed R Evid Serv 189 (8th Cir 1996); *State v. Ware,* 338 NW 2d 707 (Ia 1983); *State v. Noel,* 157 NJ 141, 723 A 2d 602 (1999); *State v. Grube,* 126 Idaho 377, 883 P 2d 1069 (1994); Kiely, 235; and "Bullet Lead Analysis," §36.2, 728–729.

30. *United States v. Mikos,* No. 02 CR 137, 2003 WL 22922197 (ND Ill 2003).

31. National Research Council of the National Academy of Sciences, Committee on Scientific Assessment of Bullet Lead Elemental Composition Comparison, *Forensic Analysis: Weighing Bullet Lead Evidence* (2004), retrieved December 31, 2009, from http://books.nap.edu/openbook/0309090792/html/index.html.

32. Federal Bureau of Investigation (FBI) Press Release, *National Academy of Sciences Releases FBI-Commissioned Study on Bullet Lead Analysis* (February 10, 2004), retrieved December 31, 2009, from http://www.fbi.gov/pressrel/pressrel04/bullet021004.htm.

33. FBI Press Release, *FBI Laboratory Announces Discontinuation of Bullet Lead Analysis* (September 10, 2005), retrieved December 31, 2009, from http://www.fbi .gov/pressrel/pressrel05/bullet_lead_analysis.htm; and see Charles Piller, "FBI Abandons Controversial Bullet-Matching Technique," *Los Angeles Times,* Sept. 2, 2005, A38.

34. "Bullet Lead Analysis," 731.

35. See, for example, *Ragland v. Com.,* 191 SW 3d 569 (Ky 2006).

36. See, for example, *Clemons v. State,* 392 Md 339, 896 A 2d 1059 (2006).

37. John J. Lentini, "Fires, Arson and Explosions—Scientific Status," in *Modern Scientific Evidence: The Law and Science of Expert Testimony,* ed. David L. Faigman, Michael J. Saks, Joseph Sanders, and Edward K. Cheng (Eagen, Minn.: Thomson/ West, 2009), §39.21, 205.

38. *Michigan Millers Mut. Ins. Corp. v. Benfield,* 140 F 3d 915, 49 Fed R Evid Serv 549 (11th Cir 1998).

39. *Carmichael v. Samyang Tire, Inc.,* 131 F 3d 1433, 48 Fed R Evid Serv 334 (11th Cir 1997), rev'd *sub nom Kumho Tire Co., Ltd. v. Carmichael,* 526 U.S. 137 (1999).

40. Ibid.

41. National Fire Protection Association (NFPA), *Guide for Fire and Explosion Investigation* (Pub. No. 921 2008). Retrieved for purchase January 1, 2009, from http:// www.nfp.org.

42. See Lentini, §38.2, 109.

43. See, for example, *Travelers Property & Casualty Corp. v. General Electric Co.* 150 F Supp 2d 360 (D Conn 2001); *Royal Ins. Co. of America v. Joseph Daniel Const., Inc.* 208 F Supp 2d 423 (SD NY 2002); *American Family Ins. Group v. JVC Americas Corp.,* 2001 WL 1618454 (D Minn 2001); *Allstate In. Co. v. Hugh Cole Builder, Inc.* 137 F Supp 2d 1283 (MD Ala 2001); *Ziegler v. Fisher-Price, Inc.,* 2003 WL 1889021 (ND Ia 2003); *Booth v. Black & Decker, Inc.,* 166 F Supp 2d 215 (ED Pa 2001); *Tunnell v. Ford Motor Co.* 320 F Supp 2d 707 (WD Va 2004).

44. Lentini, §39.23.

45. Ibid. See Francis Brannigan, ed., *Fire Investigation Handbook* (Washington, D.C.: U.S. Bureau of Commerce, National Bureau of Standards, 1980), 134, retrieved January 1, 2009, from http://fire.nist.gov/bfrlpubs/fire80/PDF/f80004.pdf.

46. See *U.S. v. Marji,* 158 F 3d 60 (2d Cir 1998), upholding the use of a dog alert evidence to assist in accelerant detection.

47. American Society for Testing Materials (ASTM), *Standard Practice for Sampling of Headspace Vapors from Fire Debris Samples,* ASTM E1388-05 (2005), retrieved for purchase January 1, 2009, from http://webstore.ansi.org/RecordDetail .aspx?sku=ASTM+E1388-05.

48. ASTM, *Standard Test Method for Ignitable Liquid Residues in Extracts from Fire Debris Samples by Gas Chromatography-Mass Spectrometry,* ASTM E1618-06E1 (2006), retrieved for purchase January 1, 2009, from http://webstore.ansi.org/RecordDetail .aspx?sku=ASTM+E1618-06e1.

49. Lentini, §39.52.

50. National Research Council of the National Academy of Sciences, 173.

51. *Weisgram v. Marley* 169 F.3d 514 (8th Cir. 1999), aff'd, 528 U.S. 440 (2000).

52. See, for example, *Pride v. BIC Corp.,* 218 F 3d 566 (6th Cir 2000); *Werner v. Pittway Corp.* 90 F Supp 2d 1018 (WD Wis 2000); *Comer v. American Elec. Power,* 63 Supp 2d 927 (ND Ind 1999); *Knotts v. Black & Decker, Inc.,* 204 F Supp 2d 1029 (ND Ohio 2002); *Truck Ins. Exchange v. MagneTek, Inc.,* 360 F 3d 1206 (10th Cir 2004).

53. *Allstate Ins. Co. v. Hugh Cole Builder, Inc.,* 137 F Supp 2d 1283 (MD Ala 2001).

54. See, for example, *Zeigler v. Fisher-Price, Inc.,* 261 F Supp 2d 1047 (ND Iowa 2003); *Zeigler v. Fisher-Price, Inc.,* 302 F Supp 2d 999 (ND Ia 2004); *Hynes v. Energy*

West, Inc. 211 F 3d 1193 (10th Cir 2000); *Thurman v. Missouri Gas Energy*, 107 F Supp 2d 1046 (WD Mo 2000).

55. Margaret A. Berger, *Expert Testimony in Criminal Proceedings: Questions Daubert Does Not Answer*, 33 Seton Hall L Rev 1125 (2003); Keith A. Findley, *Innocents at Risk: Adversary Imbalance, Forensic Science, and the Search for Truth*, 38 Seton Hall L Rev 893, 929–950 (2008), retrieved January 1, 2009, from http://ssrn.com/abstract=1144886; Jennifer L. Groscup et al., *The Effects of Daubert on the Admissibility of Expert Testimony in State and Federal Criminal Cases*, 8 Psychol Pub Pol'y & L 339 (2002); Peter J. Neufeld, *The (Near) Irrelevance of Daubert to Criminal Justice and Some Suggestions for Reform*, 95 Am J Pub Health 107 (2005); D. Michael Risinger, *Navigating Expert Reliability: Are Criminal Standards of Certainty Being Left on the Dock?* 64 Alb L Rev 99 (2000).

56. *U.S. v. Norris*, 217 F 3d 262 (5th Cir 2000).

57. *U.S. v. Gardner*, 213 F 3d 1049 (7th Cir 2000).

58. *U.S. v. Diaz*, 300 F 3d 66 (1st Cir 2002).

59. *Comm. v. Goodman*, 54 Mass App Ct 385, 765 NE 2d 792 (2002).

60. *State v. Campbell*, 2002 WL 398029 (Ohio Ct App 1st Dist 2002).

61. T. Paulette Sutton, "Presumptive Testing for Blood," in *Scientific and Legal Applications of Bloodstain Pattern Analysis*, ed. Stuart H. James (Boca Raton, Fla.: CRC Press, 1991).

62. See L. T. Lytle and D. G. Hedgecock, *Chemiluminescence in the Visualization of Forensic Bloodstains*, 23 J Forensic Sci 550 (1978).

63. Terence I. Quickenden and J. I. Creamer, *A Study of Common Interferences with the Forensic Luminol Test for Blood*, 16 J Bioluminescence Chemiluminescence 295 (2001); Dale L. Laux, *Effects of Luminol on the Subsequent Analysis of Bloodstains*, 36 J Forensic Sci 1512 (1991); *Rivera v. State*, 2005 WL 16193 (Tex Ct App 2005); see Kiely, 390.

64. *State v. Canaan*, 265 Kan 835, 964 P 2d 681 (1998); *State v. Maynard*, 954 SW 2d 624 (Mo Ct App 1997).

65. *Ayers v. State*, 334 Ark 258 , 975 SW 2d 88 (1998).

66. Terence I. Quickenden and Paul D. Cooper, *Increasing the Specificity of the Forensic Luminol Test for Blood*, 16 Luminesence 251 (2001), retrieved January 1, 2009, from http://mason.gmu.edu/~pcooper6/papers/1.pdf.

67. Stuart H. James, Paul E. Kish, and T. Paulette Sutton, *Principles of Bloodstain Pattern Analysis: Theory and Practice* (Boca Raton, Fla.: CRC Press, 2005), 1–2.

68. William C. Fischer, "Defining the 'Address' of Bloodstains and Other Evidence at the Crime Scene," in *Scientific and Legal Applications of Bloodstain Pattern Analysis*, ed. Stuart H. James (Boca Raton, Fla.: CRC Press, 1991), 1–2.

69. For a detailed history of forensic blood and blood pattern analysis, see James, Kish, and Sutton, 3-6; and see also Anita Wonder, *Blood Dynamics* (St. Louis: Academic Press, 2001).

70. International Association for Identification, *Bloodstain Pattern Examiner Certification Requirements*, retrieved January 2, 2009, from http://www.theiai.org/certifications/bloodstain/requirements.php.

71. Scientific Working Group on Bloodstain Pattern Analysis, *Guidelines for the Minimum Educational and Training Requirements for Bloodstain Pattern Analysts,* retrieved January 2, 2009, from http://www.fbi.gov/hq/lab/fsc/backissu/jan2008/standards/2008_01_standards01.htm.

72. National Research Council of the National Academy of Sciences, 178.

73. Ibid., 178–179.

74. See generally Kiely, 398–405.

75. *Holmes v. State,* 135 SW 3d 178 (Tex Ct App 2004).

Chapter 7: The "Whether" Question: Social Science Evidence in Criminal Cases

1. Brandon L. Garrett, *Judging Innocence,* 108 Colum L Rev 55, 125 (2008).

2. Krista L. Duncan, Note, *"Lies, Damned Lies, and Statistics"? Psychological Syndrome Evidence in the Courtroom after* Daubert, 71 Ind L J 753, 760–761, 765–766 (1996).

3. See Dara Loren Steele, Note, *Expert Testimony: Seeking an Appropriate Admissibility Standard for Behavioral Science in Child Sexual Abuse Prosecutions,* 48 Duke L J 933, 970 (1998).

4. Ibid., 968.

5. *Carmichael v. Samyang Tire, Inc.,* 131 F 3d 1433, 1435 (11th Cir 1997), *cert granted sub nom Kumho Tire Co. v. Carmichael,* 526 U.S. 137 (1999).

6. Ibid.

7. *Kumho Tire Co. v. Carmichael,* 526 U.S. 137 (1999), at 157–158 (quoting *Gen. Elec. Co. v. Joiner,* 522 U.S. 136, 146 [1997]).

8. Some of the earlier distinctions were made in *United States v. Bighead,* 128 F 3d 1329, 1330 (9th Cir 1997); *United States v. Cordoba,* 104 F 3d 225, 230 (9th Cir 1997); and *Berry v. City of Detroit,* 25 F 3d 1342, 1349 (6th Cir 1994).

9. *People v. Beckley,* 434 Mich 691, 456 NW 2d 391 (1990).

10. *Gilbert v. Daimler Chrysler Corp.,* 470 Mich 749, 685 NW 2d 391, 409 (2004).

11. Mich R Evid 702.

12. *United States v. Downing,* 753 F 2d 1224 (3d Cir 1985).

13. See, for example, David L. Faigman, *The Evidentiary Status of Social Science under* Daubert: *Is It "Scientific," "Technical," or "Other" Knowledge,* 1 Psychol, Pub Pol'y & L, 960 (1995); Teresa Renaker, *Evidentiary Legerdemain: Deciding When Daubert Should Apply to Social Science Evidence,* 84 Cal L Rev 1657 (1996).

14. See, for example, James Richardson and Gerald Ginsberg, "'Brainwashing' Evidence in Light of *Daubert,*" in *Law and Science: Current Legal Issues,* ed. Helen Reece, (New York: Oxford University Press, 1998); David T. Moore, *Scientific Consensus & Expert Testimony: Lessons from the Judas Priest Trial,* 17 Am Psy L News 3 (1997).

15. "Not surprisingly, when social science-based testimony is subjected to the *Frye* test or to the *Daubert* factors, that testimony fails either standard." Steele, 956.

16. *Newkirk v. Commonwealth,* 937 SW 2d 690, 695 (Ky 1996) (holding that child sexual abuse syndrome evidence offered for any use would fail to meet the standards

set forth in either *Frye* or *Daubert*); *State v. Foret,* 628 So 2d 1116, 1127 (La 1993) (holding that child sexual abuse accommodation syndrome fails *Daubert* because it is not scientifically reliable); *Commonwealth v. Dunkle,* 602 A 2d 830, 832 (Pa. 1992) (holding that syndrome evidence does not meet *Frye* standards); *Fowler v. State,* 958 SW 2d 853, 864 (Tex App 1997) (holding that testimony regarding domestic violence might satisfy state equivalent of *Daubert* and therefore be admissible, but that it did not meet the reliability requirements here).

17. In an empirical study of the so-called *CSI* effect, jurors demonstrated that they had high expectations that the prosecutor would produce scientific evidence *but* that they were nevertheless willing to find a defendant guilty without any scientific evidence if the government had eyewitness testimony. The demand for scientific evidence as a prerequisite for a guilty verdict was prominent only in rape cases, or where the government was relying on circumstantial evidence. Donald E. Shelton, Young S. Kim, and Gregg Barak, *A Study of Juror Expectations and Demands for Scientific Evidence: Does the "CSI Effect" Exist?* 9 Vanderbilt J Ent & Tech L 334 at 363–364 (2006); Donald Shelton, *The CSI Effect: Does It Exist?* Nat'l Inst Just J, Mar. 2008, 1, 5 (2008), retrieved January 3, 2010, from http://www.ojp.usdoj.gov/nij/journals/259/csi-effect.htm; Donald E. Shelton, Young S. Kim, and Gregg Barak, *An Indirect-Effects Model of Mediated Adjudication: The CSI Myth, the Tech Effect, and Metropolitan Jurors' Expectations for Scientific Evidence,* 12 Vand J Ent & Tech L 1 (2009), retrieved January 3, 2010, from http://law.vanderbilt.edu/publications/journal-entertainment-technology-law/archive/index.aspx.

18. See Brian L. Cutler and Steven D. Penrod, *Mistaken Identification: The Eyewitness, Psychology, and the Law* 6–7 (1995); Neil Brewer, Nathan Weber, and Carolyn Semmler, "Eyewitness Identification," in *Psychology and Law,* ed. Neil Brewer and Kipling D. Williams (New York: Guilford, 2005); David L. Faigman, Michael J. Saks, Joseph Sanders, and Edward K. Cheng, eds., *Modern Scientific Evidence: The Law and Science of Expert Testimony* (Eagen, Minn.: Thomson/West, 2009), § 16: 1 *et seq.*; Elizabeth F. Loftus et al., *Eyewitness Testimony: Civil and Criminal,* ed. 4 (Alexandria, Va.: Lexus Law Publishing, 2007), § 4-18, 112; John C. Brigham and Robert K. Bothwell, *The Ability of Prospective Jurors to Estimate the Accuracy of Eyewitness Identifications,* 7 Law & Hum Behav 19 (1983).

19. Jane Campbell Moriarty, *Psychological and Scientific Evidence in Criminal Trials* (Eagen, Minn.: Thomson/West, 2009), §13:54.

20. Janet Reno, introduction to *Eyewitness Evidence: A Guide For Law Enforcement,* by National Institute of Justice and U.S. Department of Justice (Washington, D.C.: U.S. Department of Justice, 1999), iii–iv, retrieved January 3, 2009, from http://www.ncjrs.gov/pdffiles1/nij/178240.pdf.

21. *United States v. Holloway,* 971 F 2d 675, 679 (11th Cir 1992).

22. See *State v. Goldsby,* 650 P 2d 952, 954 (Or Ct App 1982); *Commonwealth v. Simmons,* 662 A 2d 621, 631 (Pa 1995); *State v. McKinney* 74 SW 2d 291, 302 (Tenn 2002), *cert. denied,* 537 U.S. 926 (2002); *State v. Coley,* 32 SW 3d 831, 832 (Tenn 2000).

23. *United States v. Smith,* 122 F 3d 1355,1358 (11th Cir 1997).

24. See, for example, *United States V. Downing,* 753 F 2d 1224, 1232 (3d Cir 1985); *United States V. Smith,* 736 F 2d 1103, 1107–1108 (6th Cir 1984); *State v. Chapple,* 660

P 2d 1208, 1218–1219 (Ariz 1983) *(en banc)*; *Echavarria v. State,* 839 P 2d 589, 597 (Nev 1992); *State v. Hill,* 463 NW 2d 674, 676–678 (SD 1990); *Pierce v. State,* 777 SW 2d 399, 414–416 (Tex Crim App 1989) *(en banc).*

25. See, for example, *United States v. Martin,* 391 F 3d 949, 953–954 (8th Cir 2004); *United States v. Hicks,* 103 F 3d 837, 847 (9th Cir 1996); *United States v. Kime,* 99 F 3d 870, 884 (8th Cir 1996); *United States v. Larkin,* 978 F 2d 964, 971 (7th Cir 1992); *State v. Higgins,* 898 So 2d 1219, 1240 (La 2005).

26. *United States v. Moore,* 786 F 2d 1308, 1312 (5th Cir 1986); see also *United States v. Mathis,* 264 F 3d 321, 335–342 (3d Cir 2001) (providing a detailed analysis of whether an expert's testimony should have been admitted), *cert. denied,* 535 U.S. 908 (2002); *United States v. Langan,* 263 F 3d 613, 624 (6th Cir 2001) (allowing the jury to weigh eyewitness testimony without the aid of any expert); *People v. Lee,* 750 NE 2d 63, 66–67 (NY 2001) (holding the inclusion of eyewitness expert testimony was not an abuse of discretion); *People v. Radcliffe,* 764 NYS 2d 773, 775 (Sup. Ct. 2003) (identifying the traditional safeguards of eyewitness testimony).

27. The Innocence Project, *Eyewitness Identification Reform,* retrieved January 3, 2010, from http://www.innocenceproject.org/understand/Eyewitness-Misidentification.php.

28. "Studies show that professional [psychiatry and psychology] clinicians do not in fact make more accurate clinical judgments than laypersons. . . . We began by asking whether expert witnesses achieve reasonable certainty to aid the trier of fact. The scientific evidence clearly suggests that clinicians fail to satisfy either legal standard for expertise." David Faust and Jay Ziskin, *The Expert Witness in Psychology and Psychiatry,* 241 Science 31, 32, 34 (July 1, 1988).

29. See generally Andrew Cohen, Note, *The Unreliability of Expert Testimony on the Typical Characteristics of Sexual Abuse Victims,* 74 Geo L J 429 (1985) (analyzing the use and admissibility of expert testimony in sexual abuse cases).

30. See, for example, *People v. Peterson,* 450 Mich 349, 537 NW 2d 857 (1995); *People v. Beckley,* 434 Mich 691, 456 NW 2d 391 (1990).

31. Sophia I. Gatowski et al., *The Globalization of Behavioral Science Evidence about Battered Women: A Theory of Production and Diffusion,* 15 Behavioral Sci L 285, 296 (1997).

32. American Psychiatric Association, Appendix C, in *Diagnostic and Statistical Manual of Mental Disorders,* ed. 4 (Arlington, Va.: American Psychiatric Association, 1994).

33. Dirk Lorenzen, *The Admissibility of Expert Psychological Testimony in Cases Involving the Sexual Misuse of a Child,* 42 U Miami L Rev 1033 (1988), 1046–1048 (citing J. P. Chaplin, *Dictionary of Psychology* 529 [St. Louis: San Val, 1985]).

34. Ibid., 1048; Steele, 942–946.

35. Lenore E. Walker, *The Battered Woman* (New York: Harper, 1979); Lenore E. Walker, *The Battered Woman Syndrome* (New York: Springer, 1984).

36. National Institute of Justice, U.S. Department of Justice, NCJ 160972, *The Validity and Use of Evidence Concerning Battering and Its Effects in Criminal Trials: Report Responding to Section 40507 of the Violence Against Women Act* (1996), 20–22, retrieved January 3, 2010, from http://www.ncjrs.gov/pdffiles/batter.pdf.

37. Lenore E. Walker, *Terrifying Love: Why Battered Women Kill and How Society Responds* (New York: HarperCollins, 1989), 48–49; Michael McGrath, "Psychological Aspects of Victimology," in *Forensic Victimology: Examining Violent Crime Victims in Investigative and Legal Contexts,* ed. Brent E. Turvey and Wayne Petherick (St. Louis: Academic Press, 2009), 229, 241 (indicating that the four general characteristics of battered woman syndrome are often attributed to Walker's *The Battered Woman Syndrome* but that no such characteristics are in fact found in that text); and see Walker, *The Battered Woman Syndrome*, 95–97.

38. *Arcoren v. United States,* 929 F 2d 1235 (8th Cir 1991); *People v. Brown,* 94 P 3d 574 (Cal 2004); *Thompson v. State,* 416 SE 2d 755 (Ga Ct App 1992).

39. *Parrish v. State,* 514 SE 2d 458 (Ga Ct App 1999); *People v. Howard,* 712 NE 2d 380 (Ill Ct App 1999); *State v. Pargeon,* 582 NE 2d 665 (Ohio Ct App 1991); *Ryan v. State,* 988 P 2d 46 (Wyo 1999).

40. Faigman, Saks, Sanders, and Cheng, §13:1 *et seq.*

41. See, for example, *People v. Christel,* 449 Mich 578, 537 NW 2d 194 (1995).

42. David L. Faigman, Note, *The Battered Woman Syndrome and Self-Defense: A Legal and Empirical Dissent,* 72 Va L Rev 619 (1986).

43. *Fowler v. State,* 958 SW 2d 853 (Tex App 1997).

44. Faigman, Saks, Sanders, and Cheng, §15:1.

45. Ann Burgess and Linda Holmstrom, *Rape Trauma Syndrome,* 131 Am J Psychiatry 981 (1974); and see *People v. Taylor,* 75 NYS 2d 277, 552 NE 2d 131 (1990).

46. *Commonwealth v. Federico,* 425 Mass 844, 683 NE 2d 1035 (1997); *People v. Seaman,* 657 NYS 2d 242 (1997); *State v. Kinney,* 171 Vt 239, 762 A 2d 833 (2000).

47. *State v. Taylor,* 633 SW 2d 235 (Mo 1984); *State v. Chul Yun Kim,* 318 NC 614, 350 SE 2d 347 (1986); *State v. Alberico,* 116 NM 156, 861 P 2d 192 (1993).

48. *United States v. Smith,* No. 96-5385, 1998 WL 136564, at *2 (6th Cir Mar 19, 1998); *People v. Burkett,* No. 254996, 2005 WL 2401634, at *4–5 (Mich Ct App Sept 29, 2005); *People v. Stull,* 127 Mich App 14, 338 NW 2d 403 (1983).

49. See *State v. Moran,* 728 P 2d 248 (Ariz 1986); *People v. Bledsoe,* 681 P 2d 291 (Cal 1984) *(en banc)*; *People v. Fasy,* 829 P 2d 1314 (Colo 1992) *(en banc)*; *State v. Spigarolo,* 556 A 2d 112 (Conn 1989); *Townsend v. State,* 734 P 2d 705 (Nev 1987); *State v. J.Q.,* 617 A 2d 1196 (NJ 1993); *People v. Thompson,* 699 NYS 2d 770 (App Div 1999); *State v. Hall,* 412 SE 2d 883 (NC 1992); *State v. Middleton,* 657 P 2d 1215 (Or 1983); *State v. Jensen,* 432 NW 2d 913 (Wis 1988); and *Chapman v. State,* 18 P 3d 1164 (Wyo 2001).

50. Shirley A. Dobbin and Sophia I. Gatowski, "The Social Production of Rape Trauma Syndrome as Science and as Evidence," in *Science in Court: Issues in Law and Society* (Farnham, UK: Ashgate, 1998), 140.

51. Steele, 944.

52. Roland C. Summit, *The Child Sexual Abuse Accommodation Syndrome,* 7 Child Abuse & Neglect 177, 181 (1983).

53. For an excellent description of the history and judicial reactions to the child sexual abuse syndrome, see generally Steele, 933–973.

54. Council on Scientific Affairs, *AMA Diagnostic and Treatment Guidelines Concerning Child Abuse and Neglect,* 254 1. Am Med Ass'n 796, 798 (1985); see also *People*

v. Peterson, 450 Mich 349, 537 NW 2d 857 (1995) (citing with approval the behavioral signs in the American Medical Association's guidelines); and *State v. J.Q.,* 617 A 2d 1196 (NJ 1993), at 1201–1202.

55. For a discussion on the use of expert testimony in child sexual abuse cases, see generally Lisa R. Askowitz and Michael H. Graham, *The Reliability of Expert Psychological Testimony in Child Sexual Abuse Prosecutions,* 15 Cardozo L Rev 2027 (1994); John E. B. Myers et al., *Expert Testimony in Child Sexual Abuse Litigation,* 68 Neb L Rev 1 (1989); and Veronica Serrato, Note, *Expert Testimony in Child Sexual Abuse Prosecutions: A Spectrum of Uses,* 68 Boston U L Rev 155 (1988).

56. *People v. Peterson,* 450 Mich 349, 537 NW 2d 857 (1995).

57. *Newkirk v. Commonwealth,* 937 SW 2d 690 (Ky 1996) (finding that child sexual abuse syndrome offered for any use would fail to meet the standards set forth in either *Frye* or *Daubert*); *State v. Foret,* 628 So 2d 1116 (La 1993) (finding that child sexual abuse accommodation syndrome fails *Daubert* because it is not scientifically reliable); *Commonwealth v. Dunkle,* 602 A 2d 830 (Pa 1992) (finding that syndrome evidence does not meet *Frye* standards).

Chapter 8: Jurors and Forensic Science Evidence

1. For a listing of a few of the multitude of media reports of the *CSI* effect see Donald E. Shelton, Young S. Kim, and Gregg Barak, *A Study of Juror Expectations and Demands Concerning Scientific Evidence: Does the "CSI Effect" Exist?* 9 Vand J Ent & Tech L 331, 363–364 (2006) (citations omitted) (footnote omitted).

2. "To a prosecutor surprised, or just disappointed, by an acquittal, the CSI Effect presents a ready, appealing explanation." Simon A. Cole and Rachel Dioso-Villa, CSI *and Its Effects: Media, Juries, and the Burden of Proof,* 41 New Eng L Rev 435 (2007), at 463.

3. Ibid., 464. Cole and Dioso-Villa explain, "Both sides may be seen as trying to influence the jury pool by getting the media to propagate the story that their side is being increasingly disadvantaged by the CSI Effect. In other words, litigators seek to benefit from media stories that claim that the other side has been unfairly benefited by television programming."

4. Shelton, Kim, and Barak, 363–364; and Donald E. Shelton, Young S. Kim, and Gregg Barak, *An Indirect-Effects Model of Mediated Adjudication: The* CSI *Myth, the Tech Effect, and Metropolitan Jurors' Expectations for Scientific Evidence,* 12 Vand J Ent & Tech L 1 (2009). For a further analysis of the 2006 study data, see Young S. Kim, Gregg Barak, and Donald E. Shelton, *Examining the "CSI-effect" in the Cases of Circumstantial Evidence and Eyewitness Testimony: Multivariate and Path Analyses,* 37 J Crim Justice 452 (2009).

5. "We conclude that there is little support for the gravest of the CSI Effects, which is that jurors who watch *CSI* are wrongfully acquitting in cases lacking forensic evidence or that they are wrongfully convicting based on an unrealistic belief in the infallibility of forensic science." Cole and Dioso-Villa, 436.

6. George Gerbner et al., "Growing Up with Television: Cultivation Processes," in *Media Effects: Advances in Theory and Research,* ed. Jennings Bryant and Dolf Zill-

mann (New York: Routledge, 2002), 43–44; George Gerbner and Larry Gross, *Living with Television: The Violence Profile*, 26 J Comm 173 (1976).

7. Gerbner and Gross, 191.

8. See Steven D. Stark, *Perry Mason Meets Sonny Crockett: The History of Lawyers and the Police as Television Heroes*, 42 U Miami L Rev 229, 229–235 (1988); Steven Keslowitz, Note, The Simpsons, 24, *and the Law: How Homer Simpson and Jack Bauer Influence Congressional Lawmaking and Judicial Reasoning*, 29 Cardozo L Rev 2787, 2787–2798 (2007).

9. See John Dimmick, Yan Chen, and Zhan Li, *Competition Between the Internet and Traditional News Media: The Gratification-Opportunities Niche Dimension*, 17 J Media Econ 19, 27 (2004); The Pew Research Center, press release, *Social Networking and Online Videos Take Off: Internet's Broader Role in Campaign 2008* (Jan. 11, 2008), retrieved January 7, 2010, from http://people-press.org/reports/pdf/384.pdf (indicating that the number of people who get political information from the Internet, as opposed to television, almost doubled between 2004 and 2008).

10. David Ray Papke, *The Impact of Popular Culture on American Perceptions of the Courts*, 82 Ind L J 1225, 1226–1228 (2007).

11. Shelton, Kim, and Barak, 368.

12. Cole and Dioso-Villa suggest that what prosecutors really mean is that jurors may be rejecting the adversarial system in favor of more scientific truth finding. "Writ larger, this perhaps speaks to law's more fundamental anxiety about science encroaching on the law's role as a truth-making institution. Perhaps this, then, is the real CSI Effect." Cole and Dioso-Villa, 469.

13. Margaret R. Hinkle, *Criminal Practice in Suffolk Superior Court*, Boston Bar J (Nov./Dec. 2007), 6, 7.

14. Joel D. Lieberman, Courtney A. Carrell, Terance D. Miethe, and Daniel A. Krauss, *Gold Versus Platinum: Do Jurors Recognize the Superiority and Limitations of DNA Evidence Compared to Other Types of Forensic Evidence?* 14 Psychology, Pub Pol'y & L 27 (2008), 32. Shelton, Kim, and Barak also found that 22 percent of jurors expect to see DNA evidence in all criminal cases, with that number expanding to 46 percent in murder cases and 73 percent in rape cases.

15. Lieberman, Carrell, Miethe, and Krauss, 52.

16. Sarah Keturah Deutsch and Gray Cavender, CSI *and Forensic Realism*, 15 J Crim Just & Popular Culture 34, 34 (2008), retrieved January 7, 2010, from http://www.albany.edu/scj/jcjpc/vol15is1/Deutsch_Cavender.pdf.

17. Edward J. Imwinkelried, "The Relative Priority That Should Be Assigned to Trial Stage DNA Issues," in *DNA and the Criminal Justice System: The Technology of Justice*, ed. David Lazer (Cambridge, Mass.: MIT Press, 2004), 97.

18. *State v. Cooke*, 914 A 2d 1078, 1082 (Del Super Ct 2007).

19. Ibid., 1080.

20. *U.S. v. Fields*, 483 F 3d 313 (5th Cir 2007).

21. *People v. Marquez*, No. B184697, 2006 WL 2665509, at *4–*5 & n.5 (Cal Ct App Sept 18, 2006).

22. *People v. Smith*, No. 271036, 2007 WL 4248571, at *5 (Mich Ct App Dec 4, 2007).

23. *State v. Latham*, No. 92,521, 2005 WL 1619235, at *2 (Kan Ct App Nov 1, 2005).

24. *State v. Taylor*, No. 06CA009000, 2008 WL 834437, at *3–*4 (Ohio Ct App March 31, 2008).

25. *U.S. v. Harrington*, 204 F. App'x 784 (11th Cir 2006).

26. *Batson v. Kentucky*, 476 U.S. 79 (1986) (holding that exclusion of jurors based on race violates the Equal Protection Clause of the United States Constitution).

27. *United States v. Hendrix*, 509 F 3d 362 (7th Cir 2007).

28. *State v. Carson*, No. C-040042, 2005 WL 497290 (Ohio Ct App March 4, 2005).

29. See, for example, *Wells v. Ricks*, No. 07 Civ 6982(CM)(AJP), 2008 WL 506294, at *28–*30, *33 (SDNY Feb 26, 2008) (reading detective novels or watching *CSI* is a race-neutral basis for excluding a juror); *People v. Reyes*, No. E040509, 2007 WL 4427856, at *9–*11 (Cal Ct App Dec 19, 2007) (responding to prosecutor's suggestion that the case "would not be like the *CSI* television show," juror indicated that she thought "it would be harder to evaluate the case just on testimony"; this was found to be a race-neutral ground for excluding Hispanics); *People v. Henderson*, No. A102395, 2004 WL 2526448, at *4–*5 (Cal Ct App Nov 9, 2004) (holding juror's statement that *CSI* "shows how they get evidence that they do and things like that" was a race-neutral ground for exclusion [internal quotation marks omitted]).

30. *Boatswain v. State*, No. 408, 2004, 2005 WL 1000565 (Del April 27, 2005).

31. *Mathis v. State*, No. 25, 2006, 2006 WL 2434741, at *4 (Del 2006) (delivering closing argument, the prosecutor told the jury: "Now, keep in mind when you're listening to the testimony from the witness stand this is not CSI Miami, it's not Law and Order. Nobody involved in this case, no one in this room is an actor. These are real people.").

32. *Morgan v. State*, 922 A 2d 395 (Del 2007).

33. Ibid., 402–403. The court held that, unlike *Boatswain*, there had not been a timely objection, and therefore did not require reversal on that ground. See also *State v. Snowden*, Nos. 04-07-2546, 03-09-3175, 2007 WL 1119339, at *4 (NJ Super Ct App Div April 17, 2007) *(per curiam)* (finding a lack of evidentiary basis for prosecution arguments).

34. See, for example, *State v. Hill*, No. A05-570, 2006 WL 1320075, at *3–*5 (Minn Ct App May 16, 2006) (finding harmless error); *State v. Minor*, No. C-060043, 2007 WL 196504, at *3 (Ohio Ct App Jan 26, 2007).

35. *People v. Compean*, No. A111367, 2007 WL 1567603, at *8 (Cal Ct App May 31, 2007).

36. *State v. Pittman*, No. 04-03-00373, 2007 WL 4482159 (NJ Super Ct App Div Dec. 26, 2007).

37. *State v. Strong*, 142 SW 3d 702, 724–725 (Mo 2004) *(en banc)* (citing *State v. Christeson*, 50 SW 3d 251, 268–269 [Mo 2001] [*en banc*]). The holding apparently presumes that jurors have a common knowledge about the length of criminal investigation or that *CSI* has assumed such popularity that it can now be considered "popular knowledge."

38. *State v. Snowden*, Nos. 04-07-2546, 03-09-3175, 2007 WL 1119339, at *4 (NJ Super Ct App Div April 17, 2007) (holding that the prosecutor was legitimately re-

sponding to a defense argument that mistakes had been made in the investigation); see also *United States v. Duronio*, No. 02-0933 (JAG), 2006 WL 3591259, at *3 (DNJ Dec 11, 2006) (holding the statement that the defense attorney's "favorite television program" must be *CSI* was not an *ad hominem* attack on counsel, but was a permissible response to the defense argument that fingerprints were not found on a computer); *State v. Ash*, No. A07-0761, 2008 WL 2965555, at *7 (Minn Ct App Oct 21, 2008) (citing *State v. Walsh*, 495 NW 2d 602, 607 [Minn 1993] (holding that the prosecutor's closing statement, asking the jury not to hold the state to a burden like *CSI* was not improper).

39. *State v. Goetz*, 191 P 3d 489, 517 (Mont 2008).

40. *State v. McKinney*, No. 2007-T-0004, 2008 WL 2582860 (Ohio Ct App June 27, 2008).

41. Ibid. A similar objection as to character and relevance was rejected in *People v. Brooks*, No. F051251, 2008 WL 2897093, at *15 (Cal Ct App July 29, 2008).

42. See, for example, *Cox v. State*, 966 So 2d 337, 353–354 (Fla 2007) (citing *Holland v. State*, 916 So 2d 750, 758 [Fla 2005]; *Gordon v. State*, 863 So 2d 1215, 1223 [Fla 2003]) (holding that it was not ineffective representation for failing to object to expert testimony that DNA evidence could be wiped from a murder weapon was "preposterous" because "anybody else with walking-around sense would think the same thing . . . in this day and age of watching CSI").

43. *United States v. Saldarriaga*, 204 F 3d 50 (2d Cir 2000).

44. *United States v. Mason*, 954 F 2d 219, 222 (4th Cir 1992).

45. *Evans v. State*, 922 A 2d 620 (Md Ct Spec App 2007).

46. Ibid., 628.

47. Ibid., 633.

Chapter 9: Conclusions: Where Do We Go from Here?

1. Michael J. Saks, *The Past and Future of Forensic Science and the Courts*, 93 Judicature 94 (2009), 94.

2. Richard Silberglitt, Philip S. Antón, David R. Howell, and Anny Wong, *The Global Technology Revolution 2020: In-Depth Analyses: Bio/Nano/Materials/Information Trends, Drivers, Barriers, and Social Implications*, (2006) xxvi, retrieved January 9, 2009, http://www.rand.org/pubs/technical_reports/2006/RAND_TR303.sum.pdf.

3. See the further discussion of the impact of these developments on popular culture and the court system in Donald E. Shelton, Young S. Kim, and Gregg Barak, *A Study of Juror Expectations and Demands for Scientific Evidence: Does the "CSI Effect" Exist?* 9 Vanderbilt J Ent & Tech L 334 (2006), at 362–365.

4. Saks, 95.

5. Professor Saks also suggested that the National Academy of Sciences report must be a separate factor as well. "The NRC Report might come to be viewed as yet another event pushing the non-science forensic sciences toward the construction of sound scientific moorings." Ibid., 95

6. *Daubert v. Merrell Dow Pharm., Inc.*, 43 F 3d 1311 (1995), at 1317–1318. And see the discussion of this position in the context of criminal cases in Peter J. Neufeld, *The*

(Near) Irrelevance of Daubert *to Criminal Justice and Some Suggestions for Reform,* 95 Am J Pub Health 107 (2005), retrieved April 12, 2010, from http://www.defendingscience.org/upload/NeufeldDAUBERT.pdf.

7. Brandon L. Garrett and Peter J. Neufeld, *Invalid Forensic Science Testimony and Wrongful Convictions,* 95 Va L Rev 1 (2009), 14–15.

8. *Science, State, Justice, Commerce, and Related Agencies Appropriations Act of 2006,* PL No. 109–108, 119 Stat 2290 (2005); S Rep No 109–88, 46 (2005); National Research Council of the National Academy of Sciences, *Strengthening Forensic Science in the United States: A Path Forward* (Washington, D.C.: National Academies Press, 2009), 1–2.

9. National Research Council of the National Academy of Science, 53.

10. National Research Council of the National Academy of Science, 19–33. The recommendations are set forth in the appendix.

11. Ibid., 22–23; see appendix.

12. American Academy of Forensic Sciences, *AAFS Position Statement in Response to the NAS Report,* 39 AAFS Academy News 4 (November 2009), retrieved January 9, 2009, from http://www.aafs.org/pdf/AAFS_Position_Statement_for_Press_Distribution_090409.pdf.

13. Thomas L. Bohan, *President's Message,* 39 AAFS Academy News 1 (November 2009).

14. See American Academy of Forensic Sciences, supra.

15. Bohan, 35.

16. See, for example, Peter E. Peterson et al., *Latent Prints: A Perspective on the State of the Science,* 11 Forensic Sci Comm, No. 4 (October 2009), retrieved January 9, 2009, from http://www.fbi.gov/hq/lab/fsc/current/review/2009_10_review01.htm.

17. Barry A. J. Fisher, *Legislative Corner,* 39 AAFS Academy News 3 (November 2009).

18. *U.S. v. Rose,* No. CCB-08-0149 (D Md, December 8, 2009), retrieved December 27, 2009, from http://www.mdd.uscourts.gov/Opinions/Opinions/Brian%20Rose%20Mem-FINAL.pdf; see Chapter IX C *infra.*

19. Ibid., citing Hon. Harry T. Edwards, *Statement before U.S. Senate Judiciary Committee* (Mar 18, 2009).

20. Hon. Harry T. Edwards, *Statement before U.S. Senate Judiciary Committee* (Mar 18, 2009), 10, retrieved January 9, 2009, from http://judiciary.senate.gov/pdf/09-03-18EdwardsTestimony.pdf.

21. *U.S. v. Mouzone,* Criminal No. WDQ-08-086, United States District Court (D Maryland, October 29, 2009).

22. *U.S. v. Prokupek,* Case No. 8:08CR183, United States District Court (D Nebraska, August 14, 2009).

23. Donald E. Shelton, Young S. Kim, and Gregg Barak, *An Indirect-Effects Model of Mediated Adjudication: The* CSI *Myth, the Tech Effect, and Metropolitan Jurors' Expectations for Scientific Evidence,* 12 Vand J Ent & Tech L 1 (2009); and see Chapter XVI *infra.*

24. Ibid.

25. Ibid.

26. D. Michael Risinger, *Navigating Expert Reliability: Are Criminal Standards of Certainty Being Left on the Dock?* 64 Alb L Rev 99 (2000).

27. Lloyd Dixon and Brian Gill, *Changes in the Standards for Admitting Expert Evidence in Federal Civil Cases Since the* Daubert *Decision* (Santa Monica, Calif.: Rand, 2001); Carol Krafka et al., *Judge and Attorney Experiences, Practices, and Concerns Regarding Expert Testimony in Federal Civil Trials,* 8 Psychol, Pub Pol'y & L 309 (2002), retrieved January 9, 2009, from http://files.ali-aba.org/thumbs/datastorage/skoobesruoc/pdf/CJ081-CH05_thumb.pdf.

28. David L. Faigman, Michael J. Saks, Joseph Sanders, and Edward K. Cheng. *Modern Scientific Evidence: The Law and Science of Expert Testimony* (Eagen, Minn.: Thomson/West, 2009), §1:35.

29. Risinger, 99.

30. Neufeld.

31. Jennifer L. Groscup et al., *The Effects of* Daubert *on the Admissibility of Expert Testimony in State and Federal Criminal Cases,* 8 Psychol Pub Pol'y & L 339 (2002), at 345–346.

32. Neufeld, 110.

33. See Faigman, Saks, Sanders, and Cheng, §1:35.

34. Groscup et al., 364.

35. Faigman, Saks, Sanders, Cheng, §1:35, 112.

36. Chris Guthrie, *Misjudging,* 7 Nev L J 420 (2007), 438–440, citing *The Hearing of Samuel A. Alito, Jr.'s Nomination to the Supreme Court,* Hearing Before the S Judiciary Comm, 109th Cong 56 (2006).

37. Rodney J. Uphoff, *On Misjudging and Its Implications for Criminal Defendants, Their Lawyers and the Criminal Justice System,* 7 Nev L J 521 (2007), 532; and see Fredric N. Tulsky, "How Judges Favor the Prosecution," *Mercury News* (February 12, 2007), retrieved January 9, 2009, from http://www.mercurynews.com/search/ci_5128172?IADID=Search-www.mercurynews.com-www.mercurynews.com (claiming that "in a fourth of all jury cases, a review finds, members of the bench apply their tremendous powers in ways that hurt defendants").

38. Michael J. Saks, *The Past and Future of Forensic Science and the Courts,* 93 Judicature 94 (2009), 97.

39. Ari Shapiro, "Foolproof Forensics? The Jury Is Still Out," *National Public Radio,* August 24, 2009. Retrieved January 10, 2010, from http://www.npr.org/templates/story/story.php?storyId=112111657.

40. Ibid., quoting Scott Burns, Executive Director of the National District Attorneys Association.

41. Uphoff, 547

42. William J. Brennan, Jr., *Reason, Passion and "The Progress of the Law,"* 10 Cardozo L Rev 3 (1988).

43. Federal Rule of Evidence 803 (18), *Learned Treatises.*

44. National Research Council of the National Academy of Sciences, 7.

Index

About the Author

The Hon. **Donald E. Shelton**, Ph.D., is a rare combination of active jurist with scholar, writer, and academic. A trial judge for over twenty years, he serves as chief judge of the court system in Ann Arbor, Michigan, and has presided over many high-profile criminal and civil trials. In 2007, Judge Shelton received the Frank J. Kelley Distinguished Public Servant Award presented by the State Bar of Michigan. Prior to becoming a judge, he was an accomplished trial attorney.

In addition to his law degree, Judge Shelton has a master's degree in criminology and criminal justice, and is one of only seven American judges with a Ph.D. in judicial studies. He is also an active professor on the adjunct faculty in both criminology and political science at Eastern Michigan University.

Judge Shelton is the author of several legal texts and has written for and lectured at numerous academic and professional organizations throughout the United States. One of his primary interests is the impact of technology on the judicial system, and especially on jurors. He has conducted a significant amount of empirical research in the field and is the author of the "*CSI* Effect" chapter in the book *Battleground: Criminal Justice.*